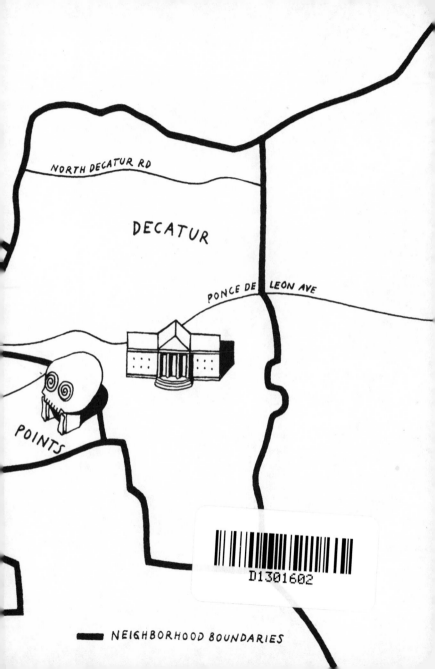

NORTH DECATUR RD

DECATUR

PONCE DE LEON AVE

POINTS

NEIGHBORHOOD BOUNDARIES

# atlanta

december '95

m—

here's a handy little
guide to your new
home town...

enjoy!

C—

# atlanta

by Jordan Simon and
Jeff Clark

with maps by Ingo Fast

**Longstreet**
**Atlanta, Georgia**

**edge guides**

Published by Longstreet Press
A subsidiary of Cox Newspapers,
A subsidiary of Cox Enterprises, Inc.
2140 Newmarket Parkway
Suite 122
Marietta, Georgia 30067

Printed in the United States of America
First Printing, 1999

Chapters by Jordan Simon: Introduction, Midtown, Downtown,
Buckhead, and Virginia Highland. Chapters by Jeff Clark, with
additions and editing by Jordan Simon: Decatur, Little Five
Points, East Atlanta, and South Buckhead.

Book design by Sue Canavan

A Balliett & Fitzgerald Book
editors: Rachel Aydt, Vijay Balakrishnan
production editor: Sue Canavan
copy editor: Meagan Backus
proofreader: Donna Stonecipher
associate editors: Kristen Couse, Aram Song

ISBN: 1-56352-517-8
Library of Congress Catalog Card Number 98-066367

# table of contents

# introduction

Atlanta is lovely, lively, cosmopolitan, and growing at a remarkable pace. It is the proud, at times preening, capital of the "New South." Many Fortune 500 companies have corporate or regional headquarters here, and the influx of young professionals and even artists from around the world has given Atlanta a complexion far more variegated than bland "new modern" cities like Dallas, Orlando, and Phoenix. The 1996 Centennial Olympics triggered a massive urban renewal campaign that saw greenspaces and artworks sprout throughout Downtown and Midtown. Urban hipsters are regentrifying decaying in-town neighborhoods. Corporate fat cats have been fattened, and upmarket restaurants thrive. Malls, office buildings, stadium complexes, tabernacles, and hotels are under constant construction, prompting locals to joke that "the building crane is the state bird." National publications consistently rank it as one of the top cities in which to live, work, and raise a family. And for all that, Atlanta is as beautiful and image-conscious as an aging Southern beauty queen making constant visits to the plastic surgeon, then seeking validation from her therapist and her third husband-to-be.

An anecdote told by the great writer-humorist Calvin Trillin on "The Tonight Show" back in the late 1970s illustrates both Atlanta's penchant for self-importance and its shaky sense of identity. He related a conversation with an Atlanta native concerning Soviet ICBMs. After noting that Atlanta wasn't on the list of top 10 U.S. targets, the Atlantan blustered, "But we most certainly should be on that list! Wait! What am I saying???"

Atlanta has a multiple-personality disorder—which of course makes it all the more fascinating. There's a subliminal tension, as it struggles to preserve Southern charm while assimilating all the transplants and displaying the aggressiveness and energy of a large international city. Just like the ongoing feminist debate, Atlanta is a belle wondering if she can have it all: corporate and country club culture, not to mention a cutting-edge arts scene. Those gleaming new skyscrapers reduce the precious greenspace that locals have come to take for granted, while superhighways curl tendrils into the green countryside, through historic antebellum towns like Roswell and Marietta.

Many locals like to proclaim Atlanta the New York of the South, which betrays a certain insecurity. It's really more like L.A. There's the sunny, laid-back personality, the sheer urban sprawl, the sidewalk cafe mentality, and of course that car culture status thing. Locals, although they adore the Braves, even leave Turner Field by the seventh inning, much as Angelenos flee Dodger Stadium, to escape traffic.

Atlanta has also built a tradition of tolerance and inclusiveness. Sure, bubbas exist in droves a short drive away in, say, Gwinnett County (generally, the farther you go from the city limits, the tighter the Bible Belt cinches its buckle). But you can forget those ancient images of pissant Southern backwaters replete with corrupt sheriffs, where the apotheosis of culture is the top high school cheerleading routine. Gays and lesbians have found a haven in neighborhoods like Midtown and Decatur. When Cobb County (a conservative bastion, half redneck and half blue-blood) passed a resolution denouncing the gay lifestyle, many prominent in-town leaders rallied to the lavender cause. And while many Atlantans look down their noses (or hold them) at the thought of the neo-punks and slackers in areas like Little Five Points, most residents are proud of Atlanta's diversity.

In 1959, then-mayor Bill Hartsfield, mindful of promoting Atlanta's modern status, coined an odd phrase: "Atlanta, the city too busy to hate." Today, to be true, race remains a troubling issue with even some ultra-liberal whites. Most Atlantans remain slightly defensive and sensitive. Behind the closed doors of elegant dinner parties you'll hear talk of dividing Fulton County into north (upper-middle-class white) and south (mostly black and poorer), so the haves won't bear a disproportionate tax burden of caring for the have-nots.

The flip side is that *Ebony* magazine rated Atlanta the number one place for African-Americans to live. The top-notch black colleges like Spelman and Morehouse overflow with students. Many opportunities for education and corporate-ladder climbing abound for blacks and whites alike. Atlantans can all point proudly to such distinguished citizens as former mayor Andrew Young and current mayor Bill Campbell. But for all the rise of a black middle class, many still remain "south side" (Downtown, East Atlanta, West End), which has traditionally been, for lack of a better word, the ghetto. The expansion has been up the east side suburbs like Stone Mountain, Clarkson, and Tucker, which are now experiencing the "white flight" phenomenon. Upper-middle-class blacks have gradually moved "north" into Decatur, Midtown, Morningside, Dunwoody, even tentatively putting down roots into whitebread, ultra-posh South Buckhead. Still, International Boulevard serves as a relatively clear-cut border.

Which brings up a term you'll hear constantly in Atlanta: OTP versus ITP. OTP, or Outside The Perimeter, refers to the communities lying beyond the ring of I-285. In the 1980s, OTP was hot indeed, as young professionals wanted to escape urban squalor to raise families. But now, it's trendy to live ITP, which has something of the snob appeal of the city versus the 'burbs. People are renovating the beautiful turn-of-the-century mansions of East Atlanta and Grant Park, the craftsman bungalows of Virginia Highland and South Buckhead, even the warehouse lofts in Downtown. So chic is the loft sensibility, in fact, that Atlanta's most upscale address, Buckhead, is building warehouse repro-ductions whose lofts have been purchased before con-struction has even started.

Perhaps it's fitting in Turner-land to describe the neigh-borhoods in television terms. The aforementioned Buckhead is "Dynasty," "Dallas," and "Designing Women," with the staid older crowd in their mansions, yet a younger, brash "Melrose Place" contingent animating its bar scene. Mid-town, which boasts the largest gay population, as well as Atlanta's toniest address, Ansley Park, is "Soap" meets "Tales of the City" meets "Will and Grace." Virginia Highland, Atlanta's arty answer to New York's SoHo, is sensitive yuppie "Ally McBeal." Meanwhile, the more cutting-edge alterna-tive nabe, Little Five Points (aka L5P) with multiple-pierced, tattooed types on the prowl, is an NC-17 cable access show.

East Atlanta, with its combination of younger middle-class whites, and gays renovating old homes and poorer blacks and whites, is like a show on the WB, "Moesha" meets "Roseanne." Decatur is "Ellen": more openly lesbian than Disney permitted, yet not overly demonstrative, with a nice mix of suburban and urban types, from students frequenting coffeehouses to the "upwardly mobile-home" crowd. And Downtown, still the business and convention center, is, well, CNN.

No matter where they live, many people play in other neighborhoods. Buckhead gets the nod for its bars (for both the frat and yuppie sets) and fine dining and shopping. Virginia Highland is another hip hopping happening eat/shop 'hood for yupsters with less attitude. Midtown and L5P feature the top music and dance clubs. Of course, some folks avoid entire neighborhoods. About the only thing the old guard in Buckhead and L5P folk agree on is nicknaming the frat-party atmosphere of central Buckhead, "Butthead." One resident of East Atlanta (an urban frontier) comments flippantly that in ritzy Buckhead "everyone looks the same; it's like watching twins out on a date." But Buckhead's grande dames are ironically among the first to praise the artistic diversity of L5P. Go figure.

It just goes to show that in Atlanta, no matter what your background or what you believe, anyone can be a member of some club. And if Atlanta sometimes remains uptight about its image, this city also knows how to unwind. The living here is easy (if you don't steam over the traffic at rush hour). Martinis may be preferred over mint juleps, but this is still the South, sugar. So relax and "set a spell." Even as Atlanta itself zooms onward and upward.

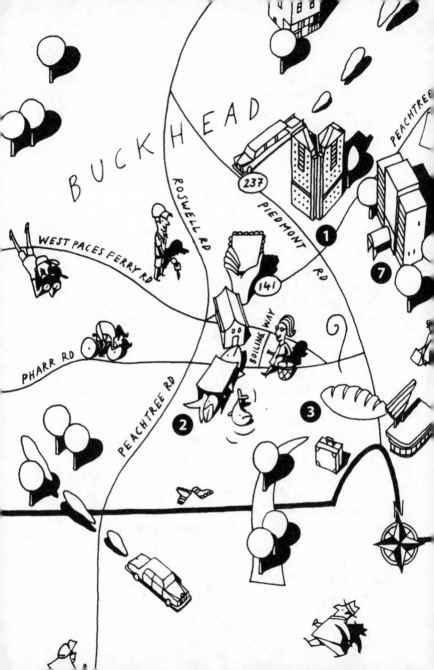

# buckhead

Denizens and detractors alike refer
to Buckhead as the
Beverly Hills of Atlanta.
It's the Lexus nexus of
conspicuous
consumption (and local
center for the men
Man-In-Full Tom
Wolfe once termed
"masters of the universe" and
their "social X-ray" wives). A
superficial glance reveals a popu-
lace infected with affluenza,
decked out in Prada and Versace,

LENOX RD

turn page for map key

for whom liposuction can be a way of life. Yes, Buckhead has its posturing, but it's got the best damn posture you're gonna see.

Its residential areas rank among America's loveliest. The two deluxe shopping malls, Phipps Plaza and Lenox Square, feature valet parking. The lots are a sea of Lexuses and Land Rovers, ubiquitous Beamers and the ultra-trendy new Beetles. Shade trees line the twisting roads, while few hedges obscure the view of the showplaces (most of the annual Decorator's Showhouses are located in Buckhead, at grand manors like Villa Juanita and White Oaks). Indeed, the mansions themselves seem to preen like fashion models, awaiting their *Architectural Digest* and *House & Garden* photo shoots. Queen Anne, neo-Gothic, and red brick sit chic-by-jowl with hacienda, Tudor, and Italianate palazzo residences along the quieter roads, while even main arteries like Piedmont Road feature some dreadfully tasteful faux-Victorian housing and office developments. You name it, Buckhead is an architectural hodgepodge of showmanship and one-up-manship. Snooty/snotty quotient? The Buckhead Homeowners Association would never allow anything so tacky as a yard sale.

In this respect, Buckhead serves as the perfect model for Atlanta itself: upwardly mobile, impeccably manicured, and obsessively driven (by status, success, and the symbols thereof). Those who believe the "New South" stands for

| map key | | |
|---|---|---|
| 1 | Grand Hyatt | 4 Buckhead Diner |
| 2 | Atlanta Fish Market | 5 Lenox Square |
| 3 | Buckhead Bread Company | 6 Phipps Plaza |
| | | 7 Swissôtel |

nouveau riche will certainly find ammunition here. Bigger is definitely better. One Ansley Park (the original "Uptown" district of Atlanta, and still old-money) matron dismisses Buckhead casually: "Oh, my husband used to hunt deer there 40 years ago. How do you think it got its name?" (Actually, local legend declares that the first resident, one Henry Irby, was an avid hunter back in the 1840s.) And residents are sensitive about social standing. As one Buckhead doyenne lets drop, in competitive reference to the Piedmont Driving Club (Margaret Mitchell's country club, located in Midtown's Piedmont Park), "Sugar, I belong to the Cherokee Club, and it may not be our oldest club, but it has the longest waiting list!" (To which another member sniffs, "How did SHE get in? Oh, must have been a family membership . . .") That typifies Buckhead's extraordinary combination of Southern-fried hospitality and Southern-fried hypocrisy. Not for nothing was "Designing Women" set in Atlanta . . . and that's a decade behind the times.

Yet Buckhead's serene facade is just that. Scratch its surface and you'll discover more contradictory Buckheads. Many people live in, aspire to live in, or travel to Buckhead to bask in its posh, Rodeo Drive mentality. Yet its nightspots also attract the card-able crowd who persist in treating the central area as one extended frat party, foaming, spilling, frothing messily and happily from one "stumbling bar" to the next. Atlanta's finest young specimens of manhood can often be found peeing in an alley only a few blocks from the piss-elegant Atlanta History Center.

But it would be unfair to dismiss Buckhead solely as the enclave of the upper-middle-class "booboisie." Buckhead's growth by leaps and bounds mirrors Atlanta's increasing importance in the corporate world. Like the rest of town, fewer than half of Buckhead's residents are "natives." And what this neighborhood lacks in true "New York 400" social prestige, it makes up for in sheer Fortune 500 power. Skyscrapers and shopping malls sprout like fungi; construction is omnipresent. The scenery changes constantly: Office buildings resembling glittering glaciers, black Vuarnet lenses, and geometric ziggurats surrender to a series of strip malls that unexpectedly open up into delightful green-spaces. It's intensely suburban and urban at the same time.

Traffic is so bad on Buckhead's clogged arteries, locals cheerily resign themselves to "the world's largest parking lot," only to sigh a few minutes—and inches—later. It's rather jarring to find Atlanta Historic Markers sitting incongruously next to strip malls, car dealerships, drive-thru dry-cleaning shops, and empty lots. But this is Atlanta, a city that prides itself on keeping up appearances (and keeping up with the Joneses). The main drags are beautifully landscaped and canopied with trees. The day after a storm, the gardening crews will be out at apartments and office buildings all over the neighborhood replacing the flowers and plants, making everything "just so" again.

The streamlining serves as an implicit reminder of Buckhead's uniform population: young, white, straight, well-educated, and pretty. Buckhead's final irony is that in a city that prides itself on defining the "New South," it remains so white-bread. Buckhead probably has more preps and debs and hyper-tanned leggy blondes than the rest of town, and it remains eerily segregated. You see remarkably few African-Americans, living, going out at night, or even working here, unless they're a celeb like Peabo Bryson or the occasional "Brooks Brother" (whose flagship store, tellingly, is in Downtown). The one exception is Lenox Square Mall, where a MARTA stop brings many African-Americans from Atlanta's south side.

Perhaps it's fitting then that the heart of Buckhead is uncannily shaped like the state of Georgia: bounded by Chastain Memorial Park on the north, Northside Avenue on the west, Wieuca Road/Roxboro Road on the east, and Wesley Road/Sidney Marcus Boulevard to the south. Defining Buckhead's amorphous borders isn't easy. Technically, it could include Peachtree Battle (a less upmarket suburban/strip-mall area abutting Midtown to the south); it could certainly extend east to the ethnic street fair that is Buford Highway. But nearly everything quintessentially Buckhead is located within these margins. And the center for shopping, dining, and bar-hopping, the Buckhead Triangle where Roswell Road, Peachtree Road, and West Paces Ferry Road meet, is actually walkable in a town where drivers goggle at pedestrians. Take a stroll or drive in this "neck of the woods" and immerse yourself in the good life.

# eating/coffee

Recent surveys indicate that 47 percent of Atlantans dine out or get takeout nightly; the percentage is likely even higher in Buckhead. If the neighborhood isn't quite the culinary hotbed Atlantans advertise, it certainly is warming up on the national scene. Buckhead's reputation as a gastronomic temple can be traced primarily to two enterprising owner/chefs. Guenter Seeger, who oversaw the renowned Ritz-Carlton Buckhead kitchen (dining in the restaurant there is still a sublime night out), is credited with putting Atlanta on the culinary map. But don't overlook the indefatigable Pano Karatassos and his chef/partner Paul Albrecht, who run the Buckhead Life Group, 11 of Atlanta's leading eateries, each unique in cuisine and concept, and all dramatic, sumptuous, and glamorous.

Given its homogeneous population, Buckhead offers a surprising diversity of cuisines and an amazingly good price-to-quality ratio. Of course, this remains an area where nothing succeeds like excess. Buckhead features a vast array of loud yuppieterias with model (in every way) wait staffs, and tony old-fashioned boîtes whose menus were frozen in the Kennedy era. Many uppity upmarket spots are ironically located in strip and shopping malls. This is not to say that Buckhead doesn't have its inexpensive restaurants, many serving gussied-up pub grub (menus with 20-word variations on burgers and Buffalo wings). There are even a few cheap ethnic eateries, but bar-restaurant-taverns remain your best bet not to go bust.

**Cost Range** per entree
$/under 10 dollars
$$/10–15 dollars
$$$/15–20 dollars
$$$$/20+ dollars

**american...** The **Buckhead Diner** (3073 Piedmont Rd. 404/262-3336 $$-$$$) offers dazzling reinventions of comfort food (veal-and-wild-mushroom "meatloaf" with garlic mashed potatoes; homemade potato chips with

Maytag blue cheese, poblano grits) and also classics with a down-home twist (chocolate chip crème brûlée) in a Hollywood-set diner decorated in exotic hardwoods and chrome, neon, colored glass, Art Deco swan lamps, and silver, evoking both turn-of-the-century railroad dining cars and the slick lines and colors of 1950s jukeboxes. This deliriously retro pastiche is eternally jam-packed; expect a wait (it peaks around 10 p.m.). Meanwhile, you can try the intriguing wine selections (by the glass) at the polished granite bar or even make a meal of their luscious appetizers, like salmon carpaccio with honey lime vodka sauce.

A perfect example of Buckhead culinary ostentation is **John Harvard's Brew House** (3041 *Peachtree Rd.* 404/ 816–2739 $$). It's not exactly your classic pub grub: fried calamari accompanied by shallot balsamic vinaigrette and pomodoro sauce, artichoke with lager-steeped cheese dip, or roasted cod with rock shrimp. They also have a superlative selection of single malts, as well as more than 100,000 ales, stouts, lagers, porters, etc. The blond wood decor and potted plants are enlivened by saucy murals and jokey stained glass depicting legends from Paul Revere and JFK to Margaret Mitchell and Jerry Garcia. Regulars can stow their steins here, lending new meaning to the term mug shot.

**OK Cafe** (1284 *W. Paces Ferry Rd.*, *N.E.* 404/233–2888 $) duplicates an old-style roadhouse diner, with leatherette banquettes, formica tables, a 1950s jukebox that features Peggy Lee and Tony Bennett, gum-cracking "Flo" waitresses, folk art, and guilt-free fat-laden blue-plate standbys like meatloaf, six-cheese macaroni and 24-hour-a-day breakfast items that keep it hopping. But at peak hours be prepared to wait.

### caribbean... La Fonda Latina (2813 *Peachtree Rd.* 404/816–8311 $–$$), an offshoot of the Fellini's Pizza empire, offers this recipe for success: wild colors (banana-tree murals adorn the exterior), sizzling salsa (music mix and sauces alike), as hip a crowd as Buckhead can muster, and fab food (*arroz con pollo*, jerk chicken) at south-of-the-border prices.

### coffeehouses... J. Martinez & Company (3230A *Peachtree Rd.* 404/231–5465) is quite simply one of America's finest purveyors of coffee. John Martinez's family has grown superlative coffee in Jamaica's renowned Blue Mountains for generations, and he imports only the finest "estate" (think not just wine appellations but individual vineyards) beans from around the world. Although 95 percent of their business is mail order, there are a few tables in the elegant space, where you can relax over a Kona or Sumatran Mandheling and nibble on biscotti. Luxuriating in this aromatic oasis, you'll agree with John's observation that coffee is "man's most affordable luxury," an irony in a city where people drink iced tea.

### continental/prix fixe... At $48, a meal at Bacchanalia (3125 *Piedmont Rd.* 404/365–0410 $$$$), considered by many to be Atlanta's finest restaurant, is a steal. Set in a dollhouse-like mint-and-maroon, gabled and shingled brick Victorian cottage, you feel like you're dining in the home of chef/owners Anne Quattrano and Cliff Harrison, especially if you're seated near the swooningly romantic fireplace. The dishes are simple yet exquisite, a virtual U.N. of culinary influences, including mini rack of

lamb with sun-dried-tomato sauce or blue-crab fritters with avocado, citrus, and essence of Thai peppers. The standout dessert is probably the signature Valrhona chocolate cake with vanilla-bean ice cream. It's the perfect place to pop the question—or let someone down easy.

But the master in Atlanta remains Guenter Seeger, whose **Seeger's** (*111 W. Paces Ferry Rd. 404/846–9779 $$$$*) offers a Zen dining experience, in which everything, from colors to textures, blends together magically and effortlessly. Witness the haunting, vaguely Russian Expressionist portrait of a lady in red overseeing the plush cherry banquettes in one corner, or the way the "electric-light" artworks play off the unfinished brick. The food, designed to please both eye and palate, dazzles. Seeger improvises with flair: One dinner might include pumpkin gnocchi with sage and ginger; grilled turbot with fennel *coulis* and wild ramps (a relative of the onion); and a lip-smacking, mouthwatering passion-fruit *topfen* with basil sorbet. Wherever possible, he uses organic, indigenous ingredients, deals with local purveyors, and cures his own meats in-house; local items like pecan oil, Vidalia onions, and Georgia goat cheese usually grace any given menu. Dinners are $58 to $75, and worth every penny.

The formerly tired **Hedgerose** (*490 E. Paces Ferry Rd. 404/233–7673 $$$$*) recently received a complete overhaul, from menu to decor. Martin Gagne is one of Atlanta's great unsung chefs; his ambitious prix fixe and à la carte menus are a deft fusion of Asian, French, and regional influences. Beautifully presented standouts include duck *foie gras* served seasonally with shallot marmalade and wild-blueberry pancakes. The surroundings are unorthodox: The

Greco-Roman Contemporary room oddly juxtaposes track lighting and blond wood walls with arches and engraved Attic columns, warm brick fireplaces with chilly abstract art. Even though the tuxedoed wait staff are hospitable, the decor makes the room more forbidding than it should be.

**french...** Operated by Maguy Le Coze of Le Bernardin fame, **Brasserie Le Coze** (3393 *Peachtree Rd., Lenox Square* 404/266–1440 $$$) is noted for its delectable seafood, and is nearly as good as the legendary New York restaurant, at half the price. The room is a loving evocation of a Belle Epoque Parisian cafe, gleaming with brass, etched glass, lace curtains, dark wood paneling, hand-painted Provençal tilework, metallic angels, floor-to-ceiling mirrors, and photos of sultry French flirts like Simone Signoret. Standouts include a classic meaty monkfish braised in red wine, soy, and ginger, and a delicately flaky skate swimming in brown-butter caper sauce.

**fusion...** Elegantly balancing plush banquettes, mother-of-pearl inlaid tables, 19th-century Chinese antiques with Phillippe Starck chairs and polished stainless steel, the ambience at the red-hot **Fusebox** (3085 *Piedmont* Rd. 404/233–3383) is lively yet mysteriously serene. Executive chef Troy Thompson and culinary director Guenter Seeger inventively synthesize the best of the East and the West with dishes such as a delicate Panko squid immersed in a spicy fresh gazpacho, or desserts such as gingered fruit soup with chamomile. In addition to the superlative fare, Fusebox also offers lovely private rooms for banquets and a marble-top bar with large windows facing the street—ideal for lounging.

**italian...** **Fellini's Pizza** (2809 *Peachtree* Rd. 404/266–0082 $), one in a chain of six scattered throughout the metro area, makes classic thin-crust pies that are delectably gooey. The restaurant's interior is splashed with vivid circus colors; the patio overlooks a fountain festooned with frolicking seraphs and gargoyles. Equally popular with families and grad students, it's the perfect place to watch the parade along Peachtree.

**Azio** (220 *Pharr* Rd. 404/233–7626 $$) occupies a hip, slick warehouse-y space; low-cal woodburning oven pizzas (try the blue corn) and simple pastas lure a diverse crowd encompassing Nietzsche-sporting students and society matrons. The patio affords splendid Downtown views.

**Metropolitan Pizza Lounge** (3055 *Bolling Way* 404/264–0135 $) certainly qualifies as the hippest pizza joint in Buckhead, with cool Deco-style murals of debauched women in Fauvist hues. There's also good ol' rockabilly bands and swing dancing, karaoke Tuesdays, Pizza-a-Go-Go Wednesdays (the DJ spins '70s funk, R&B, and disco hits). Topping the topping charts are BBQ Chicken (including smoked gouda, cilantro, and red onion) and the Neptune (Gulf shrimp and pesto). There's even a pool table in back, and no attitude.

**Ciao Bella** (309 *Pharr* Rd. 404/261–6013 $$–$$$) is homier than most Buckhead Italian restaurants, right down to the garlic wreaths hanging everywhere and the cozy fireplace area. The menu savvily sticks to the tried and true, like chicken sauteed with capers, black olives, and anchovies, and fettuccine in shiitake/porcini cream sauce. It's a very popular, affordable date place where you don't have to shout to make your feelings known.

**japanese...** There are several worthy sushi parlors, but **Genki** (3188 *Roswell Rd.* 404/869–8319 **$$**) surpasses them all for value, not to mention fun. Even on a chilly gray day, the deck's preferable to the bargain-basement, plain-bulbed interior. It's not unusual to find sozzled young Bucks attempting to navigate their chopsticks, going on kamikaze Sake Bomber missions (a hot cup of sake plunged in a mug of frosty Sapporo beer), or even starting an udon fight with the next table. **Soto** (3330 *Piedmont Rd.* 404/233–2005 **$$–$$$**) is far more restrained, from the harsh lighting and sterile earth tones of the sushi bar to the poker-faced sushi masters. Yet the fish is divine, including lobster tempura and broiled sea bass in miso and sake.

**mexican/southwestern...** Dallas' large, jolly Kevin Rathbun is a rising culinary star, with his own TV show; everything about his Atlanta showplace, **Nava** (3060 *Peachtree Rd.* 404/240–1984 **$$$**), is larger than life, and boldly colored and textured, from food to decor. *Nava* means "hillside" in Spanish, and the space is theatrically staggered on three levels; they even brought wood and dirt from Santa Fe for authenticity. The sumptuous setting is filled with Native American vases and artwork set in their own dramatically lighted niches. The food is just as artful, from the fresh-baked breads (served in a wire horse-shaped basket) flavored with the likes of sunflower or coriander, to architectural desserts like the crème brûlée napoléon in phyllo. Rathbun's dishes take a subtle approach: the Suncorn Crusted Snapper or the Lobster Taco with Cascabel Cream Sauce sneak up on the palate. Oh, and the margaritas are marvelous, with such unusual flavors as prickly pear.

**Bajarito's** (3877 *Peachtree Rd.* 404/239–WRAP $–$$)
serves designer burritos "from around the world," such as
the Thai Peanut Chicken Burrito (a spinach tortilla envelop-
ing ginger-lime cabbage, mango-chipotle puree, cucumber, and cilantro-lime rice) or the Grilled Mediterranean
Eggplant Burrito (a virtual ratatouille filling). They emulate
Wolfgang Puck and his gourmet pizzas in spirit and daring,
with an eye toward pleasing the calorie- and cholesterol-
conscious. Even the mellow decor is cross-cultural, with a
striking 60-foot mural of an abstract land- and seascape
with a long mirrored wave (Chinese *feng shui*), aubergine-
stained walls (Provence) . . . and surfing videos for that laid-
back California cool.

The utterly unmemorable chain **Rio Bravo Cantina**
(3172 *Roswell Rd.* 404/262–7431 $–$$) at least serves up
kick-ass margaritas and decent fajitas, attracting hordes of
recent college grads celebrating being legal, especially
during raucous Friday happy hours.

## southern/ribs...
Yep, you can get real smothered ribs
at **Feeder's Barbecue** (264 *Pharr Rd.* 404/869–8979 $–$$).
It's the genuine article, little more than a shack with a
porch, a wooden bar with maroon naugahyde stools, and
family-style seating. Sauces are on the sweet side, but the
ribs and chicken are tender. It also offers pretty decent
comedy improv on Thursdays, and blues or good old-
fashioned rock 'n' roll on weekends.

**The Horseradish Grill** (4230 *Powers Ferry Rd.* 404/255–
7277 $$–$$$) specializes in haute Southern cuisine: quail
over creamy stone grits with country ham and mushroom
gravy, braised beef shortribs slow-cooked with green toma-

toes and a whiskey peppercorn sauce, peanut and cracker-crumb trout with port and onion confit. The menu and matching rustic-elegant setting lures a well-heeled clientele.

**steaks/seafood...** Heavy hitters lick theirs at **Chops** (*70 W. Paces Ferry Rd.* 404/262–2675 **$$$–$$$$**), where the setting is modern (herringbone coffered ceilings, brass lamps, towering redwood columns, carved glass, mixed-wood bar, black marble floors, open kitchen) and the three-pound porterhouse comes out like a gorgeous slab of abstract sculpture. Steaks are flown in from Iowa and Montana and cured in-house. The seafood is also superb; the downstairs, in fact, has been transformed into the all-seafood Lobster Bar, which resembles a soaring 1920s train station. It's so state-of-the-art that a filtration system recycles the cigar stench.

This restaurant's name, **PRIME** (*3393 Peachtree Rd., Lenox Square* 404/812–0555 **$$$**), could refer to both the grade-A meats and the Type-A clientele. Tom Catherill serves sensational steak and sushi in a lofty space (big semi-circular banquettes face the Ritz, and Da Vinci-esque "flying machines" dangle from the cathedral ceilings). The aggressively modern, brash decor fits the suit-and-tie youngbloods who go into shark-feeding frenzies over free sushi Fridays 5–7 p.m. As juicy as the meats are, the Asian-influenced seafood is even better: Witness melting sea bass in shitake miso broth counterpointed by crunchy daikon sprouts and gossamer shrimp dumplings.

**Steamhouse Lounge** (*3041 Bolling Way* 404/233–7980 **$–$$**), is a jamming little bar whose patio sits invitingly under a 400-year-old spreading oak. The goofy nautical decor includes ships' steering wheels, fishing nets, and a neon oyster shell proclaiming "we shuck 'em, you suck 'em"; it's also legendary among Buckhead seafood lovers for its smashing, velvety lobster bisque.

## takeout/on the run... The Buckhead Bread Company/Corner Cafe (3070 Piedmont Rd. 404/240–1978 $–$$) is divided in half between a spectacular bakery (sticky cinnamon rolls, rosemary eight-grain loaves) and a casual European-style cafe where you can savor hearty soups like potato leek with fried mashed potatoes, sandwiches made with those sensational breads, and even basic yet lustily flavored fish and meats served with ultra-fresh veggies. The 16,500-square-foot **EatZi's Market and Bakery** (3221 Peachtree Rd. 404/237–8646 $–$$) is envisioned on an even grander scale: the theater of food. The owner even insists on blasting opera—usually Verdi or Puccini—through well-lit, well-stocked aisles bursting with cheeses from St. André to Stilton; up to 50 homemade breads like scrumptious chili-cheese; meals grilled-to-order; marinades; even sushi. Chefs chant like old fishmongers from their stations, "Succulent, golden-roasted chicken!" "Melting, flaky sesame-crusted sea bass!"

## tapas... That lovely Spanish institution of nibbles, or tapas, is alive and well in Buckhead. **Tu Tu Tango** (220 Pharr Rd. 404/841–6222 $$–$$$) defines "eclectic" in every sense. The wild decor includes painted gourds, Valentine-red mosaic work and rotating artworks generally so hideous you'd swear they were a put-on if you couldn't see the artists at work. The entertainment careens from (fake) fire-

eaters to equally faux belly dancers. And the food veers from *ropa vieja* (shredded beef) to ratatouille—and that's just the R's. It may also be the only place in town to offer alligator meat on a regular basis. **Eclipse di Luna** (*764 Miami Circle 404/846–0449 $*) sits in Atlanta's poshest antiques enclave, and is terrifically priced (tapas, from fried calamari or garlic shrimp to risotto, are $2.95 apiece). The international wine list is just as affordable, with selections under $20. Pulsating salsa and merengue vie with animated chatter, creating a noisy but festive ambience. The funky decor incorporates metal trunks, paper mobiles, and chairs dangling from the ceiling.

# bars

Buckhead bars are boisterous. Not for nothing are they called "stumbling bars" around Buckhead's West and East Villages, where the streets resemble one big keg party. Some older residents of the neighborhood call the scene "Butthead." How bad is the drinking? A converted ambulance, called the "Buckhead Coach," circulates through the streets and is available for hire; it has a bar in back. The energy almost rivals Bourbon Street on Friday and Saturday nights (minus the go cups and Dixieland), with babes beckoning from balconied windows and beefy ex-jocks, looking ready to initiate you into their fraternity, slapping you on the back. To a certain extent, the bars along Bolling Way and Peachtree Road are virtually indistinguishable.

Weekend nights, Buckhead is at its most diverse: that is to say, from white collar to redneck, white limos too long to be tasteful and pick-up trucks with Gwinnett County tags and fluffy dice. Alcohol is the drug of choice; the neighborhood is too clean-cut for anything injected, and there's more pimple- than pill-popping. It's also hormones on the prowl, man and woman alike seemingly equal in their intensity. But Buckhead is also heaven if you're in your 20s and make an income approaching six figures. The freshly graduated cruise the fancy microbreweries and the J.Crew set cruise each other. Indeed, the warren of streets around East Village Mall constitutes the perfect maze for the rat-race crowd.

Which isn't to say there aren't more sedate options, though these tend to be intimate restaurant lounges and posh hotel bars for the older, easily Viagra-vated crowd. Some of these places are class, as in ruling all the way, with latter-day Scarletts flouncing about in DKNY and aging roués who emulate Rhett Butler. That's the blue-blood, blue-blazered, blue-chip-on-their-shoulder crowd (Candace Bushnell's "toxic bachelors" come freshly minted here); it takes forever to gain their trust, let alone access to their trust funds.

But the rest of Buckhead isn't jaded. A couple of buds, a few Buds, plenty of cigarettes, and the plainest bar is transformed into Party Central. Nearly all the restaurants offer thriving bar scenes (and for that matter, nearly every bar has a kitchen and cheap eats). The bonus, surprisingly, is that drinks, even in the toniest places, are comparatively inexpensive. Atlanta is an affordable town when it comes to food and entertainment, and Buckhead is no exception.

The prototypical Buckhead bar is **Lulu's Bait Shack (3057 *Peachtree Rd.* 404/262–5220)**, where trolling, reeling off lines—and pouring down linebacker-sized 96-ounce

"Fishbowls" (choice of Gator Bite, Croc Bite, Hurricane)—
are the favorite activities for the Phi Delta Psi-chotic crowd.
The decor is clichéd—oars, neon beer signs, license
plates—as is the undistinguished live music several nights
a week, best enjoyed on the spacious deck.

At the other extreme, the lavish interior of **fadó** (3035
*Peachtree Rd. 404/841–0066*) duplicates both the facade and
inside of a Dublin pub. The earnestly faux decor is as
impeccably manicured as the clientele. But yupsters lap it
up. (Telling lack of authenticity: It's easier to get a decent
single malt than an aged Jamie or Bush . . . the place is too
classy for "Oi-rish" whiskey.)

A third classic Buckhead-style bar is **Havana Club** (247
*Buckhead Ave., N.E. 404/869–8484*), where the attractive
space—industrial ceilings, natural wicker chairs, maize
walls, cushy sofas, wrought-iron lamps, tobacco theme
galore (cigar boxes, ads, and labels mounted on walls)—
matches the sleek patrons. The cigar room/humidor is
larger than the tiny dance floor. The club is a big deal for the
music and fashion industries, where one-"Upmann"ship
is practiced by moguls-in-the-making.

**The Lodge** (248 *Buckhead Ave., N.E. 404/233–3345*) is
immediately recognizable by the sculpture (whatchamacal-
lit is more accurate) of a large red hand outside. It's your
classic sports bar: neon beer signs, old baseball photos, aging
high school football heroes and cheerleaders. The rooftop
bar has a fine view of Downtown, as well as a dance floor
(mostly disco revisited and Top 40). And for two bucks you
can place a bucket in a chute and guide it to try to catch your
own lobster. Daily specials like fried catfish go for $6.95.

They pour in and out of **The Atlanta BeerGarten**

**(3013 Peachtree Rd. 404/261–9898)**, most notable for its stab at decor: an overwhelmingly green motif, from booths to lamps to pool-table felt to ferns, and rusting farm implements hanging everywhere. It really cranks up Thursday through Saturday nights with live acoustic sets on the expansive patio.

**Mako's Cantina** (3065 Peachtree Rd. 404/846–8096) offers a subtle example of Buckhead attitude. Couldn't be more casual in feel and look: big ol' barn with a wood-plank floor covered in sawdust, a crystal disco ball, kilted bartenders, blasting Van Morrison for frat boys and sorority girls reliving their pledges, and a pathetic excuse of a "cigar lounge." Yet incongruously, a sign prohibits athletic logo wear, sunglasses or goggles, ripped jeans, tank tops, or vests. Still, it's one of Buckhead's less uptight—and more mixed—spots.

**Panini's** (3069 Peachtree Rd. 404/816–1116) and its downstairs sibling **Orchestra Pit** (3069 Peachtree Rd. 404/459–9929) are cozy hangouts with brick walls and wood floors. Upstairs, the "kitchen never closes" (meaning sandwiches and hoagies are always available if you have the "munchies") while 21 TV screens and more than 50 beers make the "Pit" an informal sports hangout; like most of the stumbling bars, they offer live bands, pool, and foosball.

A flame mural wraps around the vast **World Bar** (3071 Peachtree St. 404/266–0627), where the clientele could hardly be called global. Two-dollar drinks, a great music mix, and the largest dance floor in Buckhead keep it jammed and jamming.

**The Bar** (250 E. Paces Ferry Rd. 404/841–0033) is as divey as the name suggests: The foaming-at-the-mouth crowd perch on beer barrels, dance on the bar, plaster up sports posters, and chug domestic brewskis by the half yard ($6 per slam dunk).

**CJ's Landing** (270 *Buckhead Ave.* 404/237–7657) seems like the standard setup, with Harp and Guinness neon signs and minimalist woody decor, but provides surprisingly good reggae in the "cave" and acoustic guitar on the "deck."

**Pat Hurley's Backyard** (280 *Buckhead Ave.* 404/261–3422) is a refreshing tonic: Real, money-impaired people flock here. Highway signs, murals of "partying dogs" and bras provide the decor. The music mix ranges from Neneh Cherry to the Red Hot Chili Peppers, though dance ditties are more typically "Celebrate" and "Come on Eileen" (and everyone sings along). Slammers and beers are the order of the day (and night) at this rambunctious, resolutely un-chic spot.

**Buckhead Billiards** (200 *Pharr Rd.* 404/237–3705) is similarly unpretentious, just a cue-and-brew spot, with sporting events blasting from several big-screen TVs.

A totally different respite is the throwback **Churchill Arms** (3223 *Cain's Hill Place* 404/233–5633), a near-authentic English pub replete with dartboards, Bass on tap, and a 50-ish crowd singing "Johnny Boy" and "Sunny" along with the jukebox.

The older moneyed crowd repairs to its own hangouts. The seniors of the Junior League set—wearing pearl chokers and lingering over afternoon tea—and the power brokers going for broke frequent **The Ritz-Carlton** (3434 *Peachtree Rd., N.E.* 404/237–2700). This is THE place where affairs of all kinds are consummated: on the rocks with a tryst. Tables are discreetly spaced apart (with enough

nooks and turns to confound prying eyes and ears). The
decor is suitably English-manor, with tapestries, piano bar,
and plush armchairs and settees; but you wouldn't be sur-
prised, given the air of staid intrigue, if Miss Marple made
an appearance.

An eclectic, show-offy crowd, including writers and the
people who underwrite them, belly up to the bar at **Beluga**
(3115 Piedmont Rd. 404/869–1090) to order caviar and cham-
pagne. **Goldfinger's** (3081 E. Shadowlawn Ave. 404/
627–8464) is where to take out the Eurotrash, the stogie
stooges, and those who consider James Bond the height of
elegance and decadence. There's plenty of Bond memorabilia, secluded nooks, and a laser-swept dance floor where
30- and 40-somethings pretend to appreciate house.

The A list also makes a beeline to the opulently old-world
**Pano & Paul's** (1232 W. Paces Ferry Rd., N.W. 404/261–3662)
and **103 West** (103 W. Paces Ferry Rd. 404/233–5993), both
celebrity haunts designed in haute bordello decor as conceived by Disney via Nero. A mature, well-heeled crowd
comes to these two places for expertly prepared foie gras,
fried lobster tails, rack of lamb, and ostrich. But their more
subdued yet plush lounges are lesser-known, supremely
civilized places to imbibe. And you can order oysters and
caviar if you've got a mind (and a wallet) to.

# music/clubs

Though Buckhead has plenty of hangouts catering to the
young, rich, and restless, hipper types have long migrated
toward L5P, Virginia Highland, Midtown, and even Down-

town, for entertainment. Hence, Buckhead's club scene is far more relaxed than you'd expect. Sure, there are a few intimidating bouncers (actually they resemble Secret Service agents, with black suits and walkie-talkies), but few venues overflow with creepy nightcrawlers and fashion fascists. It's low-key but high-energy. You won't see anything spikier than ladies poured into spandex looking as if they're auditioning to replace Ginger Spice. What the Buckhead club scene sorely lacks is a sense of irony. The venues would need only klieg lights to resemble a model shoot-'em-out, while the gorgeous waxworks stand and pose or dance in place, flailing their arms like demented sushi chefs.

One observation: Despite the Atlantan penchant for flash, Buckhead loathes anything with a hint of (white) trash. Hence, the surprising demise of the gorgeous Country Star, part-owned by Reba McEntire. But then Country & Western crooning, line dancing, and spangles hit a little too close to (down-)home and roots; it probably would have thrived anywhere else in a town that flaunts its Hard Rocks and Planet Hollywoods. Buckhead doesn't like being lumped in with the lumpen proletariat.

**Tongue and Groove** (3055 *Peachtree Rd.* 404/261–2325) is the closest Buckhead (and Atlanta) gets to steel-hand-on-velvet-rope. The exhibitionistic crowd is unself-consciously exhibitionistic. This is the place to watch local sportscasters with hair replacements hit on lithe, leggy Uma-lookalikes. Specialty nights include Salsa for Gringos on Wednesdays and Ultra Lounge Thursdays with swing and big band; both feature dance lessons. No surprise, you get art openings and fashion shows as well. The decor is beyond striking: pressed-tin ceilings, exposed pipes, billowing posters, handblown gas lamps, mosaic tile bars, screens embedded in walls, and murals. The guys all wear unstructured Armani jackets, swirling their wine glasses as they boogie to the bathrooms; the girls wear clingy black numbers; the DJs get a funky white groove thing going. For all the hipper-than-thou touches (trendoid quotient: a sushi bar adjoins the dance floor) it actually resembles an inflated prom night.

**Bellbottoms** (225 Pharr Rd. 404/816–9669) is just what it sounds like, a complete throwback to the '70s, replete with lighted dance floor, dry-ice fog, disco balls, lava lamps, and gogo cages: A psychedelic, groovy combo of *Saturday Night Fever* (minus the polyester) and "Laugh-In" (minus the tongue-in-cheek).

The triplex **Chili Pepper** (208 Pharr Rd. 404/812–9266) is most notable for its whacked-out, metallic, space-agey interior, including a batting-cage coat check. But DJ Dean Coleman has a loyal, even rabid following for his right-eous hi-energy dance mix Saturdays. Local celeb sightings are frequent in the VIP Lounge; the Downtown views from the Sky Lounge, which offers live music on weekends, are excellent. Thursdays bring out the barely legal crowd, while the Midnight Marauders turn Tuesdays into a hap-pening hip-hop scene.

If you need to be carded, you'll probably be carted off from soigné **Otto's** (265 E. Paces Ferry Rd. 404/233–1133). Thirty-plus is the comfort zone at this piano bar/dance club lifted from the '70s (with attractively up-lifted crowd that remembers disco's halcyon days). The warren of rooms favors overstuffed banquettes, leopard-skin seats, "silver lamé" bar stools, Japanese paper-lantern lamps, and recessed lighting. There's a cigar room, a wood-paneled library with a fireplace, flickering lamps—and real books. The youngsters (anyone under 35) also congregate here when they're in the mood for phenomenal local blues bands.

Want something more sedate? Crosby imitators croon at **Dante's Down the Hatch** (3380 *Peachtree Rd.* 404/266–1600), most notable for its hokey yet fun nautical theme, replete with a "sunken galleon" and real live crocodiles. Hardly an inferno (or paradiso) of activity, though the jazz trios can play the oldies but goodies.

Even the name **Johnny's Hideaway** (3771 *Roswell Rd.* 404/233–8026) sounds like something from a Sinatra tune. Guess what? They may spin the latter-day Boss for a change of pace, but Frank (and Dino and Elvis) still rule the dance floor. Waiters in bow ties, men with ill-fitting toupees cutting some rug, bouffants and beehives, honest-to-God touch dancing, and a suburban crowd celebrating their silver anniversaries all remind you that baby boomers have grownup kids of their own. Johnny Esposito still greets every guest after nearly 20 years. Don't flinch if he kisses your hand; he's just being gentlemanly.

# buying stuff

Gucci-gucci-goo could well be the Buckhead motto; the neighborhood is a paean to our consumer society. You can sow your wild "hautes" in such areas as Miami Circle (one priceless—and pricey—gallery and antique store after another), or in those famed malls, Phipps Plaza and Lenox Square. Atlanta is a boomtown, and Buckhead folk spend as if there's no such thing as going bust. With rare exception, Buckhead is not a place for bargains. It's a bull market where shoppers roam the ritzy-glitzy boutiques and bull-doze through china (and silver and fur) shops. Remember, you're in major Junior/Ivy League territory, where a gold Am-Ex can provoke a look of disdain. So forget the flea-market mentality when shopping here. Unless one of the department stores advertises a sale, this is the place to search out one-of-a-kind pieces at unkind prices.

**antiques...** Home to Atlanta's most venerated antiques dealers, Miami Circle beckons like a crooked come-hither finger off Piedmont Road. Expect high quality and high prices; some showrooms are open only to the trade and those decorators pick them clean. **J. Tribble Antiques** (764 Miami Circle 404/846–1156) features Italian mirrors, 19th-century porcelain, and contemporary folk art (one example: Rosie Clark's "Moo-ed Music," a painting of a cow with musical horns), as well as custom-crafted urns and fireplace facades. **Tibetan Traditions** (764 Miami Circle 404/816–5510) tantalizes with Tantric art (of the yoga and sexual-endurance variety), glorious woven rugs and tapestries, and shimmering jewelry. It's not-for-profit, and most of its proceeds benefit Tibetans in exile, refreshing in a neighbor-hood that generally puts Tony Lama before the Dalai Lama. **Maison de Provence** (764 Miami Circle 404/364–0205) and **Reed & Reed** (764 Miami Circle 404/364–9665) both specialize in French country antiques; the latter also carries English furnishings and a vast array of garden statuary and benches in its maze of rooms. **The Gables Antiques** (711 Miami Circle 404/231–0734) features an extraordinary selection of china and porcelain from England and Asia. **The Flying Crane Gallery** (715 Miami Circle 404/467–8482) specializes in beguiling accessories like kimonos and obis, Frank McGee's walnut and dogwood sculptures as curvaceous as Henry Moore bronzes, Raymond Waites china, and hand-tooled leather items exquisite enough to be family heirlooms.

**books/records...** One house split down the middle provides a tantalizing snapshot of Buckhead's contradictions: Old South versus New Atlanta. On the left side, **Antiquarian Books and Bindery** (2855 Piedmont Rd. 404/814–0220) sports a large sign reading "Old Bibles restored," the appealing aroma of old leather, a sizable rare-book selection, and a clientele that runs toward elderly men with gloriously carved walking sticks and florid moustaches. On the right, the window display of **Oxford Comics & Games** (2855 Piedmont Rd. 404/233–8632) runs toward cut-outs of Marilyn Monroe and her billowing skirt from The Seven Year Itch and the Robot from "Lost in Space." The stacks of cool collectibles include a plethora of movie posters, old and new comics, and videos from Spawn to "Speed Racer."

Otherwise, Buckhead is not noted for its specialty book and music emporia. This is superstore and chain land, though the enormous **Borders** (3637 Peachtree Rd. 404/237–0707) and **Barnes & Noble** (2900 Peachtree Rd. 404/261–7747) both feature ticket outlets for local concerts and events, plush armchairs for checking out the selections, and a good reading roster. The soulless but well-stocked musical equivalents are, of course, **Tower Records** (3500

"*Around Lenox Drive*" 404/264–1217) and **HMV** (3393 *Peachtree Rd. Lenox Square* 404/816–8383), both of which also offer concert tickets. Tower is generally considered somewhat cooler, sponsoring in-store concerts by acts like DJ Honda. Budding musicians might lick their chops at the **Atlanta Guitar Center** (3199 *Maple Dr.* 404/231–5214), a family-run outfit where fellow strummers will help you find the perfect instrument.

**clothes...** **Orvis** (3255 *Peachtree Rd.* 404/841–0093) is a sporting tradition back in Vermont, and a cockeyed shrine to the outdoors. You'll find everything from waders to pith helmets, faux Guatemalan shirts, bejeweled puppy pillows, fly tackle lamps, rubber fishhead puppets, and of course a color wheel of golf apparel. Young suits striving to be the (Hugo) Boss should amble next door to **Men's Warehouse** (3255 *Peachtree Rd.* 404/264–0421) for bargain menswear ranging from Beene to Cardin. Mostly odds, ends, and remainders from the warehouses, it's the closest you'll come to a factory outlet in central Buckhead. Of course, if you prefer fawning, obsequious staffers ready to whip out their measuring tapes, run to **Oxford Street Designer Men's Wear** (3031 *Peachtree Rd., N.E.* 404/262–1486), which carries Armani to Zegna. The staff at **Guffey's** (3340 *Peachtree Rd., N.E.* 404/231–0044) are more likely to dish out guff if you check for price tags on the very conservative lines (Oxford, Cole-Haan, Robert Talbott) here, where even off-the-rack racks up the cost.

Career women and disaffected re-belles make a statement at **Almanac** (22A *E. Andrews Dr.* 404/266–1188): They CAN have it all, from street wear to evening-wear, jeans to jewelry. Here's where younger Buckhead misses mix and match, bending the rules of the couturier's art. **Razzle Dazzle** (49 Ioby Dr. 404/233–6940) specializes in brisk, trim, no-nonsense contemporary designs for women who've set goals and know how to attain them; it's the best casual wear in Buckhead, with bargain basement prices on used Levi's. If you want to go *au naturel* (as in natural fibers), **The Bilthouse** (414 E. Paces Ferry Rd. 404/816–7702) built its reputation on flowing linen and cotton shifts that are both attractive and practical. **Atlanta Beach** (3145 Peachtree Rd. 404/239–0612) is the antithesis of a day at the beach: classical music (you'd think "Song of the Humpback Whale" was a natural, not Pachabel), soft non-UV lighting, plush carpeting, and aromatherapy wafting through the air while you try on your Calvin Klein or Robbin Piccone two-piece. They also sell stylish wraps, lotions, bonnets, and sunglasses. Want to get all dolled up? Then head over to **Cornelia Powell Antiques** (271-B E. Paces Ferry Rd. 404/365–8511), which should be nicknamed Victorian Secret for its frilly, beribboned antique clothes, from tea dresses to christening gowns. But if you've always wanted to look like a debutante or simply the demure mother of the bride, **Susan Lee** (56 E. Andrews Dr. 404/365–0693) is one big swirl of chiffon and taffeta. Scarlett herself couldn't have done better with all the draperies in Buckhead.

## home decor... Melange et Cie (3211 Cain's Hill Place 404/266–3375) recycles "vintage" clothes and accessories into newly minted furnishings, such as pillowcases hand-stitched from old hankies. You'll also find Moroccan teapots, English bath gels, and the unique children's furni-

ture designs (a "barn" bed straight from Old MacDonald's, anyone?) of owners Cheryl Echols and Natalie Brown. **Jeff Jones Design** (25 Bennett St. 404/350–0711) is a treasure trove of objects saved from the wrecker's ball: gargoyles, capitals, friezes galore, that make for dazzling accents in the home or yard. It also carries some fairly priced furnishings (with an especially good selection of Shaker and Mennonite classics). **The Potted Plant** (3165 E. Shadowlawn Ave. 404/233–7080) is the latest venture of Ryan Gainey, Atlanta's garden guru (and consultant to Buckhead's big–lawn crowd). It features everything from patio furnishings to table settings to gardening accessories to flowerpots; Ryan uses a team of in-house artists to decorate, embellish, paint, and glaze each unique item. And **C'est Moi** (3198 Paces Ferry Place 404/467–0095) is a charming little store specializing in Provençal accessories. Even the building's facade imitates an Avignon storefront, with stucco walls and hand-painted shutters. Inside, you can find delightful pottery, exquisite linens, wine glasses, tabletop accessories, adorable little wooden bunnies for the mantel, and dried floral arrangements.

**jewelry and silver...** A diamond the size of a Christmas ornament, anyone? The biggies like Tiffany, Cartier, and H. Stern occupy the malls, but **Richters** (87 W. Paces Ferry Rd. 404/262–2070) has built up a reputation and a longstanding clientele for period antique and fine estate baubles, bangles, and beads from Edwardian to Art Deco. **Jules Jewels** (283 Buckhead Ave. 404/261–5510) offers truly original silver and gold tchotchkes along with "fun art" that can only be described as Gustav Klimt meets

## big food

Forget the Big Apple, Atlanta is the big cheese when it comes to "food art" on public display. Most notable is the Big Fish outside the **Atlanta Fish Market** *(265 Pharr Rd.)*, a leviathan 65-foot steel-and-copper sculpture of a salmon trout pirouetting on its tail. Other factoids: The fish is 100 feet long, three stories tall, weighs 50 tons (more fish than the restaurant has sold in its three years of existence), and was even considered for inclusion in the *Guinness Book of World Records* under a new category: largest fish sculpture. The ultra-fresh fish served inside is small fry by comparison. Not quite as imposing is the Big Chicken, a 30-foot clucker out-side the Marietta KFC that's been used as a local landmark for years (radio ads trumpet "just down the road" or "across the street" from the Big Chicken). And rumor has it one city father quipped, "Once it was a bunch of cockledoodle-doody, but now it's a feather in our cap."

Hanna-Barbera in an unlikely outpost of the original Vir-ginia Highland store.

Resale silver, "all secondhand," is the deal at **The Beverly Bremer Silver Shop** (3164 *Peachtree* Rd., N.E. 404/261–4009). This is Buckhead at its most . . . Buck-headed. It boasts an incredible selection of Tiffany, Sheffield, Strasbourg. Want a silver tray the size of a table?

Paloma Picasso originals? A choice of more than 100 tea sets at any given time? You weren't born with a silver spoon in your mouth? No problem: Drool over hundreds of shoe boxes crammed with flatware odds and ends at sterlingly low prices.

**smoke...** **La Havanita** (3061 Peachtree Rd. 404/846–0765) features Dominican tobacco, Connecticut wrappers, and "authentic" Cuban rollers. Stogies are excellent, and, this being Buckhead, you can even find Belgian chocolate cigars, cognac-steeped Don Julios, and Mike Ditka's personal cigar series (he's a partner). **Edward's Pipe Shop** (3137 Piedmont Rd. 404/233–8082) is owned by a genuine good ol' boy, who sits comfortably in his chair chewing the fat and the tobacco. Great place for fine tobaccos by the pouch, wondrously fashioned pipes from briar to meerschaum (brands like GDB, Rivera, and Peterson) and accessories like Dunhill lighters.

**shopping malls...** The big two, **Phipps Plaza** (3500 Peachtree Rd., N.E.  404/262–0992) and **Lenox Square** (3393 Peachtree Rd. 404/233–6767), are just down the block from one another (though everyone drives between them, even on perfect spring days: After all, as the saying goes, "the best place to park is valet.") Both sport the kind of endless marble floors that make you itch to rollerblade, slaloming around the potted plants, fountains, and proper shoppers. If you shouted, you'd doubtless hear an echo. Lenox is anchored by Neiman Marcus; specialty stores include Nicole Miller, Cartier, FAO Schwarz, Banana Republic, and St. John by Marie Gray (who perfected that aging debutante style). It also offers a few more offbeat boutiques and galleries, including **Gaillard's (404/350–9191)**, showcasing Penny Vincent-George's Zimbabwean-inspired hand-painted pottery, which combines *art naïf* with Cézanne in its startling colors and serene landscape-as-still-life portraits of the veldt.

Phipps is even more shiny, resembling a deluxe hotel lobby with crystal chandeliers, both square cherry wood and graceful white columns, two rotundas, and a domed skylight. Lord & Taylor, Saks Fifth Avenue, Gucci, Abercrombie & Fitch, Jaeger, Dolce & Gabbana, Gianni Versace, Pierre Deux, and Tiffany & Co. set the tone. The concessions to the middle class include outposts such as A|X (Armani Exchange), Doubleday Book Store, Nike Town, and the requisite umpteen-plex cinema. Phipps also offers concierge, babysitting, personal shopping, and fax services.

# sleeping

Even the most prestigious Buckhead accommodations (most, including the Big Four—Ritz-Carlton, Grand Hyatt, Swissôtel, J.W. Marriott—are concentrated near the big shopping plazas) offer surprising bargains, especially on weekends, when the business crowds depart. The area has a smattering of small inns, too, and even the occasional low-on-the-totem-pole motel, but the bulk is business hotels, from high-rise to "suite" deals. Just don't expect that funky little B&B with the dotty owner reminiscing over sherry about the *Gone with the Wind* premiere.

**Cost Range** for double occupancy per night on a weeknight. Call to verify prices.

$/under 75 dollars

$$/75–125 dollars

$$$/125–175 dollars

$$$$/175+ dollars

**Grand Hyatt** (3300 *Peachtree Rd.*, N.E. 404/365–8100 **$$$$**) was originally built as the Nikko, and still attracts a sizable Japanese clientele, as well as young couples looking for a romantic in-town weekend retreat. The GH is as soothing a place as you'll find amid the Buckhead bustle, thanks to the 9,000 square feet of traditional Japanese gardens outside, which conform to the principle of providing a range of environments from hills to riverscapes. (It's maintained by a gardener who flies over from Japan several times yearly.) The rooms are oversized, with all conceivable business amenities; there's also a Baby Hyatt for families, a full-scale health club with sauna, whirlpool, and massage service, an outdoor hibiscus-lined pool, free shuttles to Lenox and Phipps malls, a business center, and the widest range of packages in Buckhead. Jazz brunches at its restaurant, Cassis, are a neighborhood staple.

**J.W. Marriott** (3300 *Lenox Rd.*, N.E. 404/262–3344 **$$$–$$$$**) opens right onto Lenox Square. A synthesis of retreat and business hotel, it epitomizes Buckhead at its most gracious (the uncommonly peaceful lounge is the ultimate comfy drinking spot, with grandfather clocks, oriental prints, brass lamps, crystal chandeliers, and plush burgundy armchairs). Everything is perfectly pitched, from the imposing yet restrained lobby with majestic silver-leaf coffered ceiling, to the good-sized rooms with their period reproduction flair, including Chippendale-inspired pieces, mahogany armoires, gilt-framed paintings of palatial Buckhead mansions, and green marble in the bathrooms.

**The Ritz-Carlton Buckhead** (3434 *Peachtree Rd., N.E.* **404/237–2700 $$$$**), the grande dame of Atlanta hotels, is an oasis of civility, hypocrisy, and everything we love about the South. Exquisite in every way, from the beautifully outfitted staff to the superlative setting, all mahogany, Chinese porcelain vases, hunting prints, genuine 18th- and 19th-century portraits, marble fireplaces (some from German castles), Waterford crystal chandeliers, and handwoven tapestries throughout the "museum-like" public rooms. The smallish but cozy lodgings are Laura Ashley gone Ralph Lauren: frilly and fussy yet masculine. And not only has the signature dining room remained an Atlanta power base, but the more casual cafe serves delectable French fare with flair. Still, this ain't the place to stay if you are easily intimidated. The staff is ultra-polite, but you get the feeling they're sizing you up and down like country-club directors.

The words "striking and spare yet fun public space" sum up **Swissôtel** (3391 *Peachtree Rd.* 404/365–0065 $$$–$$$$) perfectly. There's nothing neutral about this hotel: The look veers from "Jackson Pollock drip" chairs and leopard skin settees to De Kooning clones to the genuine Stellas, Rosenquists, and Henri Cartier-Bresson photos on the walls. Modern Danish meets the firm of Biedermeier, Bauhaus and Gaudí in the geometric lines, sinuous curves, and contrast of woods against black marble and sheets of glass.

Though tariffs at the Big Four are quite competitive (the

Ritz-Carlton offers weekend rates starting at $150 double), Buckhead offers lower-priced options. **Wyndham Garden** (3340 *Peachtree Rd.* 404/231–1234 **$$$**) needs a face-lift, but unexpected elegance—dark wood paneling, crystal chandeliers, and parquet floors—lurks behind its dowdy concrete facade. The carpets, curtains and walls are mostly in faded, or rather muted, colors, but if you want a tony address (the enclave it sits in, Tower Place, even has security guards patrolling the premises) without stratospheric prices, it's ideal "slum" sleeping.

**Terrace Garden Inn** (3405 *Lenox Rd.* 404/261–9250 **$$–$$$$**) may lack the panache of the Big Four just around the corner, but it lives by the two classic hotel mantras: "location location location" and "service with a smile." The sizable lodgings may try a bit too hard to duplicate French Provincial, with colonial touches like four-poster beds in several rooms. The lovely, leafy split-level cafe is a fairly priced, civilized hotel restaurant, while the lounge is as intimate as a ski lodge with its stone-and-copper fireplace. Other facilities, like a state-of-the-art health club and a charming pool with cavorting dolphin fountains please discriminating Euros on a budget.

The Terrace Garden has a little sister, **The Lenox Inn** (3387 *Lenox Rd.* 404/261–5500 **$–$$$**), which enjoys sibling privileges. The pristine motel rooms offer 18th-century repro furnishings, Spectravision TV, steambaths in king-size-bed units, and lots of freebies from local calls to local papers to an airport shuttle.

**Embassy Suites** (3285 *Peachtree Rd.* 404/261–7733 **$$$$**) offers reasonably stylish, centrally located digs hosting a high percentage of families and smaller business conventions. The space is surprisingly attractive: a typical glass atrium setup overlooking a lush interior garden. Suites are sizable, with mahogany and marble accents, light floral prints and still-life artworks. They also offer a full restaurant and both indoor and outdoor pools.

**Summerfield Suites** (*505 Pharr Rd. 404/262–7880 $$$$*) is an affordable, appealing option for families. Perfectly located on the residential fringe, a couple of (serene) blocks away from the bar-hopping madness; there's even a little-known city park [see **doing stuff**] where the kids can get up a ball game or tennis match. The one-bedroom suites are also thoughtfully handicapped-accessible, a surprising rarity in many genteel Atlanta hotels.

Despite its unprepossessing location next to a Mazda dealership, **Marriott Residence Inn** (*2960 Piedmont Rd. 404/239–0677 $$$*) is a pleasant, low-key alternative just a few blocks from the action over on Pharr and Peachtree roads. It resembles an oversized private home in neutral taste. Units are fresh, enormous, and fully equipped with kitchens and washer-dryers. Many have fireplaces. Little extras include barbecue grills and basketball, tennis, and volleyball courts in addition to the requisite pool.

Finally, if you seek an intimate, "European-style" hostelry, there's **The Beverly Hills Inn** (*65 Sheridan Dr. 404/233–8520 $$*), a 1920s apartment building now housing 18 individually decorated rooms with hardwood floors, Oriental rugs, and antique love seats and armoires; some have balconies and kitchenettes. Continental breakfast is served in a tranquil garden room. It doth protest its civility much, and you half-expect to see a lissome debutante appear in a cloud of chiffon in the conservatory, but it's a reasonable, small alternative for the B&B set. True B&B-philes might be shocked by **The Buckhead Bed & Breakfast Inn** (*70 Lenox Pointe Rd. 404/261–8284 $$*), which has the temerity to be located at a major intersection. But pass the portals of the colonnaded building and you'd almost believe you're in a bona fide plantation great house. Each room, either with vaulted ceilings or dormers, is uniquely decorated; beds range from four-posters to brass to sleigh. But bowing to the biz market, units all have a writing desk, fax/modem capability, and TV hidden in the armoire. The elegant dining room is a Chippendale off the old block (or Louis XIV on the block); a peaceful, fully stocked bar with fireplace is available to guests.

# doing stuff

Buckhead, with one major exception, doesn't offer the usual tourist attractions. Of course, merely driving through the tree-lined residential areas, admiring the upscale real estate (the most impressive streets are West Paces Ferry Road, Valley Road, and Habersham Road), or people-watching in the ritzy shopping malls and restaurants qualifies as sightseeing. Oddly enough, for all its greenspaces, Buckhead isn't big on public parks; then again, most residents belong to private golf courses and country clubs, or have a tennis court and pool out back.

**The Atlanta History Center** (*130 W. Paces Ferry Rd. 404/814–4000*) is a beautifully mounted apologia to the Southern legacy of slavery and segregation. In many respects, it's a model summation of the city's turbulent past, with 32 acres of gardens and woodlands, plus period recreations of a 19th-century blacksmith's shop and corn crib, and two structures on the National Register of Historic Places: The 1840 Tullie Smith farmhouse and the grandiose 1928 Swan House—with a magnificent decorative arts collection and a frilly little restaurant and gift shop, both popular with blue-haired bluebloods—also occupy the grounds. A compellingly self-congratulatory air pervades the ultra-contemporary museum space, providing not revisionist history, but interpretation. The videos, exhibits, timelines, and interactive exhibits are all impressively researched and laid out. But as you pass through the various displays, with labels such as "Urban Geography" and "Moral Frontiers," honeyed voices on tape rather hypocritically discuss racial harmony. The black history sections seem to place Martin Luther King Jr.'s efforts and Henry Aaron's breaking the home-run record on equal footing; they're filled with photos of white leaders embracing their African-American counterparts, suggesting that the white business community supported African-American entrepreneurial efforts as far back as the teens of this century (for another perspective, walk through Downtown's Sweet Auburn District). The docents in period dress are avid volunteers, blissfully ignorant of the implicit irony of a museum that both trumpets "the capital of the New South" and wistfully celebrates the good old days.

**Frankie Allen Park** (*Pharr Rd. at Bagley St.*) is a little-known oasis in central Buckhead with free public tennis courts and baseball fields, used primarily by families that are merely well-off.

And the big greenspace—Chastain Park—is technically just north of Buckhead. Beautifully laid out, with everything from public tennis courts to riding stables to an Olympic-sized swimming pool, it also includes North Fulton Golf Course, which is hilly and scenic, with spreading oaks lining the fairways—but not terribly challenging.

## galleries... Fay Gold Gallery (247 Buckhead Ave., N.E. 404/233–3843) is the pioneer in the Atlantan art movement, and Fay is to Atlanta what Mary Boone is to New York. Her enormous space houses very expensive local artists and national names taking their act on the road, as well as print, poster, and litho retrospectives of modern masters like Toulouse-Lautrec (avoid the openings: her idea of canapés is Goldfish crackers). A more subdued atmosphere (and price level) is supplied by **Christina Gallery** (271 E. Paces Ferry Rd. 404/240–0301), which displays everything from concrete slabs masquerading as sculpture to designer beaded and glazed ceramic jewelry. **Art With an Attitude** (309 E. Paces Ferry Rd. 404/842–1913) is something of a misnomer, unless it refers to the patrons. Still, they rep some Southeastern up-and-comers; they do notably better with abstract than with representational art. If you're looking for something recycled, a "found" object, or the most expensive but elegant crafts in Atlanta, sign in at **The Signature Shop** (3267 Rosewell Rd. 404/237–4426), where humble materials such as paper, glass, wood, fiber, and clay are spun into artistic and financial gold. **E. Thomas Gavin Studio** (3115B Maple Dr. 404/239–9228) is an enchanting hodgepodge of anything that catches the owner's eye during his travels: Dalí

prints (those melting watches) wickedly stare down imposing 19th-century grandfather clocks, and works of younger artists animate the walls in a riot of color and passion. Best of all is the tender care given to chipped porcelain and stemware. If you chat with Gavin, his eyes glitter like rhinestones as he explains the story behind each piece brought in for restoration, a Waterford goblet that's a gift from a cherished late aunt or the cracked old plate from a detergent box that someone's father ate dinner off of every night.

If you're feeling creative yourself, saunter over to two pottery stores. **The Painted Biscuit** (247 Buckhead Ave. NE 404/869–0411) is a do-it-yourself studio where you fire your own ceramic ware. You pick out one of various house designs (mostly cutesy, examples are displayed in the windows) or create your own, then they do the final glaze. T-shirts and candles, too. **Wired and Fired** (279 E. Paces Ferry Rd. 404/842–1919) is a less ostentatious, ostensibly more serious version; it even holds regular pottery classes that make for a pleasant escape from the glazed-and dazed-looking hordes rambling outside.

**spectating...**While a glut of bars, restaurants, and clubs offer live music, Buckhead doesn't have major concert venues. Readings are confined to celebrity signings at the superstores and performance art means the mwah-mwah scene at gallery openings.

Still, just outside Buckhead is the 7,000-seat **Chastain Park Amphitheater** (Pool Rd. and Stella Dr. 404/733–4800), Atlanta's loveliest venue. Concerts by acts as diverse as the Atlanta Symphony Orchestra, Kansas, Arlo Guthrie, Gladys Knight, and Julio Iglesias have taken place here, as well as special concerts like Save Tibet (which brought Sheryl Crow and Grant Lee Buffalo). The audiences alone are worth a peek. Some corporations purchase the front sections (replete with fixed seats and folding tables) and provide elaborate spreads for their movers and shakers. The picnics range from fried chicken and cole slaw on paper plates to linen-draped folding tables graced with candelabras.

The other primary concert venue is **The Roxy** (3110 *Roswell Rd. 404/233–7699*), a slightly dilapidated, converted depression-era movie theater, whose offerings run the gamut from touring acts (Robin Trower, Graham Nash) to live boxing.

# body

Welcome to the land of the slim-hipper-than-thou and the collagen-enhanced straight out of college, where bodies are wrapped, not pierced. Can you say makeover? Atlanta supports five major glossy city magazines; three seem devoted obsessively to the body beautiful (and the accoutrements such as gowns and jewelry), regularly including supplements on skin care, plastic-surgery advertorials, and gushy articles along the lines of "My Hairdresser Is a True Artiste." The most egregious are *The Season* (one long list of debutante balls and charity functions), *Jezebel*, and *Peachtree*. Dermabrasion, liposuction, and rhinoplasty are practically rites of passage here. And the nip-and-tuck biz isn't likely to go bust anytime soon, either. Buckhead is emphatically NOT big hair, but it is big-name stylists.

**Carter Barnes** (3500 *Peachtree Rd. 404/233–0047*) is the hoity-toity salon, where regulars are offered a glass of wine upon entering. It's a prime place to spot three generations of true Southern Jeze-belles catting like high-toned Steel Magnolias. Consistently vying in the Triple Crown clotheshorse sweepstakes is **Jamison Shaw Hairdressers** (**3330 Piedmont Rd. 404/262–3777**), whose unquestioned star Pascal Bensimon—formerly director of Manhattan's prestigious Jacques Dessange Salon—goes out on the lecture circuit. The ads gush, "A woman's face is like a painting. Her face is the light and her hair is the shadow. We are the artists and she is our muse." The way his clients (including Fran Tarkenton and Mayor Bill Campbell's wife Sharon) speak reverently of him, you'd swear **Giorgio Ponce de Leon** (**3655 Roswell Rd. 404/364–0195**) had discovered the Fountain of Youth (it spouts Aveda and Biolage); or maybe it's just the hope of rubbing tresses with the music world's stars, since he's an official Grammy stylist. If you're worried about being taken when they take a little off the sides, **Van Michael Salon** (**39 W. Paces Ferry Rd. 404/237–4664**) and **Scott Cole Salon** (**2865 Piedmont Rd. 404/237–4970**) occupy more restrained, lower-profile spaces. Both are noted for good conservative cuts, fine colorists and manicurists, a younger, hipper clientele, and (comparatively) reasonable prices. **The Purple Door** (**3229 Paces Ferry Pl. 404/262–7800**) caters almost exclusively to upmarket African-Americans; hairdresser Dwight is universally considered to be a whiz with kinky hair (wavy-haired white gays flock to him, too). **Nails and Tan** (**310 Pharr Rd. 404/261–0475**) draws leather-skinned, lacquered divorcées, who can't quite afford a nip and tuck job, to a tacky strip mall. A find for excellent silk wraps at a decent price, though.

The two top day spas are **Spa Sydell** (3060 *Peachtree Rd.* 404/237–2505) and **Claiborne's** (3391 *Peachtree Rd.* 404/ 239–9191). The former is a fave of the Buckhead Women's League (the charity chairs); the latter attracts more out-of-towners thanks to its Swissôtel location. Claiborne's has the edge in health-club facilities, including free weights, personalized aerobic sessions, and CV equipment. The peaches-and-cream complexions are best off at Sydell's, whereas image consulting at Claiborne's is more international in scope. Both offer top-notch styling, perms, coloring, facials, waxing, pedicures, manicures, aromatherapy, body wraps (from seaweed to cellophane), and massages.

The grunge set repairs to L5P and Cheshire Bridge Road for metallic insertions and body tracery. But unbelievably, the Atlanta "chain" shop, **Sacred Heart Tattoo and Body Piercing,** has a Buckhead branch (3232 *Roswell Rd.* 404/252–2512). Sacred Heart's owner Tony Olivas and his trained staff specialize in arty black-and-white (take that, Mr. Colorization Ted Turner) and religious-themed designs, such as Modiglianish Mod-donnas that are provocative, and even vaguely, disturbingly erotic.

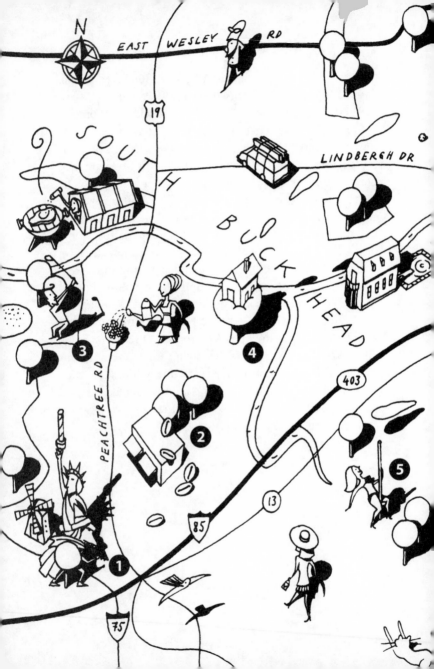

SIDNEY MARCUS BLVD

PEACHTREE CREEK

CHESHIRE BRIDGE RD

# south buckhead

Some neighborhoods, utterly lacking in identity except by comparison to surrounding areas, exist almost in spite of themselves. One example is the aggregate of sleepy, semi-suburban communities south of Buckhead and northwest of Midtown—Peachtree Hills, Peachtree Battle, Collier Hills, and Brookwood Hills—which are slowly being transformed into "South Buckhead," or "SoBuck."

turn page for map key

Judging strictly by the main arteries, Peachtree and Piedmont roads, seemingly one long shiny strip mall, you could be forgiven for thinking this is the kind of place you traverse on your way to or from somewhere more inviting. Actually, ever more yupscale restaurants, shops, and salons rise and fall here with dizzying speed. As Buckhead's business and nightlife boomed in the '80s and '90s, the heat quotient crackled ever southward, gobbling up any and all real estate along the coveted Peachtree Road and turning the entire shaft into a de facto extension of Buckhead itself. Fortunately, the quiet, old, tree-lined neighborhoods noted above still exist, nestled off to the east and west of Peachtree Road's traffic and noise.

Local wags have dubbed the combination of semi-upmarket dining and shopping options and pockets of pleasing, rather high-priced real estate "Buckhead in diapers": an ironic reference to the many second-generation Buckheader yuppies taking their baby steps in home ownership, following in the footsteps of their higher-income parents. After all, where's a self-respecting young Turk— make that two-income couple with tots—to move? Whether you're a native of Atlanta or a corporate transplant, you want some cachet (okay, Elton John lives in one of the futuristic high-rise bunkers along Peachtree, called Park Place). You want proximity to a strip of activity, nightlife, and shopping, but not if it impinges on your

| map key | | |
|---|---|---|
| 1 | R. Thomas's Deluxe Grill | 4 Treehouse Restaurant |
| 2 | Cafe Intermezzo | & Pub |
| 3 | Bobby Jones Golf | 5 The Gold Club |
| | Course | |

cozy "country-in-the-city" lifestyle. A home ITP (Inside The Perimeter), close to the major business areas, is increasingly desirable. It's even the sole white-bread nabe in which some members of the African-American upper-middle class have made inroads (albeit very few), rather than continuing their ascent up Atlanta's east side.

And that's how a bunch of tranquil little areas became the Frankenstein's monster of Atlantan real estate. "SoBuck is entry-level Buckhead," admits one resident. "It will never quite have the poshness and snob appeal." Though transitional in terms of status and paycheck, it's still a marker of success, and an upgrade is expected down the road—or rather up the road, to Buckhead itself. Of course, the boundaries separating Buckhead proper from its upstart sibling are nebulous: Lindbergh Drive, perhaps Wesley Avenue on the north, Northside Drive on the west, Piedmont Avenue on the east, and the I-75/I-85 juggernaut to the south, all bisected by the slash of commercialism on Peachtree Road. You can actually tell from the residential architecture, which, though varied, offers nothing crafted on the truly grand scale of Buckhead, Ansley Park, Druid Hills, or even Marietta. You have postwar ranch-style houses and stone-and-brick apartment buildings along Lindbergh Drive; the sterile skyscraping condominium complexes along Peachtree Road; the more stately residences and well-manicured lawns of the tree-lined Peachtree Battle neighborhood, which branches west from Peachtree Road around the 2300 block to Northside Drive. In the opposite direction, east of Peachtree Road, lie the smaller, attractively landscaped one-family dwellings of the rolling Peachtree Hills neighborhood. (Admit it, you're dazed and confused by all these different Peachtrees—so is everyone else around here.) In this area you also find the unadorned 1940s bungalows of Collier Hills above I-75. Finally, just above I-85 sit the multi-level stone-and-brick neo-neo-neo-Victorian quasi-manses of the Brookwood Hills area, which is centered around Huntington, Palisades, and Brighton roads, branching east off Peachtree near the 1800 block.

Actually, South Buckhead remains quite a nice place to live, and property values shouldn't plummet anytime soon. But it's also a fascinating example of that great '90s sociological phenomenon: The current generation won't improve upon its parents' standard of living. Indeed, more and more people are settling (in both senses of the word) here. Oh sure, this is a sanitized, prosperous, solid, upper-middle class Stepford zone; most of the houses evoke "Father Knows Best" (of course, back then an insurance salesman's salary bought a much nicer home than it does now, while the dutiful wife played homemaker). But South Buckhead is the kind of fast-vanishing neighborhod that America's Chambers of Commerce proudly used to advertise as "a great place to raise a family."

# eating/coffee

Peachtree Road has become one of the city's hottest restaurant districts, especially for those bustling theme yuppieterias that buzz noisily like horseflies for a while, then die off just as quickly. Hence, a few of our recommendations may prove as stale as yesterday's rosemary-studded seven-grain bread, though most are distinctive enough to show promise of sticking around. Fortunately, several established eateries—most sufficiently swank and lively to impress clients and dates alike—have withstood the test of time and trendiness.

**Cost Range** per entree
$/under 10 dollars
$$/10–15 dollars
$$$/15–20 dollars
$$$$/20+ dollars

**american...** Prime rib is the specialty at **MacArthur's** (2171 *Peachtree Rd.* 404/352–3400 **$$$$**) a rather conservative restaurant kowtowing to a mixed but primarily mature, moneyed crowd. The dark wood of the dimly lit vaulted interior is accented by an autumn-gold/pine-green color scheme and a more contemporary open kitchen. While the steaks and chops are choice, avoid anything that looks intriguingly inventive, such as the goopy Shrimp and Cheese Grits appetizer.

In the mood for something lighter or more light-headed? You'll swear you've stumbled upon the garden dwelling of some crazy old eccentric at **R. Thomas's Deluxe Grill** (1812 *Peachtree Rd.* 404/881–0246 **$$**). Multi-colored whirligigs spin atop poles; large birdhouses, dabs of childlike folk art, and oversized carved human figures loom everywhere; and the entire right side of the building is ceded to massive birdcages filled with squawking parrots and other exotic fowl. All this amid the stoic office buildings of heavily trafficked Peachtree Road. . . . The covered patio of this 24-hour zoo sees everyone from corporate bigwigs to grungeniks who look like they'd set off metal detectors. They chomp down on a diverse menu: hearty gourmet burgers, Chicken Piccata, and healthy grub dubbed "Food For Life." Example: the Heaping Bowl of Quinoa, a massive mix of veggies and that trendy Andean brain-like seed topped with tomato sauce for the macrobiotically inclined. Watching some vegan stare disdainfully at a drunk yupster loading up on carbs and eggs at 4 a.m. Sunday morning is worth a trip in itself.

**coffee...** **Cafe Intermezzo** (1845 *Peachtree Rd.* 404/ 355–0411 $$) is a pretentious establishment whose 22-page beverage menu mingles designer coffee drinks with over 50 liqueurs, 20 cognacs, and a bevy of single-malt scotches and ports for, as the staff purr obsequiously, "the drinking connoisseur." The regular menu offers absurdly highfalutin stuff for a java joint (Medallions of Beef Tenderloin, Black Pepper Linguini Primavera), but the display case of 100 pastries (apple pie—sorry, tarte tatin— Black Forest Cake, cannolis . . .) atones for it. Arty pony-tailed, hoop-earrings types wearing black act jaded while puffing on Davidoffs and sipping Cioccoloccino Bianco. The wait staff look as if they're auditioning to be runway models (not that they move anywhere near as briskly). Amusing people-watching, luscious pastries, astonishing beverage selection, gorgeous space (crystal chandeliers, brass tables): the perfect date place . . . for narcissists.

**continental/varied...** The delightful **Lindy's** (10 *Kings Circle* 404/231–4113 $$$) looks as if Laura Ashley had ransacked a Trollope novel for decorating ideas: fringe lampshades, plush chintz armchairs, white lacy curtains, and hand-painted furnishings abound. The patio is just as romantic. Nothing innovative on the menu: just deftly prepared standards like escargots with mushrooms or spinach-and-ricotta ravioli, whose sauces accent rather than overwhelm the fresh ingredients.

Ah, how appropriate a name is **Luna Si** (*1931 Peachtree Rd. 404/355–5993 $$$–$$$$*), owned by two Luna brothers (a third was the original chef, but he got booted for temper tantrums). The remaining siblings aren't exactly lunatics, but they are somewhat quirky for this conservative area. Their flair for creative design is evidenced by the kaleidoscopic graffiti art and multi-hued curtains that hang down to tabletop level, creating a sense of intimacy by "dividing" the space. The entrees, including signature dishes such as Chilled Bouillabaisse, Ginger-Crusted Salmon, and Grilled Chicken, are equally imaginative and immaculately prepared. Adventuresome diners should opt for the "Chef's Four-Course Tasting Menu," a sampler of that evening's more intriguing specials.

Americanized "wrap" places, whether taking their cue from Mediterranean gyros or Mexican burritos, have been all the rage in Atlanta lately, as trendy new establishments compete to "out-gourmet" their neighbors. **Shipfeifer** (*1814 Peachtree Rd. 404/875–1106 $–$$*) is recognized as the grand old patriarch of this fad. Since 1974 it has focused on zesty pita-bread gyros and Middle Eastern standards like falafel and hummus, although the selection has expanded to include such wildly popular items as jerk-chicken or portabello-mushroom wraps. The sizable lunch crowds are just as diverse.

Bearing the slogan "gourmet cuisine of the world," **Paris Market** (1833 *Peachtree Rd.* 404/351–4212 $) is a European-style bakery and delicatessen catering to discriminating palates. The shop is busiest between 7 and 9 p.m., when in-towners stop in to pick up one of over three dozen carefully prepared to-go entrees, such as Maigret of Duck and Shrimp Provençale. The lunch crowd can choose from a small but enticing selection of sandwiches and salads, as well as various cheeses, pâtés, hors d'oeuvres, and quiches. The family-run market also carries a decadent horde of fresh pies, tortes, cakes, and chocolates. Though several small tables are set up near the front of the store, the food at Paris Market is meant primarily to be take-out.

**french...** **Toulouse** (2293 *Peachtree Rd.* 404/351–9533 $$–$$$) is a gem of a brasserie: an enormous loft with a dramatic open kitchen, always percolating with life. The menu fuses Mediterranean and New American influences. A perfect example is a salad of field greens with chicken livers lightly fried in cornmeal, served with apples sauteed in butter and Calvados (Normandy meets N'awlins). And chicken and fish, rubbed with thyme and rosemary, are char-grilled to perfection in the wood-fired oven. Perhaps too noisily upbeat for a date place, but it's wonderfully chummy: It's the spot to go with pals after a breakup, or if you're trying to be friends with your ex.

**italian...** It's easy to spot owner Bob Russo at **Rocky's Brick Oven Pizza & Pasta** (1770 *Peachtree St.* 404/876–1111 $$): He's the big, burly, mustachioed Italian dude prowling around the premises, chatting up customers, sampling the food in the kitchen, or barking at one of his many employees scurrying about. His obsessive attention to detail pays off with more inventive fare than you'd expect from a joint named Rocky's. First, the pizzas (Russo practically introduced the concept of the brick oven to Atlanta): Try the traditional "real" Italian versions such as the white pizza, the "Margarita" (a thin-crusted pie with crushed tomatoes, garlic, and mozzarella), or the "Chicken Bianca Oreganato" pie (the blend of sauteed chicken breast, garlic, lemon, white wine, oregano, and mozzarella and gorgonzola cheeses approaches gourmet status). The lite opera music and flowery painted murals on the stone walls add to the "Italian village" atmosphere, while Russo's "Wall of Fame" near the front door is humorous proof of his gregarious personality and neighborhood popularity. So is the marquee outside, on which he chides local politicians. ("Shame on you, Mayor Campbell" frequently appears in big bold letters.)

**Fratelli di Napoli** (2101 B Tula St. 404/351–1533 $$–$$$$) is nearly always packed, no matter what the night or hour, with an attractive youthful crowd whose boisterous voices fill the cavernous warehouse space. Godzilla-sized family-style portions for two or more add to the jovial energetic vibe as plates clatter amid the chatter. Among the standouts are the spinach salad with toasted almonds, mushrooms, and gorgonzola dressing, Rigatoni with Vodka Sauce, and marvelously zesty, spicy Shrimp Fra Diavolo. Twice-a-month wine tastings bring in a crowd, too. Be prepared to wait.

Billy Petrucci runs the more casual **Pasta Vino** (2391 Peachtree Rd. 404/231–4946 $$). Floral patterns on the large arching windows add to the intimate (only 15 tables) room's European countryside feel. Crisp pizzas bursting with fresh flavors and colors and staples like Eggplant Parmigiana and Seafood Marinara are prepared and presented with consummate flair. And the atmosphere isn't stuffy at all for a place where the service is nearly impeccable. You never feel like you're auditioning for the style brigade.

## mexican/southwestern... Uncle Julio's Casa Grande (1860 *Peachtree Rd.* 404/350–6767 $–$$$) is part of a Texas-based chain that serves filling border-style dishes in an atmosphere carefully designed—right down to the adobe-style walls—to approximate a Mexican hacienda, albeit one inhabited by art-collecting gringo scavengers. The menu features all the standards—tacos, enchiladas, tamales—but ups the culinary ante with such unexpected items as mesquite-grilled frog legs and broiled quail. The wait staff push a house specialty drink called "The Swirl," basically a frozen margarita laced with homemade sangria and layered to look like some carnival ice cream treat. Hey, it does the trick.

**Jalisco** (2337 *Peachtree Rd.* 404/233–9244 $–$$), a tiny 20-year-old family-owned joint in a shopping center at the intersection of Peachtree Battle and Peachtree roads, gets a huge lunch business from Buckhead and Midtown office workers. The grub, while not unusual or extraordinary, sticks to your ribs and the prices are el cheapo. The most popular lunch item is the unimaginatively named "Speedy Gonzales": your basic taco, enchilada, and beans combo for under four bucks. Dinner items include various combinations of *chalupas*, burritos, and the like. The garish, nauseating yellow, green, and orange color scheme (walls, tables, chairs) calls to mind a bad trip on peyote and mescaline, but the effect is softened by tastefully arranged art prints and Mexican pottery. Still, it's fortunate that only beer and wine are served here, not tequila.

Everything at **The Cheyenne Grill** (2390 *Peachtree Rd.* 404/842–1010 $–$$$) is designed "in the spirit of the Old West." Meat lovers will feel right at home: The big items here are steaks, ribs, pork chops, and kebab. Occasional cutesy cowboyisms on the menu (the sandwiches and burgers "ride" with a "sidekick" of Texas fries, coleslaw, rice, or vegetables) bring visions of Frontierland fast food, while a special "Lil' Wranglers" 12-and-under menu drives home the point that this here's a family chuck wagon. If you're looking for a good "Quick Draw" (appetizer, get it?), try a six-pack of Armadillo Eggs—breaded and fried jalepeños stuffed with cream cheese.

For more interesting Southwestern fare, try **The Georgia Grill** (2290 *Peachtree Rd.* 404/352–3517 $$$) named not after our fair state but after the artist Georgia O'Keeffe. This quaint but not quiet bistro specializes in Santa Fe chic, i.e., artfully designed gourmet variations on burritos and quesadillas, like spicy lobster enchiladas and grilled salmon quesadillas on blue-corn tortillas. Fresh ingredients and herbs help make more ordinary selections like the veggie burrito and pork tenderloin fajitas rousing successes as well. An open kitchen adds to the lively atmosphere.

**moroccan...** **The Imperial Fez** (2285 *Peachtree Rd.* 404/351–0870 $$$$) transforms the basement of a drab, musty office building into a sheik's tent, where red and gold tasseled pillows and Persian rugs cover the floor, vivid tapestries are draped across the ceiling, and gyrating belly dancers mesmerize you into a trance. Alas, the five-course meal, including lentil soup, salad, Cornish hen appetizer, and a choice of such entrees as kebab or lamb tajine—flaky pastry layered with raisins and nuts—is tired and overcooked. Still, it's a big spot for politicos and CEOs to schmooze out-of-towners and celebs while ogling the dancers.

**seafood... Fishbone** (1874 *Peachtree Rd., N.W.* **404/367–4772 $$$**) claims to serve "the freshest fish in town"—along with several other eateries, natch. A massive 3,000-gallon aquarium "wall," filled with sharks and exotic fishies, separates the "Piranha Bar" from the main dining area, while sails strewn across the ceiling add oceanic flavor. Speaking of which, the fish (which is never kept in the kitchen for more than 24 hours) is fresh, though you're best off sticking with simple preparations. The wood-grilled varieties work best, with salmon, tuna, and mahi mahi all emerging tender and succulent. Pan-seared grouper, broiled lobster tails, fried catfish, and fried calamari also get high marks.

**vegetarian...** Stuck in an often-overlooked wing of a strip mall, **Cafe Sunflower** (2140 *Peachtree Rd.* **404/352–8859 $–$$$**) dishes out some of Atlanta's best veggie cuisine, culled from various culinary influences. Of special note is the Roasted Vegetable Pavé—asparagus, grilled portabello mushrooms, potatoes, roasted red bell peppers, tomatoes, and Parmesan cheese layered lasagna-style over a bed of sauteed kale. The scrumptious homemade rolls are eggless and seasoned with oregano, thyme, basil and sun-dried tomatoes. High walls are painted in autumn tones while dried floral arrangements in steel vases and disconcerting abstract art give the place a rustic-meets-futuristic atmosphere.

# bars

Unlike central Buckhead, where the streets are flooded with watering holes every few steps, South Buckhead has only a handful of decent bars pouring the spirits. They tend to be more laid-back, cheaper, and shabbier than their neighbors to the north. Not that that's necessarily bad, as experienced drinkers will attest. In addition to the following booze halls, many of the area's restaurants have thriving bar areas; the award for best top-shelf selection of beers, wines, liqueurs, brandies, and liquors goes to **Cafe Intermezzo** [see **eating/coffee**].

Alas, the grand old standard-bearer, The Beer Mug, will close by summer 1999 after 30 years (to be replaced by—guess what—a strip mall!), but **Ken's Tavern (2413 Piedmont Rd. 404/231–5252)** has been operating nearly as long, and looks like it's never had a makeover. The bar's finish is worn and peeling, the brick-red paint on the trim is faded, the ceiling is slightly cracked . . . nope, this ain't no snazzy Buckhead bar, and the patrons are unpretentious, too.

Neither a dingy dive nor a hoity-toity sipping spot, the standard-issue **Central City Tavern (1900 Peachtree Rd. 404/351–1957)** is an innocuous place where anyone would feel comfortable. The large, wooden bar, tables, and fixtures are scrupulously polished, while the servers are friendly and clean-cut. The food's pretty good, too, for a bar—it has a rather extensive menu of sandwiches, pastas, salads and entrees. Beer specials vie for your attention during the week.

In quiet Peachtree Hills, the genteel **Treehouse Restaurant & Pub** (*7 King's Circle 404/266–2732*) allows the SoBuck gentry to escape the rat race of Peachtree and Piedmont roads. Occupying a tiny, quaint, multi-level house, the Treehouse pours more than 70 domestic beers plus close to 30 imports, along with an impressive selection of wines and spirits. Umbrella-covered tables dot the tree-shaded front patio, where potted plants and flowers cover every available nook and cranny. Try the tasty burgers and quesadillas, nontraditional bar bites like grilled salmon sandwiches and jerk Cornish game hen, not to mention a fresh lobster special on Monday and Tuesday nights that ropes 'em in from all over the city.

# music/clubs

South Buckhead is not much of a clubbing area. The few live-music venues of decades past have been replaced by fern bars and restaurants that have little interest in giving up dining space to make room for a stage. And no dance club has come even close to catching on in the area. Oddly enough, however, a few strip joints exist on the fringes—you'll have to be satisfied with watching someone else bump and grind.

Of metro Atlanta's many nude dancing establishments, **The Gold Club** (*2416 Piedmont Rd. 404/233–1210*) is the closest to Buckhead, as evidenced by the impressive line-up

# a walk on the wild side

Cheshire Bridge Road is a nether-netherland that geographically sticks out like a sore thumb—or a middle finger stuck out at convention—from Midtown and Buckhead. Actually, licking its chops at conventioneers is more like it: This is Atlanta's ground zero for cheesy strip clubs, which alternate with car washes, sex shops, the trashier gay bars, and even a few decent long-established restaurants and respectable antiques dealers.

Imagine supping on chicken pot pie and black-eyed peas alongside blue-haired elderly couples and peroxide-blonde transvestites in the 70-year-old **Colonnade Restaurant** *(1879 Cheshire Bridge Rd. 404/874–5642 $$)*, while watching the shifty souls shuffling into nudie bar **Palomino Club** *(1888 Cheshire Bridge Rd. 404/876–9992)* across the street or right next door at the private lingerie "modeling" shop **Naughty Girls** *(1893 Cheshire Bridge Rd. 404/872–2055)*. If G-strings and camisoles are too wholesome, you can check into **The Chamber** *(just off Cheshire Bridge at 2115 Faulkner Rd. 404/248–1612)*. Masters, dominatrixes and slaves unleash their inhibitions at this primarily heterosexual S&M-themed dance club that appeals to clean-cut junior execs who bark orders during the day (but who know what they want at night). Gay fetishists, "daddies," and "bears" will find their own cubbyhole at **The Heretic** *(2069 Cheshire Bridge Rd. 404/325–3061)*.

of limos (size definitely counts here). The women are all immaculate, centerfold-quality specimens of modified female flesh—lots of boob jobs and tanning-bed addicts. The crowd consists mostly of conventioneers from out of town, investigating Atlanta's strip-king reputation firsthand, as well as bachelor parties and your usual Armani-clad yuppies. The club provides shuttle service to and from many of the Buckhead hotels—a good idea when you smell the liquor oozing from the pores of men stumbling out of here at 4 a.m.

**Tattletale** (2075 Piedmont Rd. 404/873–2294), just south of The Gold Club and I-85, offers a kinder, gentler ecdysiast experience. The women are more sociable and look unenhanced, while the bar itself is less pretentious. The usual strip club pitfalls prevail—bad talkative DJ, cheesy lighting—but the cover charge ($5) is half what you'll fork over at The Gold Club, and you'll have more fun.

The Gold Club clings to the eastern extremity of SoBuck; how appropriate, then, that **Swinging Richard's** (1715 Northside Dr. 404/355–6787) hugs the western edge. You figure it out: What's the popular nickname for Richard? Here's a hint: Richie Cunningham it ain't. The boys sometimes peel it all off for a mixed crowd of gays, suburban moms, and executive bachelorette party-goers. And hey, there are even free all-you-can-eat buffets (yes, often including mini-wieners) weekdays from 4 to 8 p.m.

# buying stuff

Unlike Buckhead proper, South Buckhead has no stylish,

high-end malls. This is the land of multi-level strip malls (of which Peachtree Battle Shopping Center is the oldest and best), while several rows of single-story storefronts dot Peachtree Road at various points. Many of these are filled with salons [see **body**] and eclectic art galleries and antique shops [see **doing stuff**]; the latter offer by far the area's most intriguing, upmarket shopping.

### art/gifts... City Art Works (2140 Peachtree Rd. 404/605–0786) specializes in one-of-a-kind functional art and gifts—although "function" seemingly consists primarily of looking cool. Painted ceramics are big here, as are pillows, candles, glassware, and dozens of different varieties of clocks, all rendered in a creative, modern, and even humorous manner. One of the clocks, for instance, is a big dog's head, the whiskers doubling as the hour and minute hands. If it all sounds a little cutesy and pointless, well . . . it is.

### books... Chapter 11 (2091 N. Decatur Rd. 404/325–1505) books are all discounted from 11 to 75 percent off list price; nor is it bankrupt when it comes to selection (though it's hardly as comprehensive as its fellow chain store Barnes & Noble). Chapter 11 also brings in prominent authors and celebs almost every week for book signings. The ultra-bright lemon-yellow color scheme is distracting but unavoidable—it covers every space not occupied by a tome or magazine. Bring your shades to read.

### cds... The **Disc-Go-Round** (2280 Peachtree Rd. 404/351–7005) franchise focuses entirely on used CDs. Unfortunately it displays little discrimination in its stock, which is

good if you're selling (it buys used discs for $1-$5), not so good if you're buying. The tons of titles include multiples of not-so-wonderful one-hit wonders like the Rembrandts and the Holy Barbarians. Most discs run between $5.95 and $7.95, although some are discounted further.

**clothes/new...** The colorful selection of clothes, accessories, and gifts at **Patrick Lindsay** (2391 *Peachtree Rd.* 404/264–9519) caters to the uptown 30ish mom types that pop in during shopping sprees; the taste is decidedly bright, carefree, and flowery. The casual clothes are almost all outfit-oriented: blouses, skirts, slacks, and so forth are put together and sold as complete combinations.

**clothes/vintage...** Some of Atlanta's finest families contribute threads to **The Thrift House of St. Philip** (2581 *Piedmont Rd.*, in the *Lindberg Plaza* 404/233–8652). Folks have been known to line up before dawn when a big shipment comes in, taking a number as if they were buying Braves playoff tix. Once inside, it's survival of the fittest, like a Loehmann's, Macy's, or Filene's Basement sale. Even Junior Leaguers have been known to fight over the goods (generally reckoned to be better than the League's own Nearly New Store in the same complex). If you like boxing matches, stop by. The referee is a take-no-prisoners broad named Rhoda Copus: Throw one too many elbows and she'll show you the hand—and the door.

**miscellaneous...** The name of Richard's Five & Dime was changed to **Richard's Variety Store** (2347 *Peachtree Rd.* 404/237–1412) a few years back, probably to describe the inventory more precisely. The store opened in 1958, and some of the stuff looks like it's been sitting here since then; the stock could qualify as artifacts. Nowhere else in town can you load up on wacky windup metal toys, Asian furniture and birdcages, women's socks and slippers, hammers and screwdrivers, glass piggy banks, greeting cards, and kitchenware. There are also four-foot wooden sculptures of ancient Chinese warriors ($1,600 plus tax takes one home), regarding which the cashier shakes her head and goes, "My boss likes 'em . . . I think they're hideous."

# sleeping

Despite all the restaurants, galleries, and businesses in SoBuck, it's not a big hotel district—yet. But as the expansion and commercialism of Buckhead continue to transform the area, more deluxe hotels and gussied-up motels should pop up. There are a couple of drab transient flophouses that at best evoke nostalgia for one's student backpacking days. The only real hotel opened in the spring of 1998, and it's designed more for the extended-stay business traveler than for the tourist who desires a central location.

**Cost Range** for double occupancy per night on a weeknight. Call to verify prices.
$/under 75 dollars
$$/75–125 dollars
$$$/125–175 dollars
$$$$/175+ dollars

**The Hawthorne Suites** (2030 *Peachtree Rd.* 404/352–3131 **$$$**) offers 80 large, furnished suites complete with kitchen, living area, and bedroom. The rooms are more luxurious than your average hotel, which, consequently, lend them to the traveler who's staying for a longer spell. With HBO, pay-per-view, a VCR, and a Nintendo setup connected to the TV, you'll be distracted from your business chores. Complimentary hot breakfast buffet and evening hors d'oeuvres fatten you up, while the on-site gym and indoor pool slim you down. It's located within walking distance of many of the better restaurants and art galleries, and it offers complimentary shuttle service anywhere within a four-mile radius.

# doing stuff

South Buckhead is home to many of Atlanta's most eclectic art galleries, which feature everything from contemporary landscape painting to interpretive sculpture to pop art to striking photography to multi-ethnic art, often within short walking distance of one another. The layouts are almost virtually identical: blindingly white walls, white track lighting, stone floors, lots of open space. The opening parties are nearly as la-di-da as those in Buckhead; if you look like you might buy something, you can probably weasel your way in. Otherwise, stick to the usual Monday through Saturday, 12 to 5 p.m., routine.

Situated inside an old warehouse across from a power generator just off Peachtree Road, **The Tula Art Center** (*75 Bennett St.* 404/351–3551) is a collective of more than a dozen galleries and studios under one roof, each with its own focus and agenda, including some of Atlanta's most cutting-edge exhibits. For example, **The Lowe Gallery (404/352–8114)** is one of the Southeast's largest galleries, with 12,000 square feet of space. Currently in its ninth year of operation, this internationally lauded space features contemporary figurative and abstract paintings and sculpture from both Southern and national artists. **The Ariel Gallery (404/352–5753)** is an artist-owned and -operated space exhibiting functional ceramics, fiber art, sculpture, and paintings, all affordably priced. **Out of the Woods Gallery** (404/351–0446) is a fine crafts source filled with pottery, wood carvings, metalwork, sculpture, and textiles from a wide swath of exotic cultures. **Opus One Gallery (404/352–9727)** offers vivid stained glass work, sculpture, and paintings in both classic and modern styles, while **The Robert Matre Gallery** (404/350–8399) features mostly figurative paintings by a variety of local and national artists.

Moving over to Peachtree Road, your concept of glass sculpture will likely be shattered at **Vespermann Glass (2140 Peachtree Rd., N.W. 404/350–9698)**. These bizarre, otherworldly, handblown creations astound with dynamic colors and multilayered textures. The sculptures tend toward the abstract, although a few whimsical items (such as a full-sized rocking chair in a recent showing) are inspired by more familiar sources. The main gallery pieces are large and ornamental, but a selection of lower-priced items like jewelry and paperweights make classy gifts for those with smaller bank accounts.

**The Sandler Hudson Gallery** (1831-A Peachtree Rd., N.E.

**404/350–8480)** specializes in contemporary works from local and regional artists in a variety of media, including photography, sculpture, and painting. There's no real theme or focus, just whatever the curators fancy; one-person shows predominate and exhibits usually change every couple of months. Not so next door at **Vaknin Schwartz Gallery** (1831 *Peachtree Rd.* 404/351–0035), where a half-dozen or more different artists are featured at any given time. The emphasis here is on photography and wild pop art.

The contemporary African sculpture in a variety of materials from mahogany to soapstone, mostly from Zimbabwe, at **Kubatana** (1841 *Peachtree Rd. N.E.* 404/355–5764), conveys a deep-seated respect for spirituality and roots. The stone carvings tend to depict humans and animals in abstracted forms. Artists from other cultures are also showcased at **Kiang Gallery** (1923 *Peachtree Rd.* 404/351–5477), where media such as photography, sculpture, painting, paper, and cloth-work are often mixed and matched in thought-provoking fashion. Meanwhile, abstract metal scupture is the focus at **Gallery Domo** (2277 *Peachtree Rd.* 404/603–8703), whose artists hail mainly from Atlanta and New York.

Other things to do in South Buckhead that don't involve eating, drinking, or spending money? Well, **Tanyard Creek Park** (off *Collier Rd., which leads west from Peachtree Rd. at the* 1900 block) is a shady, restful oasis offering a fine opportunity for a creekside picnic. There are softball and soccer fields, too. If you follow the creek across Collier, you'll find an old mill wheel. It was part of Andrew Jackson Collier's Mill, where the Battle of Peachtree Creek was fought during the Civil War.

On the north side of Collier Road lie the rolling fields of the 18-hole **Bobby Jones Golf Course** (384 *Woodward Way* 404/355–1009), a popular public facility. Try imagining the scenes of the battle that occurred over 130 years ago on these hills, and it's a sure bet you'll miss your putt.

As a last resort, you could always plant yourself in front of the population meter on the sign for the high-rise **Darlington Apartments** (2025 *Peachtree Rd.* 404/351–5474) and watch the number increase. The lighted sign, a tacky urban landmark, has been tracking metro Atlanta's population since it was in the mid-100,000s. Now it's well into the millions and rising. The number periodically increases to reflect the nonstop influx into the city. Perhaps if you wait long enough, you'll see it change. Whee!

**spectating...** There just ain't a lot of activity in South Buckhead beyond the restaurants and bars. Most partyers are just passing through for dinner before taking off for the funky clubs of Midtown or the nonstop drinking and dancing in Buckhead. There is a serious dearth of playhouses, performance centers, and movie theaters. Your choices are limited to scanning the local rags and mags for gallery openings with people-watching potential—still, there are a couple of Atlanta rarities: a true multimedia arts center and a comedy club.

Something cool may be going down at **Image Film and Video Center** (75 *Bennett St. N.W.* 404/352–4225) in the Tula Art Center. Image is a nonprofit multi-media arts center that hosts the annual Atlanta Film & Video Festival, but also presents screenings of local and non-local independent films throughout the year in a small viewing room (it

rents spaces elsewhere in the city for larger events). The
fare can range from Japanese animation to gay-coming-of-
age-in-the-South videos.

The jokes are often raunchy at **The Uptown Comedy
Corner** (2140 *Peachtree Rd.* 404/350–6990), a stylish comedy club catering to African-American audiences. No Eddie
Murphy or Chris Rock here, but it does corral some fresh,
lesser-known, touring black talents like Paul Mooney, Alturo
Shelton, Wanda Smith, and Chris Thomas. Despite the party
atmosphere that prevails, there is a strict dress code (no
shorts, jeans, or T-shirts), and this is one of the few clubs
in the city demanding a two-drink minimum. It does a big
corporate business.

# body

You won't find tattoo parlors, piercing emporia, or iron-
pumping gyms along this stretch of Peachtree Road, but
South Buckhead is home to myriad snooty salons that will
style and color your 'do, give you a massage, or perfect
your epidermis. Buffing takes precedence over getting buff.
The clientele is overwhelmingly female and, as the owner
of the typically clean, luxurious **Style Salon** (2293 *Peachtree
Rd.* 404/351–3519) puts it, "professional and upscale." In
other words, the ladies who lunch nip (and tuck) over for
snips and snippets of gossip. Staffers are usually snippy to
walk-ins and obsequious to regulars, but if you have the
dough and want to look immaculate, you'll emerge sassy
and satisfied.

**Junko Hair Studio** (2391 *Peachtree Rd.* 404/814–1827)

has a very minimal, modern look, with icy white walls, sleek track lighting and a smooth, tan hardwood floor. Owner Junko Taniguchi hails from Japan, and due to her visibility in Atlanta's Asian community, the salon attracts a lot of "professional and upscale" Japanese customers— about forty percent of its total clientele. Waxing, highlighting, facials, manicures, and the like are offered along with cuts.

Appointments are required for all services at **N'Seya Salon & Spa** (1935 *Peachtree Rd.* 404/352–7161), a high-end operation catering mainly to "professional and upscale" African-Americans. If you have a lot of time and money to blow and want to float out of the salon competely rejuvenated, submit to a full day's "Greatest Works Package," a $300 deal that includes an aromatherapy hot-oil massage, whirlpool pedicure, cut and style, facial, continental breakfast, catered lunch, and more. Swanky.

Should you tire of all the "professional, upscale" salons and just want an honest man's haircut, there's always the decades-old **Peachtree Battle Barber Shop** (2333-E *Peachtree Rd.* 404/261–9851). Reassuringly old-fashioned, it's one of those musty places where there are only a couple of traditional barber's chairs, all the snippers are older men, and you still see people bringing in little boys for their first haircut. No doubt they get a lollipop after it's all done.

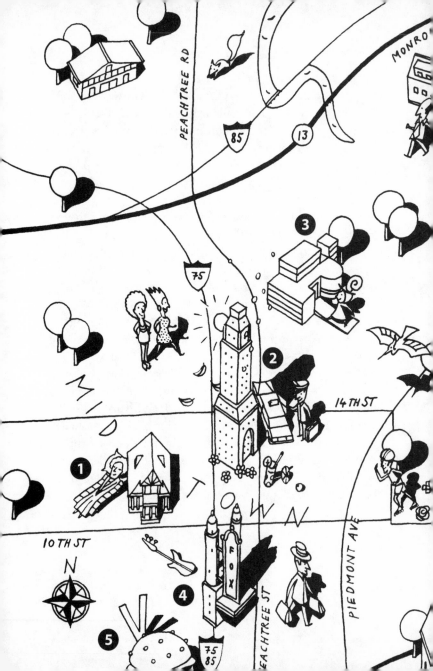

# midtown

Once upon a time long long ago, Midtown was called "Uptown," and it was Atlanta's most upscale address. Stately brick mansions and shade trees lined the major thoroughfare, Peachtree Street, while cotillions and ladies' teas were held in grand ballrooms sparkling with crystal chandeliers and diamond chokers. Remnants of this glorious past linger in the Frederick Law Olmsted–influenced Ansley Park, Atlanta's toniest real estate, and the Piedmont Driving Club, so exclusive it makes even super-exclusive Augusta seem like a melting pot.

turn page for map key

PIEDMONT AVE

6

PONCE DE LEON AVE

But when Atlanta's favorite daughter, Margaret Mitchell (a member of the Driving Club), wrote "The South shall rise again," even she couldn't have envisioned her neighborhood today. Nearly all the grand edifices along Peachtree Street were torn down and replaced by vaulting skyscrapers in Atlanta's single-minded determination to reinvent itself as a modern city in the '60s. And the current population is arguably the city's most diverse, from yuppies with 2.3 kids to flamboyant (or is that flamgirlant?) drag queens. Indeed, Midtown is thriving socially again, albeit in a thoroughly modern way, as a large part of the neighborhood has become Atlanta's gay mecca.

The gay and lesbian presence is highly visible and vocal. Rainbow flags flutter from Edwardian homes and glitzy, neon-streaked bars; RuPaul got her start at Atlanta's most infamous 24-hour club, Backstreet. Every fall, the "Armory Armettes" throw up a "Drag Roadblock" at Piedmont Avenue and Monroe Drive to raise money for local AIDS organizations (the gals are nicknamed for their costumes: May Tag is covered in tags, Flora Fluorescent just lights up the intersection). The nexus of activity is along Piedmont between 10th Street and Monroe. An Atlantan people-watching institution in summer is the Smoothie King on 10th and Piedmont, a magnet for the hunkiest guys. And Sunday brunch on Einstein's patio is a tradition: passing

| map key | | | |
|---|---|---|---|
| 1 | Margaret Mitchell House | 5 | The Varsity |
| 2 | The Four Seasons | 6 | Urban Coffee Bungalow |
| 3 | The High Museum | 7 | Ansley Mall |
| 4 | Fox Theatre | | |

cars, straight and gay alike, honk gaily at the hottest specimens on display. The scene is as liberated and "tolerant" as
the South gets.

But Midtown extends geographically and spiritually well
beyond the gay ghetto (which, incidentally, coexists with
some of Atlanta's prime cultural institutions, such as the
High Museum of Art and the Woodruff Arts Center, as well
as its most colorful night spots). As one resident winks, "Us
queens put pansies in the windowboxes; now of course families are moving in." Not to mention Tech students, buppies,
and hotshot corporate youngbloods. The neighborhood is
an amalgam of phallic office buildings, unprepossessing
apartment complexes, renovated warehouse lofts (and some
fakes), exquisite churches of every denomination, and
quiet Edwardian blocks, interspersed with pockets of green
and an amazing array of public art on display. The architecture and ambience range from the mansions along The
Prado in Ansley Park at one end to the fast-food joints and
seamy bars of Ponce de Leon Avenue (aka "The River Ponce"
for its fascinating flow of oddball human traffic) at the
other, from Richard Meier's High Museum, which looks
like the unlikely progeny of Moby Dick and a telecom satellite, to Rhodes Hall (home of the Atlanta Preservation Society), a grandiose 1904 granite mansion.

Midtown offers definitive proof that Atlanta is more than
just strip malls and strip joints juxtaposed with corporate
headquarters and glitzy homes. It's Atlanta in a nutshell
(pecan, of course), architecturally, socially, and culturally
assimilating everyone and everything that's trickled
through town over the past century. You'll see it especially
at dusk in its true spiritual center, Piedmont Park, one of

America's most beautifully laid out and maintained public parks, designed by the great landscaper Frederick Law Olmsted. That's when Atlanta comes out to walk the dog, from black stilettoed transvestites with Great Danes to imperious grande dames with faces as wrinkled as their shar-peis.

Midtown's borders are relatively clear: Ansley Park and the intersection of Piedmont and Monroe define the north. Expanding the borders a few blocks east of Monroe to Ponce de Leon Terrace sneaks in a bit of Morningside, Midtown's more residential sister nabe and its logical extension. Morningside features mostly single-family dwellings in uncertain '50s taste, older renovated buildings, hideously boxy apartment complexes—and the residents, whether gay, young parents, or old-timers, tend to be cozily "coupled." The western boundary is Howell Mill Road and Marietta Street; while not technically Midtown, this Georgia Tech campus area is an up-and-coming business/residential loft district, anchored by the trailblazing National Historic Landmark King Plow Arts Center.

Most Atlantans would locate the southern boundary of Midtown at Ralph McGill Boulevard. But the Civic Center area really reflects Downtown's hustle and bustle. North Avenue is in fact a more appropriate line of demarcation. Here residents finally took a stand against the city's wholesale modernization. The grand old Fox Theatre, one of those over-the-top Moorish-style movie palaces, was scheduled for demolition in the '70s to make room for the Bell South office building. The neighborhood rallied to "Save the Fox," and the campaign was a defining moment: "New South"Atlanta, spearheaded by Midtown's forward-thinking social quilt, was finally taking justifiable pride in its heritage. Across the street, the lavish 1911 apartment building, the Georgian Terrace (where *GWTW* held its premiere party) has been reconverted into a deluxe hotel. A new wing was added to the original structure in 1996 when it was converted from luxury apartments to a hotel. And forming a magnificent architectural triangle is "The Ponce," another gracefully symmetrical Neoclassical turn-of-the-century apartment building, as upmarket an address as "downtown" Midtown offers. The renovation of these buildings symbolizes the gradual revitalization of the down-at-high-heels area around Ponce and North, once Atlanta's Times Square, now being cleaned up (to the chagrin of some who love its colorfulness).

Hence, North Avenue also defines the neighborhood in a sociological sense. Urban studies experts speculate that it was built as a symbolic barrier to prevent blacks from moving out of the Sweet Auburn district that's to the south. After all, Ponce, just two blocks up, already had eight lanes: Why construct another mini-highway? Fittingly, as a symbol of Atlanta's continuing evolution, no overall discussion of Midtown is complete without mentioning the Freaknik phenomenon. Of the many special events and festivals that clog Midtown throughout the year, Freaknik—essentially, the Atlanta University Center's spring break in mid-April, replete with the usual partying, drinking, harassing single gals on the street—arouses the most controversy. But in truth people's feelings about it transcend sociopolitical, class, and racial barriers. Dyed-in-the-wool conservatives as well as die-hard Trotskyites cringe at the mention of the very word "Freaknik." Granted, Fort Lauderdale is no paragon of propriety. But Midtown becomes one big rave, while residents and businesspeople rant about traffic and crime. Several restaurants actually close for the entire weekend (one manager shrugs, "We lose $3,000 in business daily, but it just isn't worth the hassle; no one goes out anyway"). Despite the efforts of Afro-centric mayor Bill Campbell to brand opposition to Freaknik as racist, even middle-class blacks are embarrassed by the spectacle. It isn't Crips versus Bloods, but it's certainly rambunctious. Nonetheless, Midtown remains Atlanta's most diverse and inclusive neighborhood.

# eating/coffee

No other Atlanta neighborhood offers the quality/value ratio of Midtown's casual, eclectic restaurants. While few Midtown kitchens are as wildly innovative as eateries in Buckhead and Virginia Highland, there are several stylish, adventuresome dining outposts. Many bring creative variations on regional cuisine: Even the gourmet French and Italian eateries slyly acknowledge Southern traditions like mashed potatoes and collard greens in their recipes, giving them a down-home flavor. Otherwise, Midtown offers the apotheosis of American food, calorie- and cholesterol-laden "haute white-trash cooking" that puts meat (ribs and steaks) on your bones. You won't find much ethnic fare, though the Italian and Mexican eateries are among Atlanta's best and cheapest. There are also a few unexpected wild cards, like traditional Cubano sandwiches. Amid the hubbub, the vibe is laid-back, and the ambience conjures up images of rocking on your patio—albeit to a relaxed '90s sound mix. People tend to hang out in Midtown, whiling away the evening happily on the delightful outdoor patios, watching the world go by.

**Cost Range** per entree
$/under 10 dollars
$$/10–15 dollars
$$$/15–20 dollars
$$$$/20+ dollars

## american/southern... John Waters meets June Cleaver in the kitsch-en at **Agnes & Muriel's** (1514 Monroe Dr. 404/885–1000 $$–$$$), a professed paean to white-trash cooking named after the owners' mothers. Glenn Powell and Beth Baskin painted the walls chartreuse, lemon, and hot pink, decorated the place with '50s memorabilia and vintage Barbies, and serve the meals on mismatched china. They swear that every item on the menu comes from a Betty Crocker cookbook (meat loaf, pork T-bones with apple fritters). It's the kind of place that inspires arguments over whether macaroni and cheese is an entree or a side dish.

**The Varsity** (61 North Ave. 404/881–1706 $) is a cherished landmark: You can get car service (Nipsey Russell was once an attendant; look for his autograph), and it's THE spot for chili dogs, onion rings, and fried apple pies; is it any wonder Clinton makes pit stops here? You need a glossary to translate Varsity-speak ("walk a dog sideways, bag of rags" means hot dog, onions on the side, and bag of chips). Dig the walls in red and chrome like a '50s Chevy and the odd murals—a Great Dane picking up a poodle.

There are several rooms, each individually decorated in variations on plastic, stainless steel, and Formica; most are filled with sports fans cheering on their local teams, but also with corporate honchos sneaking a quick break from the Coca-Cola "campus" (offices) across the highway.

**Fat Matt's Rib Shack** (1811 Piedmont Ave. NE 404/607–1622 $–$$) isn't quite in Midtown (it lies a few blocks north of the unofficial Monroe/Piedmont intersection), but you'll find the whole Midtown rainbow there chowing down on mouthwatering ribs. The joint is a shrine to the blues, with photos and posters of B.B. King, Jimmy Rogers, Joe Cocker, and Beale Street, and a large mural of Mount Rushmore in the back, where the president's faces have been replaced by blues and R&B legends such as James Brown. Just as authentic as the barbecue, which is properly smoked in a pit, are the live blues (from Memphis to Delta) bands that play there (no cover). Next door is Fat Matt's Fried Chicken & Fish: same vibe, and same good vittles.

"Recover" Sunday is another Atlanta tradition. Brunch at **Einstein's** (1077 Juniper St. 404/876–7925 $$) is served in three adjoining Edwardian bungalows with a vast linked patio. It appeals to a gay/straight mix, who appreciate its shabbily suave decor and suavely shabby regulars. Besides, the cute, ditzy waiters are Atlanta's chattiest. The interiors are beguiling, each individually decorated (one with portraits of genius Albert and a math equation covering the entire wall, another with Jackson Pollock-y spray-painted tables), but the patio is the choice seating. Signature dishes include Cajun Calamari, Eggs Benedict with fried green tomatoes, Hangtown Scramble (fried oysters tossed with eggs and Asiago cheese), artichoke-and-parmesan dip, and addictive sweet-potato fries. And, the crowd is libidinous, so you're sure to satisfy at least one appetite.

When it comes down to a "best burger" survey, plenty would name **The Vortex** (878 *Peachtree St.* 404/875–1667 $–$$$), as much for its alternative vegetarian patties as its juicy cholesterol-laden hunks of heifer. But the real appeal is its weird decor and clientele, including a motorcycle, glowing skeletons, and rugs hanging from the ceiling and a melange of "types," from suit-and-tie prepsters to butch biker babes. Ignore the overpriced, uncharacteristic attempts at haute cuisine, usually so overcooked they taste like warmed-over takeout from other restaurants.

**Silver Skillet** (200 14th *St.* 404/874–1388 $) is the Atlanta diner par excellence, with grits, biscuits and gravy, and hotcakes dished out (along with advice on your love life) by big-haired, big-hearted waitresses who call just about everyone "Hon."

**asian...** **Tamarind** (80 14th *St.* 404/873–4888 $$–$$$) is sensually decorated in dark woodwork and white stucco, Thai fans, and massive jars filled with unusual ingredients, which the traditionally batik-and-silk-clad wait staff will eagerly explain. The food is delectably authentic Thai, with the ideal amount of heat and sweetness (witness the crispy-skinned boneless duck in lusty Panang curry) entertainingly presented (curried fish cakes crowned with julienne kaffir lime leaves floating in banana-leaf baskets).

Sleek **Nickimoto's** (990 *Piedmont Ave.* 404/253–2010 $$–$$$) certainly deserves the prize for most eclectic menu: Southern, Southwestern, and sushi (thankfully not combined and surprisingly good). Hence specialties include fresh sahimi at the sushi bar, whole sizzling catfish, shrimp enchiladas, stir-fried calamari, and Thai salmon (with lemongrass and coconut milk). Perhaps the novelty explains its wild popularity (there's a Buckhead location as well) with the young and powerful.

**coffeehouses...** At **Caribou Coffee** (1551 *Piedmont Ave.* 404/733–5539 $), guys come in attitude-a-blazin' for their double decaf Guatemalan Italian Roast lattes. Possibly the best gay cruising spot in Atlanta, "bar"none. (Ironically, just 50 feet down on Monroe, a straight-faced parking sign cautions, "No Cruising Zone.")

**Urban Coffee Bungalow** (1425-B *Piedmont Rd.* 404/ 892–8212 $) sports an enjoyably postmodern look, with Gaudi-esque curved steel ceiling and chairs, and nifty maize and sage walls. A fine place to pick up joe to go, along with yummy gourmet sandwiches like artichoke hummus, tuna mango, and the Mediterranean (goat cheese, basil, sun-dried tomato pesto).

**Krispy Kreme** (295 *Ponce de Leon Ave.* 404/876–7307 $), while a chain, is an Atlanta institution. In the wee hours, a tiny neon sign flashes in the window, indicating the donuts are fresh, prompting cars to brake and do U-ies, tires squealing, for midnight munchies.

**creative new southern...** **Food Studio**, in the King Plow Arts Center (887 *W. Marietta St.* 404/815–6677 $$$), makes brilliant use of the former warehouse's old brickwork and vaulted-beamed ceilings, even incorporating old plow machinery into the design. Christopher Brandt's food is just as creative, fusing Southern ingredients with global influences, from Southwestern to Mediterranean to Pacific Rim. Signature dishes include a tequila- and juniper-cured salmon carpaccio stacked between green-chili corn cakes and roasted bell peppers with pickled tomatillo and cilantro crème fraîche. The crowd is an Atlanta mosaic, from elder statesmen in suits to gay couples in form-fitting black Ts and jeans.

**South City Kitchen** (1144 *Crescent Ave.* 404/873–7358 **$$–$$$**) serves stylish upscale Southern food: scrumptious skillet-fried crab cakes with green tomato chow chow and whole-grain mustard sauce, sweet-potato ravioli, and grilled BBQ swordfish on creamy stone-ground grits. Contemporary yet traditional describes everything from the menu to the clientele to the smart decor, which seduces with rotating artworks, an atrium, and a trendily open kitchen. It's always packed, and at these prices, that's not surprising.

# french... Le Saint Amour (1620 Piedmont Ave.
404/881–0300 **$$$–$$$$**) is an adorable dollhouse cottage with uneven food. The warm interior meticulously replicates a little farmhouse, with hand-painted cabinets and tables, mismatched plates, and a cozy wood-burning fireplace in the bar. There are even touches like hanging vintage boys' suits and a library for brandies and cigars filled with steamer trunks and crates. The chefs score with creative dishes like melon "flan" wrapped in ham perched on field greens and rabbit stuffed with garlic and figs in a wild-mushroom reduction over mashed potatoes. But too often the menu settles for such bland (and overcooked) Continental staples as Dover sole *Meunière*. Nonetheless, it's Midtown's most civilized, pampering spot.

**Ciboulette** (1529 *Piedmont Ave.* 404/874–7600 **$$$–$$$$**) defines the gourmet Midtown experience. Like many fine Atlanta dining establishments, it's set in a strip mall, right by a Blockbuster Video. The interior is somewhat dowdy and clichéd, contrasting landscape art and square columns with high-tech mirrors and mosaics. The attractive wait staff are seemingly all would-be models— or counting the minutes before their hot dates. The food, however, is unimpeachable, especially the fish and game, from a bouillabaisse in fennel-leek-accented broth to venison chops with parsnip, haricot verts, and morel sauce.

## hispanic... Kool Korner (349 14th St. 404/892–4424
**$**) is a cramped grocery that makes classic Cubano sandwiches. **Las Palmeras** (368 5th St. 404/872–0846 **$–$$**) is a family-run hole-in-the-wall that shares a stucco-style one-story building with a bodega (where you buy your wine and beer). It's a wonderful low-key date place; those plastic sunflower place mats, a photo of startlingly green Cuba taken from 700 km above the earth, a mural of a beach at sunset, and peeling posters really do evoke old Havana. Chef/owner Maida Alvarez delights with *moros* (beans), *yuca*, and plantains in onion sauce; *boliche* (sausage-stuffed steak); and luscious *ropa vieja* (shredded spicy beef).

**Zócalo** (187 10th St. 404/249–7576 **$$**) is one of Midtown's most festive places. The colorful stucco shack is garlanded with Mexican basketry and ceramics; the patrons could be hanging from the rafters (if the ceiling could stand the pressure) after a couple of their kick-ass margaritas or one of the 20 special tequilas by the glass. Don't expect the usual salsa and chips, but rather genuine dishes from central Mexico like *cebollitas* (grilled green onions), and even *huitlacoche* (a special corn fungus delicacy).

**Raging Burrito** (1529-B *Piedmont Ave.* 404/885–9922 $) can't truly be called a Mexican *taqueria*, as it's Anglo-owned and features gourmet nuevo-burritos like jerk-chicken, not to mention over 25 imported and micro-brewed beers. Still, it's cheap, funky, and yet another great people-watching spot with muscled gay boys and blue-haired 60-somethings mingling cautiously.

## italian... The diverting **Big Red Tomato Bistro** (980 *Piedmont Ave.* 404/870–9881 $$) is wittily design-infected, with tomato-red tables, wood beams, vividly colored glass everywhere, and vibrant rotating artworks. The wait staff are a hoot, scatting along with Ella on the CD, dishing with wild abandon. The kitchen keeps it simple with spinach and gorgonzola ravioli, chicken piccata, and wood-fired pizzas, but also offers specialties like Vidalia onion pie, crabmeat cheesecake (smoked Gouda, parmesan, crab-meat, bacon, roasted bell peppers over wild greens with peach-walnut vinaigrette), and eggplant napoleon.

**Pasta de Pulcinella** (1027 *Peachtree St.* 404/892–6195 $$) should be renamed Pasta de Pagliacci for the clown costumes hanging amid the wood antiques and opera posters. The ambience is as casual as can be, with plenty of hip-but-not-jaded 20-somethings chowing down on pos-sibly the most creative pastas in town. Their specialty is ravioli (stuffed with everything from sausage to Granny Smith apples to portabello mushrooms). The only draw-back is that service is lackadaisical at best: You order at the counter, which doesn't exactly motivate the waiters.

**Veni Vidi Vici** (41 14th St. 404/875–8424 $$$) is Midtown's standard-bearer for Italian cuisine. The enormous room glows with pin lighting dramatically hitting each table, curved columns, towering dried floral arrangements, and stenciled oak floors, and the place seethes with perfectly coiffed power diners. The food deftly salutes various Italian cooking styles (osso buco, veal and cabbage agnolotti, perfectly creamy Piedmont style risotto, Tuscan roasts and grills—slow-roasted suckling pig crackles just right—Venetian gulf shrimp in garlic and Pinot Grigio). If you have to wait for a table—a distinct possibility—there are real boccie courts in back, or you can watch the chefs perform in the exhibition open kitchen.

## steak/seafood... A Midtown fave, **Cow Tippers** (1600 Piedmont Ave., N.E. 404/874–3469 $$–$$$) could well be described as a meat rack in more ways than one. The clientele is fairly faggy and extremely attractive. And boy, does it play up the beef/roadhouse angle. A desert mural with two yuppies running from a bull (and another bull fallen—tipped?) adorns the building. The decor inside is rustic Texas: bull horns and cowboy gear hanging on the walls. The steaks are char-broiled to perfection and quite reasonably priced. Other house specialties include prime rib, Texas Two-Step Chops (pork chops with cinnamon apple sauce), and Miss Kitty's K-bobs (chicken, shrimp, beef, or veggie). Entrees are served with heaping helpings of corn on the cob, baked potato or sweet potato, Texas fries, sauteed mushrooms, etc.

## vegetarian... Eats (600 Ponce de Leon Ave. 404/888–

**9149 $)** is decorated as thoughtfully as a factory, but the functional setting emphasizes the fresh veggie plates served daily, along with amazing jerk chicken and a variety of pastas with intense garlic bread. Nothing is over $6; even yuppies-in-training chow down here.

# bars

Straight, gay, or in-between, Midtown bars are designed for lounging and socializing, preferably with a designer martini or domestic beer in hand. The scene is neither as frenetic as that in Buckhead nor as stream-of-self-consciously arty as L5P. Midtown's feel is a little older if not wiser: "Thirtysomething" meets "Melrose Place." It isn't so much chronological age as maturity, with a dash of jaded sophistication. The guys aren't continually out on testosterone test drives and the gals' biological clocks are on snooze alarm. Most folks are unwinding after work or avoiding thinking about it over the weekend. That's not to say there aren't pickup joints, and certainly the club scene—remember, many gay bars offer drag cabarets and strip shows in the late evenings—offers its wilder moments. But Midtown just seems to invite you to kick back, enjoy the drink, the view, the people. And a crazy quilt they are. So expect to see everyone from well-heeled preppy loafers, to bewigged drag queens, to eyebrow-pierced club kids: anything from high camp to low-key.

Divine decadence is on tap throughout the evening at the posh **Martini Club** (*1140 Crescent Ave. 404/873–0794*), a renovated two-story 1920s residence filled with cushy velvet couches and tile fireplaces, and painted in lipstick colors. The well-heeled, multigendered crowd (think *The Great Gatsby* meets *Wise Blood*) can choose from over 50 oddball martinis and a prize selection of cigars, as the pianist mangles Mozart before segueing into pop, like a jazz version of, say, "Little Red Corvette."

The other lounges don't jumpstart until well after dinner. **Leopard Lounge (84 12th St. 404/875-7562)** is set in a 1920s bungalow gone '50s. It's as comfy as your eccentric uncle's ranch house living room, epitomizing down-market chic. It looks as if it were decorated by both art dealers and tripping drug dealers combined in one: leopard capitals on the columns, leopard-print wallpaper, silver-lamé-covered piping snaking through the stone walls, dolls, thrift-shop art and furnishings, and, in the small basement dance area, crimson walls. There are occasional live swing bands for the new generation of hepcats and java jivers with retro duds and slicked-back hair.

**Nomenclature Museum (44 12th St. 404/874-6344)** has similarly arched (middle)brow decor. Carnelian walls, original brickwork and piping, neon tubing at the bar, love seats galore, campy art so bad it's cool, old mill machinery. At some point, it's virtually the same crowd as the Leopard's, but slightly edgier, as witnessed by the drag acts and Sunday Erotica Nights. There are more dreadlocks, goatees, and shaved heads here; the gay men all resemble George Michael, and you might even see debutantes with Rasta-men. Look for Chuck Morgan's fabulously over-the-top Lure Lounge nights, when Atlanta really does become Manhattan for a night.

Nursing a hangover—or starting one? The oak-shaded

patio of **The Mill** (500 10th St. 404/249–0001) enjoys an enviable location, overlooking Piedmont Park at 10th and Monroe. It's the perfect place for hanging out on weekend afternoons (plenty of people bring their dogs), downing microbrews, scarfing nachos, and commenting on who has the best calves as they bike, blade, or jog by.

**Joe's on Juniper** (1049 Juniper St. 404/875–6634), which has a loyal following for its *moules marinières* and Sunday brunches, is even more notable for its selection of 30 beers on tap (and nearly 100 bottled), 40 different shooters, 10 types of burger, and nutty decor (antique tricycle suspended from rafters, neon pink flamingo). Just down the street from the immortal Einstein's, Joe's features a relaxed, fun-loving, slightly straighter crew.

Don't want a see-and-be-scene? **Prince of Wales** (1144 Piedmont Ave. 404/876–0227) is a homey English-style pub, with wood paneling, lots of greenery, and a brick garden patio. It has a terrific range of ales and stouts on draft, and a distinguished single-malt list. It's tranquil and relaxing, something slightly different for Midtown. The clientele is mostly straight sales reps and corporate sharks of both sexes, but you'll find the occasional assimilated preppy gay nursing his Bass.

**Jocks & Jills** (112 10th St. 404/873–5405) is as good or bad as the name implies: arguably Atlanta's top sports bar, part-owned by former Atlanta Hawks Doc Rivers and Scott Hastings. Lots of sports groupies hoping to brush up against their favorite athlete, corporate softball leagues hoping the same, and your usual coterie of rabid fans (trans)fixed to the large-screen TVs. Someone's guaranteed indigestion, whether from the lethal slammers, the pub grub (chicken tenders, buffalo shrimp), or their team losing. And yes, it's a pickup joint: plenty of junior execs showing saucy professional girls with sly smiles how to hold a cue stick— who's hustling whom?

**Blake's** (227 10th St. 404/892–5786) is Atlanta's foremost gay bar. The crowd is mostly pretty, preening, and conspicuously white. At least it's animated, and not quite as snotty as its rep suggests. The loud music drowns out most conversation upstairs anyway, so just stand, pose, and admire. Forget about the clubby front room, which is classic neighborhood bar with license plates and funny signs: The stools are as prized and hard to come by as Braves season tickets. Instead, go to the second-floor patio or video bar. By all means, ask if Timmy "the Sprout" (so-called for his diminutive size) is pouring. He's liberal: The plastic cups are filled with about 95 percent liquor.

The vibe is friendlier at **Burkhart's** (1492 Piedmont Ave. 404/872–4403), which is packed with the entire rainbow: brooding daddies who casually wear leather jackets; insouciant yuppies; garrulous gym queens; even faboo fag hags in black halters and vinyl boots who inevitably start a movement to the unofficial dance floor. Burkhart's offers a parade for cruising: There's a wraparound balcony for ogling and the crowd isn't the least bit stuck-up. Burkhart's also presents riotous karaoke nights and drag Gospel Girls shows at 7:30 p.m. and 10:30 p.m. on Sundays. It also displays a commendable sense of community spirit, often hanging shows of local artists to benefit AIDS coalitions and the like.

"Can't Keep a Good Hoe Down" is the theme at the rollicking country-and-western gay bar **Hoedown's** (931 Monroe Dr. 404/874–0980), which prohibits "dancing on the tables in spurs," but little else. Decor in the barn is cheeky, with cowhides on the ceilings, farm implements in suggestive positions, paintings of cowpokes leaning against fenceposts hitchin' up their jeans, and a decidedly un-P.C. cigar-store wooden Indian. Ladies are welcome too, and great dance lessons are offered by instructors who seem to be crosses between Richard Simmons and the Marlboro Man.

Leather types usually head straight for The Heretic (aka The Hairy Dick) on Cheshire Bridge Road [see **sidebar** in **south buckhead**] but the **Atlanta Eagle** (306 Ponce de Leon Ave. 404/873–2453) also lassoes them in with regular Hog and Bear meetings (if you think either term refers to animals, you don't belong), and Blackout Parties, where you literally feel your way through the door (and get felt up). There's even an in-house leather shop.

For something in between the preppy and popper sets, **Bulldogs** (893 Peachtree St. 404/872–3025) is the closest thing to a casual neighborhood bar, just a long room with pool tables, frosty beers, and a well-attended Sunday cookout on the deck. Most fashionable gays look down their noses at the crowd, which is merely attractive; Bulldogs also corrals a number of revelers staggering in after a Saturday night at Backstreet [see **music/clubs**].

The pièce de résistance in the lavender world is **My Sister's Room** (931 Monroe Dr. 404/875–6699). It's Midtown's only casually dilapidated lounge-y lesbian bar, with sprung sofas, faux gas lamps, air hockey tables, and embossed wallpaper. As the name implies, it's a lesbian spot, but anyone with a craving for 'tude-free ambience and sounds is welcome. Melissa, k.d., and the Supremes "spice" the mix along with All Saints, Paula Cole, and the soulful yet raw country-and-western balladeer Lucinda Williams.

# music/clubs

Prom queen meets drag queen in the Midtown night. Sometimes they coexist; sometimes they enjoy their own enclaves. The Midtown club scene truly redefines the term "something for everyone." Whatever your style or desire—lewd to ludicrous, Main Line to mainlining, head-bashing to headliners, alternative rock to zydeco—it's here.

Atlanta has a few 24-hour clubs; the most renowned, Backstreet, with its celebrity diva drag shows, lures about as heterogeneous a crowd as exists in town. But the scene is more than mere camp and vamp. Weekends, especially Saturdays, are a true crawl in Midtown, as most revelers hit at least three spots (including some of the bars listed above). At any given time and place, you'll observe various quintessentially '90s looks and attitudes. The terminally jaded and ironic. The disaffected bitter philosophy and Medieval English Lit majors who slave in corporate cubicles. The neo-Flower Power daughters of Lilith Fair. The cobra-tattooed, tongue-pierced heavy-metal addicts. And of course the narcissistic muscle boys and acid-tongued queens.

Midtown's scenes are saucier than Buckhead's and less fiercely posturing than L5P's. This is the nabe where folks are most likely to let their hair down. Midtown adds unpredictability and a scintilla of sleaze that continues north onto Cheshire Bridge Road. There's sexy action under stairwells and discreet sniffing in rest rooms. Still, there are no mosh pits as deranged and violent as your average Jerry Springer installment. And nose candy mostly gives way to the Nutrasweet of alphabet drugs that put the X (and Special K) in Gen-X.

Nonetheless, for all its vigor, Midtown (and Atlanta) are tame compared to international cities such as New York, Paris, even Los Angeles. Perhaps it's the lack of sheer electricity and celeb-spotting (sorry Ted, Jane, Elton, and Chipper, you can't be EVERYwhere). Go too early and the clubs may seem lethargic, but things really heat up after midnight. Few places can rival Midtown's exuberant variety: female boxing and dressy diva drag, foot-stomping grunge and toe-tapping jazz.

A young-to-immortal, male/female/straight/gay/lesbian/uncertain/trisexual crowd flocks to the tri-level **Backstreet** (845 *Peachtree St.* 404/873–1986), which advertises "Always open and pouring"and "We install and service hangovers."It's legendary for Charlie Brown's drag cabaret upstairs (featured on an HBO special), showcasing some of the South's best entertainers. Nominally a gay club, its Saturday night drag show (where RuPaul first worked it, girl!) attracts a very mixed crowd that cheers the raunchy toasts and lines up to tip the gals. Indeed, watching the divas work the ex-college Buckhead jocks trying to impress their girlfriends is worth the price of admission alone. The wild carnival atmosphere includes a Wheel of Fortune, a trophy room for bowling and softball prizes, and numerous dance floors. Where else will you find a lesbian security guard and a gay drag diva carrying on an affair of sorts?

The other big 24-hour club, the quite straight **Club**

**Anytime** (1055 *Peachtree St.* 404/607–8050) is known for its rude, crude, and tattooed dudes and dudettes: all popping muscles and eye-poppingly low halter tops. This black cavern has blue neon signage, a "starlit"ceiling, and crystal disco balls galore. Female kickboxing (and men pounding each other in non-Queensbury fashion in no-holds-barred "Rock and Brawls") lures Roman Coliseum crowds who need to work out their aggressions. Otherwise, the DJ pumps hi-energy dance tracks through the space, animating already stumbling Buckhead youths, strippers getting off work at the Gold and Cheetah clubs (and making frequent trips to the bathroom), and a few distinguished silver-haired gents hoping to get off.

Speaking of those lovely ladies. A couple of men's mags have anointed Atlanta King (or Queen) of strip joints: They're a subculture unto themselves. The highest-rent is the aptly named The Gold Club, just outside the area [see **south buckhead**]. Its closest rival, the **Cheetah Club** (887 *Spring St.* 404/892–3037) certainly isn't cheesy. Unlike The Gold Club, whose regulations are so strict one dancer calls it "Disney with boobs," the Cheetah's ladies are allowed discreet piercings or tattoos; otherwise the physical criteria are just as stringent. They have a sultrier air than their blow-dried Gold Club counterparts, and their gyrations foreshadow the seedier establishments on Cheshire Bridge Road. No Mickey Mouse operation, the Cheetah sees its share of black stretch limos. It's a big bachelor party/take-the-client-out-and-get-him . . . sozzled place. Polaroids and disposable cameras are thoughtfully offered for sale, as well as a wide variety of sex toys in the adjacent boutique.

Rather go gaga over gogo boys? **Metro** (1080 *Peachtree*

**St. 404/874–9869)** features a largely middle-aged, salivating clientele (theme nights include Toy Zone and BoyWatch) from 10 a.m. daily. The dark-dark-dark space, swept by strobe lights and flashing porn videos, has just the right touch of sleaze, with disco music throbbing incessantly and the barely legal boys dancing with glazed, dispassionate, cold eyes.

The gay **Armory** (836 Juniper St. 404/881–9280) is a true rainbow coalition, embracing blacks, Latinos, even a few senior citizens. It's official home to the Armorettes, Atlanta's

## midtown drag queens

Backstreet is legendary for Charlie Brown's drag cabaret upstairs (featured on an HBO special), which showcases some of the South's best entertainers: **Charlie Brown**, "the bitch of the south" (cyber-bitch.com is the club's Internet address); **Shawnna Brooks**, so stunning and affable she has het boys and grandmothers stuffing bucks down her panties; bodacious blond(e) **Raven** (Barbie meets Pamela Anderson meets Vegas showgirl meets tramp); and **Lily White**, "the QUEEN of all unnatural acts" (imagine doing your makeup with a Cuisinart). But don't overlook the more mainstream, *La Cage aux Folles*-y **Armory Armorettes**, who segue smoothly from the Andrews Sisters to the Supremes, with mouths like Roseanne. Or as one regular notes, "It's our answer to Yale: We have the WhiffenPOUFs!"

campiest drag queens, and the Funky Divas, Midtown's premier weeknight entertainers. The bartenders pour some of the stiffest highballs in town at lowball prices, and the DJs spin an excellent pop/dance/hip-hop mix that keeps everyone on their feet. The kind of place where Calvin Klein underwear ads are elevated to high art on the walls, it's a little trashier than Backstreet (though the boys camp it up for the occasional straights who come here to dance the night away).

**The Otherside** (1924 Piedmont Rd. 404/875–5238), just north of Midtown (im)proper, is the big lesbian dance club, but it sees its share of gay boys as well as a few rhythmic straights. The place was bombed a couple of years ago, yet had the cockiness and sense of humor to advertise itself during 1997 Gay Pride with "Have a Blast at the Otherside." It's a big ol' empty barn where you can get down to a surprisingly hip mix of funk, alternative, house, and retro (as one patron wondered hopefully during a Golden Oldies night, "Which Shirelle was the lipstick lesbian?"), as well as decent live bands on weekends.

**Kaya** (1068 Peachtree St. 404/874–4460) provides the most vibrant, varied acts in Midtown. An equally eclectic crowd (including well-toned gym rats of both sexes) bops to live bands up front, or works up an aerobic sweat on the warehouse-y, rave-ish dance floor in back (which features the best guest DJs in town). When the tracks get too intense, you can go to the cool little bistro in front, where improvisational jazz contributes to the retro-Beat feel and the nibbles (seared ahi, pan-fried crab cakes) are surprisingly tasty.

"American Bandstand" meets the mosh pit at **The Cotton Club** (1021 Peachtree St. 404/874–1993), a mid-sized venue featuring standard-issue indie garage rock, as well as name national performers like Jewel, for a mostly mangy, itchy, restless semi-punk crowd. It once favored local alternative crooners, but the clientele is losing its R.E.M.-cloned religion in favor of edgier bands like The Call, or even English neo-crooners like Swervedriver.

Too old for the mosh pit but not ready to retire? Head to **Smith's Olde Bar** (1580 *Piedmont Ave.* 404/875–1522), which has pool tables, jazz combos, and dartboards downstairs and live acoustic and alternative rock music upstairs (bands named Big Ass Truck, Brian Jonestown Massacre, and Superstar Pillow Fight), with the occasional superstar like David Bowie. It's mobbed on weekends by footloose 20-somethings reliving their "I coulda been a rocker" days.

**Yin Yang Cafe** (64 *Third St.* 404/607–0682) is Atlanta's hippest jazz boîte. The atmosphere is warm and inviting, with candlelight and exposed-brick walls hung with rotating artworks. There's a fabulous lounge area in back with plenty of couches strategically positioned for necking or debating the merits of Charlie Parker and Miles Davis. The crowd is refreshingly mixed, all races and ages (there aren't many relaxed places in Midtown where 40-somethings with late curfews can feel comfortable), and the music spans big band to acid jazz to trip-hop to funk.

# buying stuff

Midtown lacks the vast malls of Buckhead and Downtown (indeed, the only major complex is the tired Colony Square), but its chic boutique stores, many in lovingly restored Victorians, overflow with funky gifts and home accessories. The galleries strike the perfect balance between "serious" art at sobering prices and self-indulgent dabbling. Many shops feature marvelous crafts and clothes fashioned by local artists and artisans. There's also a jewel of an outlet mall, a rare beastie ITP (inside the perimeter, or within Interstate 285), called Amsterdam Outlets, which is beloved for its odd little specialty shops.

**antiques... Bel Age Galleries** (1069 Juniper St. 404/888–9307) represents the collecting mania of owner Dr. Stephen Calvert. The place overflows with every kind of trinket and novelty imaginable, from bathroom "thrones" to humidors to Gorham silver trays, as if all of northern Georgia's attics had been emptied simultaneously. On pleasant days, the sidewalk is cluttered like a garage sale, with mismatched mahogany end tables and pea-green chairs like the one in the VW commercial ("dah, dah, dah").

**arts and crafts... Twelve** (976 Piedmont Ave. 404/897–5511) specializes in whimsical handmade furnishings and unusual objets d'art in various media: glazed ceramic ware, wrought-iron Xmas tree stands, paper art, sequined pillows, urban folk art, "poetry boxes," painted mirrors, even Zen-like wheat grass and fresh flower topiaries suspended in Lucite cubes. Not to mention organic goat's milk body bath, essential oils, and chocolates. Owner John McDonald accepts custom orders for duplicates or variations on the unique pieces, and creates art events centered around different themes. **Billy Milner's Candlebar** (970 Piedmont Ave. 404/892–0977) waxes glorious over candles—

60 varieties, from new-mown hay to chocolate mint scents, decorative, votive, dripless beeswax—and candle paraphernalia (slithery, spidery wrought-iron sticks to candelabras taking decorative liberties à la Liberace). You'll also find the necessary romantic accoutrements that go with candlelight, from aromatic soaps to soothing CDs.

**Gado Gado** (549-4 *Amsterdam Ave.* 404/885–1818) sells exquisite Indonesian crafts and furnishings, ranging from handwoven Jepura *ikat* and batiks to Mancoe basketry and Balinese shadow puppets. The drop-dead furniture, including intricately carved four-poster beds and chests, is either antique or recycled teak. **Design Accents** (549-3 *Amsterdam Ave.* 404/892–9832) is a deliriously tacky shrine to plaster. The showroom resembles a rummage sale from the set of Fellini's *Satyricon*, where you can ogle owners Phillip D. Ogle's and David H. Johnson's frolicking nymphs, Michaelangelo "Davids," ram's horns, gargoyles, Pharaohs, obelisks, lions, and cherubs.

**books/records...** The leading alternative store outside L5P is **Earwax Records** (1052 *Peachtree St.* 404/875–5600). It's adorned with wildly hued graffiti; the interior resembles some futuristic *Clockwork Orange/Blade Runner*-esque film set where plastic garbage pails are used as bins for discounted CDs. It's particularly notable for its endless used (sorry, vintage) LP selections, mostly soul, funk, and reggae. Otherwise, house, techno, grunge, hip-hop, ambient, industrial—anything so cutting-edge it draws blood—rule. The very knowledgeable staff looks perpetually stoned. Speaking of alternative lifestyles, **Outwrite Book Store** (991 *Piedmont Rd.* 404/607–0082) is the

spot for queer mysteries, gay/lesbian/bisexual/transgen-
dered historic or sociological tomes, or just plain ol' net-
working with the community. Outwrite also acts as an
unofficial G/L/B/T center, dispensing advice along with a
decent cup of joe (and naturally, several flavors of iced tea)
for those new to town or just the community. Nice coffee-
klatsch feel, friendly staff, and sure, some covert cruising
does go on. For mainstream reading, you can't do better
than **Chapter 11** (1544 Piedmont Ave. 404/872–7986), part
of an Atlanta chain. Not only are best-sellers generously
discounted (30 percent), but top names like David Brink-
ley and Jimmy Carter stop in for the occasional signing,
and the staff (you'll often see them anxiously sneaking a
saucy read themselves) are exceptionally friendly and truly
discerning.

## clothing... Midtown's **Designers Warehouse** (553-3
**Amsterdam Ave. 404/873–2581**) lures a varied crowd of
ponytailed college coeds, lipstick lesbians, and African-
American execs for "church and evening suits,"with the
likes of Harvé Bernard and Barami at 30 percent to 70 percent off. **Shoemaker's Warehouse** (553-12 Amsterdam
Ave. 404/881–9301) may not sell Joan and David or Ferrag-
amo, but it has those ultra-hip New Balance running shoes,
casual Kenneth Coles, Hush Puppies, Frye boots, Stanley
Blacker men's dress shoes, and of course, stilettos in a wide
range of colors for the drag queen on a budget. The clientele is just as eclectic, but be forewarned: The staff doesn't
care if people try on half the shoes in sight in bare stinking
feet. The ultimate one-stop shop for transvestites is **Wendy-
O** (1830 Piedmont Ave. 404/249–7694), which features

delectably gaudy exotic and sensual apparel, from latex teddies to leather jocks, not to mention wigs, cosmetics, and 5-inch heels up to size 14. It's a few blocks north of Midtown proper, but very Midtown in spirit.

# sleeping

Midtown boasts Atlanta's most varied accommodations and clientele. There are upscale chains, business hotels, suite or apartment lodgings, motels, bed and breakfasts, longer-residence Victorian inns. Whether your criteria include complimentary Continental breakfasts, a concierge, convention services, cable channels, romance, history, or state-of-the-art business and fitness centers on site, you'll find it all here.

**Cost Range** for double occupancy per night on a weeknight. Call to verify prices.

$/under 75 dollars
$$/75–125 dollars
$$$/125–175 dollars
$$$$/175+ dollars

The historic **Biltmore Suites** (30 5th St., N.E. 404/ 874–0824 $$$) offers a bit of classic Atlanta stylish-funk. You can't beat the price of these fully furnished and equipped suites with lovely Art Deco fixtures. Every room is a suite, complete with a full kitchen, cable TV (with more channels than most business hotels), and at least one full bath (with marble whirlpool tub). The accents are glorious, with tracery on wallpaper, chinoiserie, hardwood floors, mahogany and cherry wood armoires, brass or four-poster beds, porcelain lamps, interior French doors or other glass walls as dividers, and exposed brick. The duplex and triplex penthouses are delightful, with spiral wood staircases. Several units can be combined for large families and extended-stay visitors. Trompe l'oeil murals in the tiny lobby (being redone at press time) suggest its former elegance (Vivien Leigh, F.D.R., and Eisenhower stayed here in its heyday). They're renovating the hotel's glamorous old ballroom (where Martin Luther King, Jr. gave speeches) and adding meeting space, so prices will likely go up slightly after the $3 million renovation.

The gorgeous **Georgian Terrace** (659 *Peachtree St.* 404/ 897–1991 **$$$**) is a former luxury apartment building where the gala party was held after the *GWTW* premiere; architects added a glass atrium new wing that duplicates the stunning spiral staircase of the original 1911 building (which is in the National Register of Historic Places). Enormous, fully equipped apartments (including washer/dryer, kitchen, and bathrooms larger than many hotel rooms) are ideal for long stays and families, with plush decor in dark wood furnishings, soft beige accents, and Moorish and Renaissance tapestry tracings. The rooftop pool offers skyline views, the fitness room is well-equipped, and the staff is courteous but a bit clueless, as it still struggles to make the transition to deluxe hotel standards and service.

Despite jacking up its prices when it joined the chain, **The Four Seasons** (75 *14th St.* 404/881–9898 **$$$$**), formerly the Occidental Grand, impresses with its air of civility unmatched in Midtown; a soaring oasis of marble and mahogany, you'd swear it was 100 years old, yet it was built in 1993. A $6.5 million renovation in 1998 mostly targeted behind-the-scenes changes, although the lounge and restaurant have been completely redone. The restaurant excels in light Mediterranean-accented food, and also prepares special menus celebrating cultural events, such as bistro-style fare to coincide with the 1998 Toulouse-Lautrec exhibit at the High Museum [see **doing stuff**]. Rooms are oversized, in sepia tones, with light florals and pastels from cream to peach; facilities include a small fitness center, a business center, a free shuttle within a five-mile radius, and proposed additions like a beauty salon/spa.

The **Wyndham Hotel Midtown** (125 10th St. 404/ 873–4800 $$$) is fashioned of Georgia red brick, accented by bronze and glass. Combining the facilities of a business hotel with the amenities and ambience of a deluxe small property, its rooms, many with charming bay windows, feature hardwood armoires, sink-into armchairs and hassocks, and expected extras like TVs, hair-dryers, and coffeemakers. The suites are sweet, with sofabeds, extra TVs and phones, and refrigerators. Top-notch facilities include a vast swimming pool and a fully equipped fitness center, plus a quiet, civilized bar offering several wines by the glass.

**Sheraton Colony Square** (188 14th St. 404/892–6000 $$–$$$) is a large, impersonal, but comfortable business hotel (which also hosts many gay/lesbian events). The look is surprisingly fresh and modern, yet earthy (De Stijl meets Southwest farmhouse): copper-inlaid paintings; halogen and paper-and-wrought-iron lamps; spackled marble coffee tables; and leatherette-look bedspreads in the suites (a good deal for families) and in many standard rooms.

There's plenty of meeting space, a pool and health club, restaurants, and a small mall, but the real attraction for arts lovers and performers is its location, across from the 14th Street Playhouse and a block from the Woodruff Arts Center [see **doing stuff**].

Refugees from the world's Ramadas will find a home at the stately **Ansley Inn (253 15th St. 404/872–9000 $$$)**, formerly the George Mews mansion. The tone of refinement is set in the lobby, with its painted wood ceilings, terra cotta floors, carved oak moldings, crystal chandeliers, fresh floral arrangements, and tile fireplace. The individually decorated rooms in restful hues like taupe, peach, and dusky rose—many with four-poster beds and fireplaces—gleam with mahogany furnishings, lace curtains, and Native American artworks or floral wreaths as accents. New owners Alan and Doris Thompson practically adopt guests and will plan your itinerary if you let them. Cable TV, climate control, private jacuzzis, irons, free local calls, and hair-dryers are among the luxe amenities at commoners' prices.

**Shellmont Bed and Breakfast (821 Piedmont Ave. 404/872–9290 $$–$$$)** is yet another lovingly restored Victorian home, vintage 1891, in the National Register of Historic Places; the exterior is so fussy and frilled-out with bows, garlands, and shells, it resembles a marzipan confection. The owners carefully researched the original colors, wainscoting, stencilling, and period furnishings, then duplicated them with Felix Unger–like obsession. Rooms feature bay or leaded-glass windows, Oriental rugs on pitch-pine floors, and wonderfully carved beds. All four rooms have TV, VCR, and private bath. An inviting verandah out back presides over a lovely garden and fish pond: Victorian Zen.

**Woodruff Bed and Breakfast** (223 *Ponce de Leon Ave.* **404/875–9449 $$–$$$**) isn't as refined as the Shellmont . . . deliberately. The three-story 1906 white brick was transformed by notorious madam Bessie Woodruff in the 1950s into a bordello. Officially licensed as a massage parlor (girls were primly garbed in virginal white nurse's uniforms), it's where many of Atlanta's movers and shakers hung out. Joan and Doug Jones pay tribute to Bessie by gracing the B&B with her name and displaying framed photos, her love letters, and most engagingly, the light boards formerly used to monitor room usage. Only two rooms share a bath (the rest are private), and the TV is banished to the parlor. Otherwise the units are an appealingly funky melange of thrift-shop throwaways and 19th-century English antiques. Some rooms offer stained-glass windows or French doors leading to private porches.

**Midtown Manor** (811 *Piedmont Ave.* **404/872–5846 $**) is a collection of three dilapidated Victorians between 5th and 6th streets. All have glorious cherry wood wainscoting and touches like jade tile fireplaces in the sitting room. The rooms are a hodgepodge; only a few have private baths, but all have unique tasteful touches like ancient washbasins used as flowerpots, fireplaces, shabby antique rockers, painted beds, great moldings, and window seats. These clash invitingly with plaid lounge chairs and ottomans and shag carpet. All feature TV, air-conditioning/heating, and phone. A microwave kitchen is available in each building and there's a coin-op washer/dryer. Since the already low prices are very negotiable with amiable GM Quinn

Richards, especially by the week or the month, extended stays (several transients and/or relocators occupy some of the 60 rooms) are common.

# doing stuff

Midtown's attractions are as varied as its residents. Possibly the best way to experience the neighborhood is to walk, noting how it changes complexion every few blocks. It offers several offbeat museums, as well as the official center of "High Art," the High Museum.

The crown jewel of Midtown is **Piedmont Park**, Atlanta's recreational and social center. Aside from offering biking, in-line skating, and jogging paths with sensational Midtown views, hard tennis courts, baseball fields, soccer fields, and a public swimming pool, it's a joy to wander through, discovering sculptures, fountains, and little ponds. The park was designed well before the advent of the skyline, yet certain times of day the light strikes the lakes just right, reflecting the high-rises. The 12th Street entrance offers a fun playscape for kids designed by Isamu Noguchi as well as the lovingly restored 1911 Ladies' Comfort Station, now a welcome center. **Skate Escape** (1086 Piedmont Ave. 404/892–1292) rents in-line skates and bikes. The park is also home to the extravagant **Atlanta Botanical Gardens** (1345 Piedmont Ave. 404/876–5859), whose 30 acres spiral from woodlands to fern glades to rose arbors to dwarf conifer forests to herb and vegetable patches. The restful oasis includes streams (and peaceful Japanese rock gardens) and statuary throughout, culminating in the magnificent glass Dorothy Chapman Fuqua Conservatory, swept by free-flying birds and housing over 7,000 exotic and endangered varieties from around the world.

**The High Museum** (1280 *Peachtree St. 404/733–4444*), notable for its Richard Meier white-on-white design and the extravagant Calder stabile on the lawn, possesses a fine collection of 19th- and 20th-century American paintings, prints, decorative arts, and photographs (a superb 1998 special exhibit highlighted Walker Evans). Traveling exhibitions lately have leaned toward European masters like Matisse, Picasso, and Toulouse-Lautrec; other cultural institutions often plan their exhibits and performances around the High's schedule (for example the Alliance Theater performed Steve Martin's *Picasso at the Lapin Agile* during the Pablo show). Numerous gallery talks and lectures, as well as a summer art camp for kids, demonstrate its dedication to educating the community.

**The Nexus Contemporary Art Center** (535 *Means St. 404/688–2500*) has been the leading exponent of a new wave of Southern artists such as Scott Colt, Julia Fenton, and Chad Eikhoff for 25 years, and helped jumpstart the revitalization of the warehouse district with its multi-media exhibits, video presentations, and occasional performance-art pieces. Much hipper than the High, it displayed Nam June Paik and Robert Mapplethorpe when they were still considered avant-garde.

The stretch of Midtown along Peachtree between 10th and 15th streets is a veritable outdoor sculpture garden, with noteworthy works including the abstract bronze *Tai Chi* which stares down Victoria Bismarck's *Forgotten Alchemy*, a geometric, blue patina-ed bronze square teetering on a sphere. Other striking works are the steel *Sabine Women* by Dorothy Berge; Steffan Thomas's bulky copper-encased concrete *Trilon*, centerpiece of a pool and fountain; the painted metal *Olympia* by Albert Paley, and *Red* by Tad Streeter. They contrast with the more classical lines of Rodin's *L'Ombre*, the colonnaded *World Athlete's Monument*, and the ethereal yet weighty 25-foot-tall, 4.5-ton *World Events*, by Tony Cragg, an unsettling, cleverly welded spider's web entrapping 125 cast-aluminum figurines.

The renovation of the nearby **Margaret Mitchell House** (*999 Peachtree St. 404/249–7012*) was fraught with nearly as much drama and tension as *Gone With the Wind* itself. Daimler-Benz, no less, paid for the restoration of the tiny apartment building Mitchell referred to as "The Dump" where she lived in her hard-luck days. (The guides here tell you she called every place she lived in a dump. Not so, according to many locals.) Though the center reverently preserves her memory (video and photo exhibits in the main building, a recreation of her apartment, and rotating displays), the original house actually burned down twice during the restoration/recreation: arson both times. Some claim it was a deranged *GWTW* fan who believed Ms. Mitchell would have loathed her indigent period being commemorated. Of course, Atlanta had long ago demolished the original stately house of her childhood in its drive toward modernity. Airheaded "Windies" (think Trekkies with big hair) from around the world, discoursing knowledgeably on such trivia as her near-kinship to Doc Holliday, are a bonus.

Home of the Georgia Trust for Historic Preservation, **Rhodes Memorial Hall** (*1516 Peachtree St. 404/881–*

**9980)** recreates a typically privileged Mitchell-style turn-of-the-century Atlanta upbringing. The Victorian Romanesque granite structure—turrets, battlements, parapets, buttresses—was inspired by Rhineland castles, and possesses a brooding baronial feel. The sumptuous interior features mahogany- and maple-bordered oak parquet floors, a hand-carved Honduran mahogany staircase with stained-glass stairwell panels depicting "The Rise and Fall of the Confederacy," and mosaic fireplaces as well as period furnishings. Predictably, it's often rented out for banquets and weddings.

The admirable **Center for Puppetry Arts (1404 Spring St. 404/873–3089)** details the history of puppetry, showcasing contemporary and antique examples of global puppet art, from commedia dell'arte marionettes to Indonesian shadow puppets to primitive African ritual figurines to original Muppets. The exciting interactive exhibit entitled "Puppets, the Power of Wonder," allows anyone to manipulate various puppets. You and the kids can also enroll in "create your own puppet" workshops, then take in one of the magnificently staged performances.

Anyone familiar with the novels of Roy Hoffman or Alfred Uhry's plays (*Driving Miss Daisy, Last Night at Ballyhoo*) knows that Atlanta has always had a vibrant Jewish community. The impeccably laid out **William Brennan Jewish Museum (1440 Spring St. 404/873–1661)** keeps Southern Jewish culture and heritage alive, with vivid displays (extraordinary quilts stitched for synagogues), panels, and dioramas depicting scenes from classic Sabbath tables, grocery stores, and Ballyhoo (the culmination of the "season" pre–World War II at the hoity-toity Jewish country club). Chillingly effective installations include Holocaust photos embedded in broken walls; the whole effect of the museum powerfully evokes the Jewish experience from 1845 to the present. There's also a vast research library dedicated to genealogy.

Atlanta's major-league sporting venues are located in the Downtown area, but you can hop over to the Georgia Tech campus to watch the perennial ACC basketball powerhouse Yellow Jackets spin and dunk in the 10,000-seat **Alexander Memorial Coliseum** (*10th and Fowler Sts.* **404/894–5000**) or the "Rambling Wrecks" bash each other for the pigskin at 43,000-seat **Bobby Dodd Stadium** (*North Ave. west of I-85* **404/894–5447**).

**spectating...** Diverse Midtown is, fittingly, Atlanta's most versatile neighborhood for performances, offering everything from marionettes to mystery dinner theater. Lavish opera, intimate political theater, improvisational comedy, poetry readings, and the latest hot band in concert can all be found in some Midtown venue. A special note: Music Midtown, one of America's most respected festivals, takes over the area the first week of May. Though it's nominally devoted to jazz, the roster is usually delightfully diverse, encompassing gospel, rock, alternative, reggae, folk, Cajun, swing, and R&B as well. In 1998, acts ran the gamut from David Byrne, Foo Fighters, and Indigo Girls to the Duke Ellington Orchestra, Tito Puente, Dee Dee Bridgewater, and Etta James.

It doesn't matter what's on stage at the glorious **Fox Theatre** (*660 Peachtree St.* **404/881–2100; 404/873–4300**), a National Historic Landmark. The theater is a show in itself, a 1916 Shriner mosque transformed into a classic grand

'20s movie palace (America's second largest, after Radio City Music Hall): an opulent, over-the-top symphony of minarets, arabesque arches, and onion domes, and an interior *Arabian Nights* fantasia of curtains hand-sewn with sequins and rhinestones, a glittering "sky" above the audience, intricate grillwork, beams, even trompe l'oeil balconies and tents, not to mention the world's largest theater organ. It now hosts the **Atlanta Opera** (1998 saw a rendition of Giordano's *Andrea Chenier*), the **Atlanta Ballet**, and major touring shows like *Rent*.

**The Woodruff Arts Center** (1280 *Peachtree St.* **404/733–5000**) is the state-of-the-art facility hosting the **Atlanta Symphony** (with guest artists like Pinchas Zukerman, violinist Joshua Bell, and actress Claire Bloom) and the highly regarded **Alliance Theater**, which has two theaters, one standard proscenium (producing major works such as David Rabe's *A Question of Mercy* and the premieres of Alfred Uhry's Tony-winning *Last Night at Ballyhoo* and Elton John's new Disney musical *Elaborate Lives: The Legend of Aida*), the other a smaller studio space where more challenging works (meaning those by lesser-known playwrights, like Jon Marans's off-Broadway hit *Old Wicked Songs*) are performed.

Georgia Tech boasts an excellent mid-sized concert venue, **The Robert Ferst Center for the Arts** (249 *Ferst Dr.* **404/894–9600**), which books a range of leading acts from Itzhak Perlman to the Waverly Consort, an ensemble group specializing in spirituals and folk-songs of the 18th century.

**The 14th Street Playhouse** (191 *14th St.*) complex offers several "alternative" stages, each highlighting a particular ethnic group: **Jomandi** (**404/876–6346**) specializes in African-American themes, producing new plays such as *Keeping the Faith*, a musical(!) about Adam Clayton Powell, Jr., and classics like Langston Hughes's *Black Nativity*; **Theater Gael** (404/876–9762) showcases Irish, Welsh, and Scottish works (admirable recent productions include Brian Friel's *Molly Sweeney* and Sean O'Casey's *Shadow of a Gunman*) in its tiny black box; and **The Jewish Theater of the South** (770/368–7469) speaks for itself, usually with a sense of humor, choosing such fare as the Allen Sherman musical *Hello Muddah Hello Faddah*. All three offer the occasional newly commissioned work describing the ethnic experience in the South from each perspective, often incorporating oral history, such as Jomandi's tribute to Auburn Avenue (once "the richest Negro street in the world"), *Sacred Ground*.

**Actors Express** (887 W. Marietta St. 404/607–7469) lives up to its name, presenting young thespians on the fast track to success with a varied theatrical diet of new plays and revivals of classics like Shaw's *Candida*.

**Red Light Cafe** (553-1 Amsterdam Ave. 404/874–7828) offers poetry slams, readings, and folkie/acoustic concerts, as well as "finger-pickin'"Delta blues. It's the closest Atlanta gets to recreating the Beat Generation, though the look is postmodern (track lighting, brick red and eggshell walls adorned with disturbingly Schiele/Munch-ian rotating artworks and sleek black-and-white photos). The laid-back crowd lounges in torn jeans, reading alt rags and accessing the Internet.

The Center for Puppetry Arts (see above) delights kids of all ages with magical productions of stories from various traditions, like Aladdin. But it also produces some darker works, edgy latter-day variations on Punch & Judy and commedia dell'arte.

If you want a little improv mixed with intrigue, try **Agatha's Mystery Dinner Theater** (693 *Peachtree St.* **404/875–1610**). The dinner part's a dog, but the audience-participation shows are often a howl, with scenarios ranging from conventional (cantankerous old codgers and missing wills) to Agatha parodies (Marla Marple and Pork Roll Hero . . . get it?) to comical (dastardly doings in pro football).

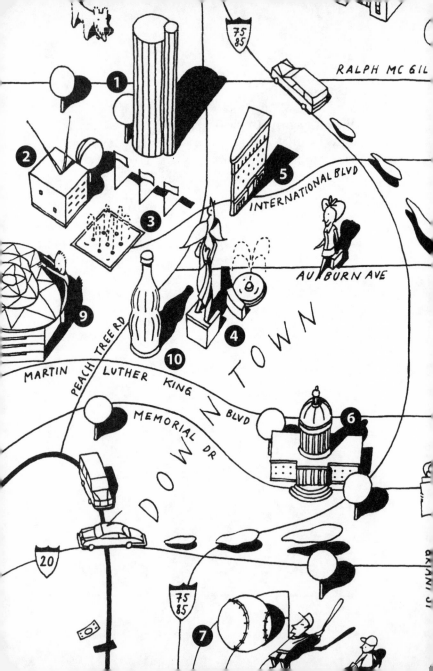

# downtown

Superficially, Atlanta's Downtown is like any other: business district, convention center and tourist magnet by day, deserted wasteland at night, save for wayward expense accounters and ATM doormen. Citizens (who live, comfortably, a mile or more away) talk of urban blight and urban renewal, of presenting a new face to the world. Like any true Southern belle, Atlanta has always sought to beautify herself, getting a face-lift, as good plastic surgeons recommend, before it's necessary. The awarding of the 1996

turn page for map key

Centennial Olympics jumpstarted Downtown's renovation with a vengeance.

The central business district along Peachtree Street was already a fascinating architectural hodgepodge. Colonnaded Neoclassical granite buildings like the Equitable, severe early-Functional Communist-bloc-style monuments such as the Sun Trust Bank, and those dated '60s futuristic cylinders pioneered by John Portman's Hyatt and Westin hotels serenely gaze at their reflections in glassy-eyed Ray-Ban skyscrapers. Only a few blocks away, Mitchell and Washington streets transport you back 75 years, with public buildings such as the gold-domed State Capitol and City Hall, stately churches, and turreted mansions.

When people refer to Downtown, they usually mean the area circumscribed by the CNN area on the west, Trinity Avenue/Memorial Drive on the south, I-75/85 on the east, and Ralph McGill Boulevard on the north. But the expanded neighborhood properly includes the entire Sweet Auburn district (with Randolph Street as the eastern edge), detouring just south of Ralph D. Abernathy Drive to include Turner Field, and bordered on the north by North Avenue, a symbolic moat dividing the old white and black parts of town.

The area is punctuated with miniature greenspaces like

| map key | | |
|---|---|---|
| | 1  Westin Hotel | 6  Georgia State Capitol |
| | 2  CNN Center | 7  Turner Field |
| | 3  Centennial Park | 8  Martin Luther King, Jr. |
| | 4  *Atlanta from the* |    Memorial |
| |    *Ashes* statue | 9  Georgia Dome |
| | 5  Flatiron Building | 10  World of Coca-Cola |

Robert W. Woodruff Park. Every empty lot is graced by saplings, courtesy of the enterprising grass roots organization Trees Atlanta, which can't leave concrete well enough alone. And artworks, many installed for the Olympics, sprout everywhere: metal sculptures that appear to have emerged from a demented trash compactor; even solid, all-too-representational quasi-fascistic figures (the austere, winged *Atlanta from the Ashes*).

This isn't even factoring in Turner Field (former Olympic Stadium now home to the Atlanta Braves) to the south, or the CNN/Centennial Park area on the western edge, where the Omni Dome was imploded in 1998. As this was being written, a state-of-the-art basketball/hockey/concert arena was being constructed which will be connected to CNN Center and Georgia World Congress Center by an atrium lined with stores and restaurants. Just when you thought the Downtown skyline was cast in stone (or glass or concrete), something new happens.

Downtown also abuts the southside, along Atlanta's ghetto; though run-down, its Sweet Auburn district, which witnessed the rise of the black middle class and was later galvanized by a homegrown preacher named Martin Luther King, Jr., is undergoing a mini renaissance, with new museums and libraries dedicated to the black experience, as well as the hulking shell of the new tabernacle, almost the size of a small sports stadium, being built by King's Ebenezer Baptist Church parish across the street from the original church.

Once purely the domain of convention hotels and office buildings, Downtown is very slowly developing as an up-and-coming residential area. Young families and professionals are renovating lofts and warehouses in dicey deserted sections, as well as small tract houses near Turner Field, while the CNN area promises to serve as a hub for future Downtown residential buildings.

Still, after dark, Downtown holds the eerie hush of sudden evacuation, conjuring thoughts of mace and Saturday-Night Specials. Several new residential spaces have risen around North Avenue, but they're virtual security compounds. Most retail development still clings to busy, bustling Peachtree Street; entrepreneurs with vision hope that by mining that strip, more people will be lured Downtown at night, creating a domino effect on its residential desirability and viability.

Just before the Olympics, mindful of safety amid fears about the high crime rate, the Downtown Improvement District introduced the "Atlanta Ambassador Force." Volunteers in outlandish outfits escort lost visitors to their destinations and proffer help with evangelical zeal; they even leave notes on windshields ("Don't leave your laptop on the seat").

# eating/coffee

There are several notable restaurants in Downtown, and they range from spicy fusion to down-home American cuisine. Otherwise, Downtown remains Conventionland, where hotel dining rooms rule (often from sky-high aeries). A few bastions of the three-martini business lunch linger. Most other restaurants think turnover, doing a brisk lunch and tourist trade with menus more gormless than gourmet. Mall food courts gobble up the rest of the market. Atlantans simply don't go Downtown to party or dine, so eateries here are better suited to a quick happy hour puupuu platter or buffalo wings with drinks after work.

**Cost Range** per entree
$/under 10 dollars
$$/10–15 dollars
$$$/15–20 dollars
$$$$/20+ dollars

## american... Max Lager's Brew Pub (320 *Peachtree St.* 404/525–4400 $–$$) occupies a beautifully converted old warehouse. The stunning upstairs features exposed brick, piping, old wrenches, murals of barley and hops, and towering copper vats. The deck offers smashing views of Downtown. Reliables include Cobb Salad, wood-fired pizzas, and whiskey shrimp in red chile tomato sauce over fettuccine. Max Lager's attracts well-groomed professionals; owner Alan Le Blanc hopes it will become a linchpin for further Downtown revitalization.

**Thelma's Rib Shack** (302 *Auburn Ave.* 404/523–0081 $), set in a teal-and-magenta shack just across from the I-75/85 underpass, is more subdued and comfortable; the ribs, collard greens, and black-eyed peas are sublime.

**Mick's** (228 *Peachtree St.* 404/688–6425 $–$$), part of a local chain, draws a diverse bunch for comfort food with a regional edge: Chicken pot pie, ribs, meatloaf, fried green tomatoes, redundantly named items like Chicken and Penne Pasta, and crayfish soup with andouille dip. Picture windows and white indoor umbrellas contribute to its airy feel.

**Johnny Rocket's** (*Underground Atlanta, 50 Upper Alabama St.* 404/525–7117 **$**) is a diner shrine, with '50s jukeboxes and red naugahyde and chrome like a snazzy '59 Impala. It advertises serving "the original hamburger," whatever that means; might as well stick to that here—it's at least superior to Mickey D's.

## portable atlanta

Looking for a take-home souvenir party pack? Try this:

***Gone With the Wind* beach towel**

**Krispy Kreme jelly donut**

**Coca-Cola keychain**

**some kudzu for your garden**

**wild mushroom grits**

**Eddie's Attic T-shirt**

**bootleg Five Rings Varsity pin** (interlocking onion rings banned by the Olympic Committee)

**Westin Hotel postcard**

**Atlanta Braves baseball cap**

**an *Atlanta Journal-Constitution***

**a CD by any of the following:** (Publisher is not responsible if these albums cause you to lose your religion): REM, the Indigo Girls, B-52s, Black Crowes, 3 lb. Thrill, Michelle Malone, Vic Chestnutt

**this book**

Amazing, isn't it, how every local outpost of **Hard Rock Cafe** (215 *Peachtree St.* 404/688–7625 $–$$) and **Planet Hollywood** (218 *Peachtree St.* 404/523–7300 $–$$) seem cookie-cutter yet distinctive. The former sports the usual Michael Jackson *Thriller* platinum album. The latter invites gawking at a Bruce Willis cop uniform, a Charlie Sheen military getup from *Hot Shots*, in addition to Tom Hanks's college football uniform from *Forrest Gump* (okay, it's a neighboring Southern state). Oh, yeah, the food. Well, every Hard Rock somehow manages to turn out hefty-heifer burgers while every Planet Hollywood dishes out fair nachos.

**asian...** **Hsu's** (192 *Peachtree Center Ave.* 404/659–2788 $$) is utterly stunning, with pagoda-style ornaments, huge Ming-y vases, and Chinese artifacts displayed dramatically in fan-shaped niches. Dishes, such as textbook Peking duck, are presented with similar flair and flourish. But deep-fried catfish in ginger scallion sauce and specials like ostrich skewers, a good ol' boy playing maitre d', blood red walls, and an upscale biz clientele make it more confused than Confucian when it comes to authenticity.

**continental...** **Dailey's** (17 *International Blvd.* 404/681–3303 $$–$$$$), set in a converted warehouse in the Central Business District, screams corporate takeover in progress. The upstairs playfully displays carousel horses alongside the exposed brick walls, but no one's clowning around—serious deals go on in between expertly prepared but doggedly Continental dishes like escargots in puff pastry with wild mushrooms and filet mignon in Cabernet butter sauce. Come here after dinner for the decadent fried ice cream, or savor the 1960s ambience downstairs—all martinis, cigars, maroon leatherette booths, and Sinatra CDs.

**fusion...** The super-hot **Mumbo Jumbo (89 Park Place 404/523–0330 $$$–$$$$)** is a feast for all the senses, with a better dance mix than most discos in town, a cozy upstairs lounge, a bar from Central Casting for the "I'm too sexy" extra crowd, and explosively witty, multitextured Gothic cathedral decor. The cavernous space retains an intimate feel, thanks to carefully spaced tables and high ceilings that absorb sound and make eavesdropping impossible. Resisting easy labels, the very talented Shaun Doty, a protegé of Atlanta über-chef Guenter Seeger, utilizes only the freshest ingredients, stewing them in their own juices, so dishes detonate with their natural flavors.

**italian...** **Azio Downtown (229 Peachtree St. 404/222–0808 $$)** is bright and breezy, with Lichtenstein-and-Warhol-meet-Matisse artworks, bright tiles and vases, and a clubby feel. Bypass the undistinguished traditional pastas in favor of spinach walnut ravioli.

# bars

Frankly, it's a case of the bland leading the bland. Most mall and hotel bars cater to the after-work happy-hour crowd carrying over the latest watercooler conversation or celebrating a Braves win; anyone bored and restless in their hotel room; just barely legal mall rats in jeans and reversed caps; or a bunch of Shriners and proctologists on the loose. Even the pickup scene needs a pick-me-up, or at least a Coca-Cola caffeine/sugar rush.

No self-respecting international city lacks a restaurant/bar with a spectacular panoramic vista. Atlanta's contribution is **Sun Dial Restaurant, Bar, and View in the Westin Hotel** (210 Peachtree St. 404/589–7506). The glass elevators that zoom up the side like a Disney ride and the views of the city and the North Georgia mountains *are* jaw-dropping.

Imagine: Atlanta has not one but two revolving eateries. **Polaris** (265 Peachtree St. 404/577–1234) sits atop the Hyatt Regency like a neon-blue flying saucer; on gloomy, foggy nights it almost holds the spooky promise of alien abduction, with the palpable loneliness of the occasional business traveler and a few pod people waiting for the mother ship to come and take them home.

You won't sight Shaq, André, Joe, or Wayne, let alone Bruce or Ah-nold at the Atlantan branches of the ubiquitous **All Star Cafe** (270 Peachtree St. 404/589–8326), **Hard Rock Cafe** (see above), or **Planet Hollywood** (see above). You're also unlikely to spot many folks over 25; it's mostly kids around the legal drinking limit, tourists who don't know any better, and perhaps, a predatory young exec hoping for a quick after-work connection.

The boisterous **Champions** (265 Peachtree St. 404/588–6017) in the Marriott Marquis is the jock's tabernacle, with more than 25 TV screens tuned to everything from curling to hurling, as well as numerous athletic video games and pool tables.

**Jocks & Jills** (CNN Center 404/688–4225) and **Hooters**

(*Underground Atlanta, 50 Upper Alabama St. 404/688–0062*) function as sports/singles bars; hormone levels increase exponentially with each sunk putt and blasted dinger. Scoring takes on double significance. These places are where people go to celebrate winning the Super Bowl pool.

Jazz trios play weeknights in the dark, plush lounge at Daileys [see **eating/coffee**], a private-men's-club-meets-Irish-pub kind of clandestine meeting place where you expect conventioneers to get fresh with their secretaries under the tables.

Sunday nights at the **Sweet Auburn Bar & Grill** (255 *Auburn Ave.* 404/523–0800) jump with Ricky Andrews and his Band ($2 "admission charge"). Otherwise, it epitomizes the neighborhood hangout, with old-timers arguing over Dr. King and younger brothers grousing about job opportunities or staring glassy-eyed into the mirrored walls.

Best happy hour (at least most cheerful) goes to **Rio Bravo Cantina** (240 *Peachtree St.* 404/524–9224) and its Margarita Madness; sop it up with decent burritos, fajitas, and nachos.

# music/clubs

Since the opulent, wigged-out Velvet was transformed into Mumbo Jumbo back in 1996 (a fair trade), Downtown has sorely lacked a dance club to galvanize the nabe at night; there's certainly nothing happening likely to make the gossip columns. So forget about boogying, unless perhaps it's a fox-trot with your grandmother or tapping your foot to a live band. In fact, the only revelers Downtown are refugees from prom night or conventions. As for music, no tribal, trip-hop, jungle, art rock, political rock, house, techno, Latin, or psycho-billy. Just jazz, rock, maybe some blues, soul, and funk in Sweet Auburn on the occasional Saturday night. Sorry.

Hard Rock Cafe [see **eating/coffee**], brings in local bands of the "college-paper-gave-us-raves-we-no-longer-play-bar-mitzvahs-and-weddings-and-we're-this-close-to-a-record-deal" variety. It merits mention in this section only because every so often someone tries to shimmy on the guitar-shaped bar. ✓ odd & wonderful

**Dante's Down the Hatch** (60 Upper Alabama St. 404/577–1800) is a replica of an 18th-century frigate, surrounded by a crocodile-filled moat and sporting nutty nautical touches like ships' steering wheels and ropes. While hardly a swinging experience, the music thankfully isn't a crock: mellow jazz standards rather than sea chanties that have drawn celebs ranging from Count Basie and Bill Cosby to Jimmy Carter.

# buying stuff

All the world's a mall and all the men and women merely shoppers. They have their exits and their entrances . . . especially those malls connecting to the CNN Center and Omni Hotel or the Marriott Marquis, Hyatt Regency, or Hilton. Virtually every mid-cost name-brand store can be found in the Downtown malls, along with a few specialty boutiques. Essentially, Downtown is one big retail and white sale, with a couple of independent la-di-da galleries, and a few funky stores selling dashikis and revolutionary manifestos.

## shopping malls/department stores... The

tri-level **Mall at Peachtree Center** (*Peachtree St. & International Blvd.* 404/654–1296) is the biggest, most elegant shopping complex south of Buckhead. It even contains nearly half of the decent restaurants in the Downtown area. **Brooks Brothers** (404/577-7221), purveying that patented "well-dressed man-nequin" look, sets the tone with parquet floors, oriental rugs, and gold doors. **Papillon** (404/525-8437) carries Versace, Jerry Garcia, and Nicole Miller toothpaste tubes. **Atlanta Tobacco and Coffee** (770/252-3626) is fragrant with imported cigars like Davidoff, Macanudo, Upmann, and Romeo y Julieta, and filled with power smokers indulging themselves or searching for the perfect business bribe. **Harmony Kingdom** (404/577-3740) specializes in tchotchkes, Swarovski crystal, and body lotions. **A Touch of Georgia** (404/577-6681) offers pecan brittle, peach preserves, and a potpourri of sachets and T-shirts celebrating the state. **B. Dalton** (404/577-2555) carries everything on the best-seller lists, as well as a fine selection of Atlanta-specific tomes. **Architectural Book Center** (404/222-9920) glorifies John Portman, the architect of the Mall at Peachtree Center, but it pays to stop in for building-block books from history to how-to. **Successories** (404/521-2040) features motivational success stories, offering seemingly every book, tape, calendar, and homespun sampler bursting with good advice, cheer, and affirmation ever made.

**The Atrium at CNN Center** (*Marietta at Techwood*

404/827–2300) is a shrine to the Atlanta Braves and Turnermania. The major outlets it houses are, predictably, **The Braves Clubhouse** (404/523–5854), with autographed bats and balls and your favorite player's jerseys, and **The Turner Store** (404/827–2100), where you can buy sweatshirts emblazoned with Turner Broadcasting logos and, since Ted owns the MGM library, classic movie tie-ins (*Gone With the Wind* beach towels!). It's a bustling space featuring fountains, endless escalators, and Olympics artwork that makes bad artwork look like Edward Hopper. An ongoing major redesign in 1998 as part of Turner's merger with Time Warner will create more office and retail space. Although the shops and eateries lack variety, they have anticipated every need, including a cineplex and even a police precinct. (Psst, Ted & Jane have an apartment in the adjacent Omni Hotel.)

Cheesy, touristy **Underground Atlanta** is a mall that tries to evoke nostalgic flair, with its pushcart vendors, old Coke billboards, exposed brick, fleur-de-lys ornamental embellishments, cast-iron columns, classic autos, even an Old Georgia Railroad car outside. Alas, the effect is destroyed by such utterly mundane modern shops as **The Gap** (404/522–0027) and **Foot Locker** (404/659–8479). There are a few intriguing boutiques, like **Kandlestix** (404/688–7102), where you can watch the candlers wasting their talents fashioning wax into frogs, swans, crescent moons, and Greco-Roman figurines.

The Downtown **Macy's** (180 *Peachtree St., N.W.* 404/221–7221) is an exquisite 1920s red brick building with surprisingly simple but stylish and striking window displays. Otherwise it's a standard Macy's.

**miscellaneous...** **Walter's Clothing** (66 *Decatur St.* **404/688–8859**) offers unbelievable buys on Hush Puppies, Reeboks, Filas, and Adidas, as well as baseball caps and sweatshirts, for the largely student and African-American clientele. There are also priceless "pimp" leather shoes the color of orange NeHi soda pop.

Head for **Lynne Farris Gallery** (105 *Grand Lobby, Hurt Building* **404/688–7311**) when you crave art in Fauvist hues, traditional landscapes, or painted screens. Prices are outrageous (not surprising, given the magnificent space in the Hurt Building). The salespeople discreetly size you up as a potential patron, making the simplest "Can I help you?" sound dismissive.

**Treehouse Records** (186A *Auburn Ave.* **404/521–9205**) appropriately features jungle, trip-hop, ska, and gospel (which often filters into the street, giving it an almost 1960s "Twilight Zone" feel).

**Tijara** (370 *Auburn Ave.* **404/753-7824**) is a Muslim store selling prayer rugs, artwork, oils and incenses, dashikis, and tomes on Black Power and the Koran.

# sleeping

Welcome to Convention(al) Land. Downtown hotels (especially those designed by John Portman, who pioneered the modern atrium concept) are partly responsible for creating one of the nation's more distinctive skylines. They're actual sightseeing attractions, with dramatic hanging sculptures in the lobbies. Small cities unto themselves, many offer 24-hour dining options, ATMs, fully equipped gyms, and access to the MARTA metro and major malls. These include the Western Hemisphere's tallest hotel, the Westin; Portman's first atrium-style effort, the Hyatt Regency, whose deliciously dated glowing blue roof screams *Independence Day* or *War of the Worlds*; and the Marriott Marquis, with its glorious atrium and plum-hued fiber sculpture hurtling 50 stories from the skylight to hang suspended just over the lobby. Of course, there are times when conventions overwhelm the big six (Westin, Marriott Marquis, Hyatt Regency, Omni, Hilton, Ritz-Carlton), but weekends as in all convention cities offer dramatically decreased special rates. Unfortunately, most of the smaller, mid-chain properties are soiled and thread-bare, or are located in slightly seedier parts of Downtown.

**Cost Range** for double occupancy per night on a weeknight. Call to verify prices.

$/under 75 dollars

$$/75–125 dollars

$$$/125–175 dollars

$$$$/175+ dollars

The class act, predictably, is **The Ritz-Carlton** (181 *Peachtree St.* **404/659–0400** **$$$–$$$$**), which, though constructed in 1984, recreates bygone opulence. The public rooms—with marble floors, Persian rugs, silk tapestries, 18th-century portraits and hunt paintings, and mahogany walls—look as if Fred and Ginger might waltz by in evening dress, or better yet, as if a "society matron" like Margaret Dumont in pearls is about to be assaulted by Groucho. A perpetual air of afternoon high tea pervades, and their restaurant serves good food for a hotel eatery. The understated yet sumptuous rooms, many with bay windows and four-poster beds, feature mahogany furnishings and marble baths; amenities include turndown service and terry robes. The courteous staff seem to have been trained to speak in cultured library whispers.

At **The Hyatt Regency,** (265 *Peachtree St.* 404/577–1234 $$–$$$$) the elevators resemble glowing pods rising to meet the startling blue rooftop restaurant spacecraft. Like all the huge hotels, the impersonal lobby is dominated by hanging gardens (a Portman signature) and enormous abstract artworks, most notably *Flora Raris*, the world's first indoor atrium sculpture, a metallic abstract flower soaring several stories. Rooms are oversized, in restful teal, dusky rose, and jade, with porcelain lamps and smart Ikea-style furnishings. Between its two towers, everything is at your disposal: a fitness center, sports and cigar bars, gourmet restaurants (Avanzare serves fine Italian), Delta airline ticket office, MARTA entrance, etc.

**The Westin Peachtree Plaza** (210 *Peachtree St.* 404/ 659–1400 $$-$$$) is the famed Portman hotel: Two glass cylinders resembling high-tech grain silos. The lobby is a perfect example of how he utilizes interior space to striking geometric effect: circles within squares, freestanding marble columns, and crystal chandeliers strategically catching the light contrast with oak bars and plush sofas. Rooms are decorated in understated pastels with walnut armoires and headboards. The Savannah Fish Company located here offers uneven seafood and indifferent service, but the stunning 100-foot waterfall makes it worth a detour. At least it's less expensive than the obligatory rotating price-gouging restaurant, Sun Dial (good for drinks though; see above).

**Suite Hotel Underground Atlanta** (54 *Peachtree St.* 404/223–5555 $$$) sounds unpromising, but it's one of Atlanta's better-kept (in all senses) hotel secrets. Though part of the cheesy Underground Atlanta complex, it's light years removed in taste. The top ten stories were added to a 1918 office building, but the interior eschews historic folderol for contemporary luxury, with cherrywood furnishings, subtle earth tones, abstract prints, and marble baths.

**Howard Johnson Suites** (330 *Peachtree St.* 404/577–1980 $$–$$$), formerly the Biltmore Peachtree, underwent a complete renovation in 1998, at which time an executive level (with data ports at work desks and bigger TVs), a corporate meeting space and a garden fountain were added. The formerly drab, dreary rooms were brightened with rich mountain colors like jade and maroon. "Suites" is an exaggeration, however: The 94 units are mostly standard large rooms, each with a microwave, coffeemaker, and fridge, and a walk-in closet with iron, ironing board, and hair dryer. It's ideally located and quite affordable; avoid it if you loathe screaming families or dazed kids in from the boonies.

Along one of the ugliest stretches in Atlanta, **The Hampton Inn** (759 *Pollard Blvd.* 404/658–1961 $) is typical of the sterile, anonymous, low-end chain properties abutting Turner Field, seemingly catering almost exclusively to Braves groupies and regional conventions. It's clean, harmless, extremely affordable, offers free continental breakfast and local calls, and boasts marvelous views of the highway. You need a car, since you're in deadsville.

# doing stuff

Downtown is Atlanta's true tourist center, with everything from museums to memorials, a baseball field to Baptist churches. Some attractions are deliriously cheesy, others urban oases. Since Downtown is so compact, just take a stroll and watch how its complexion changes from urban blemishes to stately government buildings.

The Washington/Mitchell area, with its church steeples and the Capitol's gold dome reflected in nearby skyscrapers, is a soothing respite from Peachtree's hustle-and-bustle. The Ro-cuckoo 1926 **City Hall** (68 Mitchell St. no informational tel. number), whose gilt ceiling and lavish marble staircases evoked scandalized cries when it was built—and earned it the affectionate moniker "Painted Lady"—faces a tranquil little park with a bronze statue of William Talmadge, a repro Liberty Bell, and the Sri Chinmoy Peace Tree.

Just down the block is the 1889 **State Capitol** (206 Washington St. no informational tel. number), which houses unmemorable history and agricultural museums; free tours weekdays (at 10 a.m., 11 a.m., 1 p.m., and 2 p.m.) are regrettably as boring as those used as setups for comic turns or intrigue in any generic film. Still, the 237-foot ceiling of the rotunda, lined with busts of prominent Georgians, is suitably imposing.

Ask the grizzled doorman to let you peek at the remarkable lobby of the 1930 **William Oliver Building** (32 Peachtree St. no informational tel. number), converted into prized loft apartments, with ram's-horn friezes, a dazzling mural of an abstract starry night, and ornate carved wood ceilings.

Various corporations have commissioned and installed artworks inside the **Georgia Pacific Building** (133 *Peachtree St. no informational tel. number*), including Louise Nevelson's massive all-white installation, *Dawn's Forest*. The world's largest, most complex "environmental sculpture"—white-painted wood surrounding a 25-foot column—it weighs nearly one ton. Nevelson aimed for "stillness yet scale," and the curves and angles of the hung, bolted, and stapled work are reflected in the glass doors, providing a stirring contrast to the marble floors and dark wood paneling.

You can stroll totally undisturbed in the hallways of the **Georgia State School of Art & Design** (*Decatur St. & Central Ave.* 404/651–2257), lined with student pottery, sculpture, and paintings. (It also makes a wonderfully strategic bathroom pitstop.)

A smaller branch of Midtown's High Museum of Art, **High Museum Downtown** (30 *John Wesley Dobbs Ave.* 404/577–6940) is a gleaming facility devoted to its permanent photography and folk art collections, as well as thought-provoking changing exhibits such as "The American Flag in Lakota Art." Beautifully designed with stone walls, pine floors, and towering windows suffusing the space with light, it's an airy retreat, and virtually deserted.

**SciTrek** (395 *Piedmont Ave.* 404/522–5500) features more than 150 interactive exhibits appealing to the kid in everyone. Forget "Do not Touch" signs. Everything is geared toward explaining how science affects our daily lives; clever magic and circus shows memorably dramatize concepts such as gravity, magnetics, and attraction/repulsion.

**Atlanta International Museum of Art and Design**

(285 *Peachtree St. 404/688–2467*) is an unexpected treat located in the Marriott Marquis. The changing exhibits showcase crafts and furnishings from around the world, often with a hip sensibility, such as the recent "Pop! Goes the Plastic!" tribute to '60s and '70s Playskool-colored furniture and everyday objects as curvaceous as Henry Moore sculpture.

From the sublime to the ridiculous kiddie attraction: Screaming kids you'd swear were already on a sugar rush line up outside **The World of Coca-Cola** (*55 Martin Luther King Drive 404/676–5151*), the ultimate (soda) pop culture museum. If you can get beyond the unadulterated crassness (piped-in perky theme songs—"Things go better with Coke!"—redeeming Muzak as an art form; larger-than-life Coke cans housing interactive video monitors; tacky photo ops in oversized bottles), it's rather well laid out by time frame, with zippy Coke-bottle columns, a re-creation of a classic '30s soda fountain, and a screening room and radio kiosk with all the Coke commercials. The Christmas season, with Santa Claus–shaped Coke machines lining the makeshift ice rink, is surreal. So is the vast store devoted to Coke paraphernalia (one hesitates to call it memorabilia): calendars, Xmas ornaments, ties, toy trucks, old soda glasses, Tiffany-style lamps, a stained-glass chess set, watches, even a Swarovski crystal bottle "purse" for a mere $2,200.

Boob-tube aficionados must make a pilgrimage to the leviathan **CNN Center** (*International & Marietta 404/827–2300*). The main attraction, other than waiting in line to "Talk Back Live" or possibly sighting Bernie Shaw or Ted Turner himself, is the entertaining CNN Studio Tour. The breathless 40-minute experience is the broadcasting equivalent of a thrill ride: exhibit areas filled with MGM and Cartoon Network memorabilia, a surround-sound video presentation on the foundation of the Turner empire, a glimpse of the newsroom in action, even a chance to read live feed off a teleprompter or play weatherman in front of the blue Chroma Key wall that superimposes maps and graphics.

The Center is fronted by **Centennial Park** and its famed fountain with the five interlocking Olympic rings (the play of water is entrancing). The attractive space features lighthouse columns (for the Olympic torches), phenomenal views of Downtown's skyline, an amphitheater hosting occasional concerts, an outdoor art exhibit area, a cafeteria, centennial pecan trees, and "quilt plazas" telling the Olympic story through sculpture, all linked by engraved commemorative bricks sold to finance the Games.

Overrated and underwhelming, **Underground Atlanta** (*50 Upper Alabama St.* 404/523–2311) is a brash three-level entertainment center/mall/historic renovation from the developers of Baltimore's Inner Harbor and Boston's Quincy Market that features middle-rent shops, booths, and restaurants. Housed in the complex are a vintage locomotive and **Atlanta Heritage Row** (*55 Upper Alabama St.* 404/584–7879), a multimedia history of the city. The five themed exhibits range from "The Founding of Atlanta and the Civil War" (bombs burst in the background while resonant voices declaim haunting portions of diaries à la Ken Burns' "Civil War") to "The World's Next Great City," concentrating on the development of Turner Broadcasting and Delta Airlines (you can enter the cockpit of a 1970 Convair jet).

But Underground Atlanta pales as history lesson beside a walk down Auburn Avenue, once nicknamed "the richest Negro street in the world," for its thriving all-black businesses. For many, it also possesses enormous symbolic significance as the birthplace of civil rights, spearheaded by local preacher Dr. Martin Luther King, Jr. "Sweet Auburn," as the district is known, is now somewhat dilapidated, yet the walking tour is essential Atlanta, if only for explaining the racial tensions that engulfed the city (and still simmer beneath the city's determinedly cheery, modern surface). It still resonates the spirit of with King's speeches and the sultry sounds of great entertainers like Lena Horne and Aretha Franklin, who sang at its shuttered dance halls.

Sweet Auburn's eastern sector of Auburn Avenue is frankly more involving than the western part, which comprises the Martin Luther King, Jr. National Historic District. It's a breathing slice of life, with barber shops, bars, funeral homes, soul food cafeterias, and Rasta/Revolutionist galleries. Sadly, many structures are now burnt, shuttered, or boarded up and many landmark buildings have been demolished. But interpretive signs chronicle the rise of the black middle class beginning with informative plaques about such black entrepreneurial pioneers as Peyton Allen (law office) and James Spratlin (Atlanta Steam & Dye Company) in the early 1900s.

**The Auburn Avenue Research Library** (101 *Auburn Ave.* **404/730–4001**) functions not only as a preeminent research center for African-American studies, but also as a marvelous exhibit and lecture venue.

The exemplary **APEX Museum** (135 *Auburn Ave.* **404/ 523–2739**) vividy recreates the nation's most vibrant and prosperous African-American thoroughfare at the turn of the century. The experience begins in a video room cleverly evoking a school bus. The two videos celebrate both African heritage ("I am Africa" booms the soundtrack as occasionally revisionist black history is traced as far back as Nefertiti) and the Sweet Auburn legacy (narrated in the booming and honeyed tones of Ossie Davis and Cicely Tyson, respectively). The emphasis ultimately is on the vital role the black community, including George Washington Carver, played in reinvigorating the South's dormant economy post-Reconstruction. The APEX also provides an invaluable service, enabling anyone to research genealogy in its extensive archives.

Once past the I-75/85 underpass (at Fort Street), the area changes subtly, resonating with poignant echoes of the civil rights struggle. A former Prince Hall's Mason headquarters now contains the offices of the **Southern Christian Leadership Conference** (330-4 *Auburn Ave. no informational tel. number*), founded by Dr. King. The stroll continues to the **Ebenezer Baptist Church** (*407 Auburn Ave., N.E. 404/688–7263*), where Martin Luther King, Jr. thundered at the pulpit, as his father and grandfather did before him. More than 800,000 visitors have since crammed into the church for Sunday morning services alongside the congregation. Despite many refurbishments and the odd sight of a huge video screen propped in front of the altar, the church preserves its well-worn integrity. Banners exhort "It's important that you strive and we strive toward the love of God" and "Encouraging the tithe: Growing and giving in Grace" and trumpet "Still a cornerstone of the community." The ladies who give the tour couldn't be lovelier, donations are never pushed, and the inevitable gift shop—with "I Had a Dream" T-shirts—is low-key. The church broke ground on the 1,600-seat Horizon Sanctuary tabernacle across the street in 1996; it's nice to know the donations have gone to a good cause, but the monstrosity has the unfortunate effect of diminishing King's legacy and smacking of commercialism.

**The Martin Luther King, Jr. Center for Non-Violent Social Change** (449 *Auburn Ave.* 404/524–1956) continues King's pioneering work, holding workshops on famine and illiteracy, providing day care for needy families, and inculcating non-violent leadership skills. The archive is the world's most extensive on the civil rights movement, including Dr. King's personal papers, while the memorabilia collection includes his clerical robe, hand-written sermons, and even the key to his room at the fateful Lorraine Motel in Memphis. Other rooms commemorate Gandhi and Rosa Parks; videos replay King's classic speeches. Freedom Plaza contains his white marble crypt inscribed with his stirring quote "Free at Last. Free at Last. Thank God Almighty I'm Free at Last," sitting in what can only be described as a Zen-like lap pool. The center is respectful, exquisitely designed, but rather soulless (an air of over-earnest hagiography pervades the space), though the exhibits can't help but be inspiring.

The truly moving monument to his legacy is **Dr. King's Birthplace** (39 *Boulevard, Firestation* #6 404/331–3920), a modest Queen Anne Victorian house, which showcases personal items like photos of King as a child, and has impeccably recreated period furnishings. National park rangers evoke his formative years: the loathed piano lessons, the family's nightly Bible studies in his grandfather's den, stoking coal in the cellar—giving Dr. King a movingly human face.

African-Americans are also celebrated in this city for their athletic achievements. The 70,500-seat **Georgia Dome** (1 *Georgia Dome Dr.* 404/223–9200), crowned with a cable-supported oval roof resembling a circus tent, hosts Atlanta Falcons football games, the occasional mega-rock concert, and boxing matches planned by native son Evander Holyfield.

The former Omni Dome, next to the World Congress Center, was imploded in 1998 to enable construction of a new sports and entertainment complex, connected to the CNN center by a covered atrium lined with restaurants and retail stores. It's part of the ongoing Atlanta/Ted Turner cabal to "redefine" Downtown, making it safer (if blander). The NBA Hawks and the NHL expansion Thrashers will play here starting in September 1999.

Handsome **Turner Field** (755 *Hank Aaron Dr.* 404/614–2311) is Nirvana for the Braves fan(atic). The stadium, largely brick with enormous windows and forest-green awnings (and an enormous tribute to "715," Aaron's home run record) duplicates the intimacy of old-fashioned parks, with superb sightlines from every seat. Tours of the facility, which includes the Ivan Allen Jr. Braves Museum & Hall of Fame, are offered. The original Braves home, Fulton County Stadium, aka the Chop Shop (Remember Jane Fonda tomahawking during Braves rallies?), has been converted into a parking garage/shrine: The brick pavers outlining the diamond were retained, a small park was erected on the spot where Aaron launched his record-breaking homer, while flags of every NL team flutter. Only the beer and hot-dog vendors are missing.

**spectating...** Forty years ago, Downtown was a thriving theater district; today only one of 25 venues remains (The Rialto). But since the '70s, when a death rattle was the most entertaining sound to be heard around here, life has been unexpectedly reemerging, with a few enterprising music/dance and theater spaces.

**Atlanta Civic Center** (395 Piedmont Ave. 404/523–6275) hosts everything from bodybuilding contests to Broadway touring shows in its 4,600-seat auditorium.

Shuttered in 1989, but restored by Georgia State College in 1996, the 900-seat **Rialto Center for the Performing Arts** (80 Forsyth St. 404/651–4727) is one of Atlanta's best middle-sized venues. It features original Deco flourishes, comfortable tiered seating, and superlative acoustics, while serving up refreshingly eclectic acts from the Ballet Folklorico of Bahia and Garth Fagan Dance Company to the Mingus Big Band and Juilliard's acting company.

**The Tabernacle** (152 Luckie St. 404/659–9022) has a similarly colorful history: It went from plantation house to apartment building to 1912 Baptist church, with predictably pitch-perfect acoustics. The likes of Grace Jones and LL Cool J shake the rafters in a laser and smoke swirl. Crowds appropriately range from David Bowie androgyny to homeys doing that gangsta thug thang.

In its heyday, Atlanta's version of Harlem's Apollo Theater, **The Royal Peacock** (186 Auburn Ave. 404/880–0475), presented everyone from Bessie Smith and Dinah Washington to Aretha Franklin, Della Reese, and the Supremes. It now hosts lesser-known reggae, soul, and gospel talents on a very spotty schedule. The interior is glam, with peacocks adorning the walls floor to ceiling.

**Shakespeare Tavern** (499 *Peachtree St.* 404/874–5299) isn't always true to its name, offering fare like Jean Genet's *The Maids*, Bertold Brecht's *Galileo*, and Aristophanes's *The Frogs* as often as those penned by Willie. But as that selection suggests, it's one of the more enterprising, adventuresome theaters in town.

# body

"Chop shops" can be found in the various malls, but bear in mind: No one goes out of their way to get toned or teased in the Downtown area.

**Silver Moon Barber Shop** (200 *Auburn Ave. no telephone*) is Atlanta's oldest black-owned tonsorial parlor, and although the staffers look old enough to have voted during the desegregation years, they can snip a mean fade for the boyz chillin' on the corner.

The manicures and pedicures are cheaper at the same mall's **Continental Hair Salon** (404/577–6511), and although you'd swear everyone comes out looking virtually the same, with blow-dried manes out of a douche or deodorant commercial, it's the best buy for a decent coif Downtown.

NORTH DECATUR RD

BRIARCLIFF RD

N

# virginia highland

Named for the main intersection of Virginia and North Highland avenues, the neighborhood known as Virginia Highland embodies genteel funk. Atlantans who find Little Five Points' grunge just too intense adore Virginia Highland, proudly branding it the equivalent of New York's SoHo or L.A.'s Melrose Avenue. Indeed, this formerly avant-garde area has been transformed into a thoroughly regentrified hip urban nabe, home to Atlanta's trendiest shops, galleries, and eateries. Of course, the

turn page for map key

scraggly bohemian types who pushed the envelope back in the '70s have been pushed out by higher rents.

Yet Virginia Highland remains appealingly quirky, even if it is more bean-counter than countercultural these days. The area was developed in the 1920s as a suburban enclave for the lower-middle class; today's average couple likely couldn't afford the charming craftsman bungalows, which start at $300,000. Forget the 1980s trend of moving to affluent OTP towns like Marietta and Roswell; yuppies now clamor for urban real estate. But even Downtown, with its renovated lofts currently in vogue, remains the frontier, dicey and deserted at night, with little retail development. Virginia Highland is still Atlanta's most desirable nabe for the upwardly mobile.

Part of Virginia Highland's appeal lies in its compactness: a blend of urban savvy and suburban ease. The three major pockets of activity are spread over a two-mile stretch along and just off North Highland. The rest of the neighborhood is completely residential. (As one local cracks, "The only evidence of active culture off the strip is frozen-yogurt shops.") Imagine parking, strolling to a buzzing hive of bars and boutiques that draw crowds from all over town, and then returning home to blissful quiet. It's the perfect neighborhood, the wait for a table in the latest trendy restaurant just long enough to remind you you're still in a major city.

| map key | | |
|---|---|---|
| 1 Majestic Food Shop | 3 | V. Reed Gallery |
| 2 Highland Tap Steak Cellar | 4 | Aliya/Ardavin Gallery |

The houses here are beautiful, though many are small and modest. The streets (especially those between Briarcliff Road and North Highland Avenue, like Rosedale Drive and Hudson Place) feature cottages with generous porches, fieldstone columns, and brick arches; majestic stone pillars even mark some sidewalk boundaries.

Though it has its own character, Virginia Highland also borrows elements from surrounding neighborhoods. Sharing its western border with Midtown gives it a lavender edge, with guppies galore restoring houses. To the east is the swank, tranquil neighborhood of Druid Hills, laid out by Frederick Law Olmsted in 1893, where renowned turn-of-the-century architects such as Philip Shutze, W.T. Downing, and Neel Reid contributed notable residences in a melange of architectural styles; this is where the film *Driving Miss Daisy* was shot. (A taste of Druid Hills can be found in Virginia Highland's glorious Tudor-style Callanwolde Fine Arts Center, whose evening functions bring out the black ties and silver Rolls Royces). And just to the south on Ponce (one syllable) de Leon (accent on the LEE) Avenue, the sumptuous Italianate villa that houses the Atlanta Boy Choir is a symbolic fortress between gentility and the urban frontier, standing in sharp contrast to its grittier car-wash/diner surroundings. Here, the otherwise manicured Virginia Highland hangs on to the cutting edge by its fingernails in the Poncey (Pon-see) Highlands area that now teems with new galleries and restaurants. The section directly below Ponce de Leon even merits a new nickname, SoPo, though the farther west you wander, the scruffier the neighborhood.

Virginia Highland's boundaries are relatively clear:

Though some would take it as far west as Monroe, the nabe really begins at Ponce de Leon Terrace and ends on the east at Briarcliff Road. North Avenue provides the southern boundary, and Rock Springs Road the northern. A map of the area would resemble a slightly swelled head topped by a beret.

Here you'll find a cosmopolitan blend of two-income couples, both straight and gay, and corporate neo-hippies who inhabit this kinder, gentler, more inclusive, predominantly white Yuppie-ville. Since Virginia Highland is shopping Nirvana, it's fitting to compare Atlanta's neighborhoods in sartorial terms. While Buckhead is Dior (top-of-the-line, label-conscious, and a little stuffy), at the opposite extreme, L5P is second-hand retro duds (vintage clothing would be too fancy a term). Midtown is Todd Oldham, a symphony of daring, even clashing, textures and colors, and Virginia Highland is Donna Karan: smart and sleek, with the right accessory hinting at underlying worldliness. In other words, Virginia Highland—where the urban jungle was reclaimed and tamed—offers the best of all Atlanta worlds.

# eating/coffee

Virginia Highland offers Buckhead's culinary sophistication without the high prices or, for the most part, the attitude. The quality is so uniformly high that crowds are lured from the entire metro area. With few exceptions, older standbys have maintained their standards: This is a competitive foodie nabe. For such a small area, it offers a dazzling array of savvy savory fare, including tasty Thai, bastions of fusion (or global) cuisine, and plentiful Continental and American Gothic Diner reliables for the determinedly unchic. Many eateries don't take reservations; expect long waits at peak hours. (This does, however, create some of Atlanta's hottest bar scenes on the weekends.)

**Cost Range** per entree
$/under 10 dollars
$$/10–15 dollars
$$$/15–20 dollars
$$$$/20+ dollars

**american...** If the name **Majestic Food Shop** (1031 *Ponce de Leon Ave.* 404/875–0276 $) sounds hyperbolic, stumble in around 4 a.m. after bar-hopping. First there's the comfort food—corned beef and cabbage, macaroni and cheese—that sops up any alcoholic concoction. Then there's the classic kitsch coffee-shop decor and big-haired waitresses who resemble escapees from a '50s women's prison melodrama. Finally, there's the crowd: mournful misguided sociopaths not sure which cause to rebel against, muttering street people, Social Security pension-ers from the retirement home across the street, and even a few, uh, upright citizens.

**American Roadhouse** (842 *N. Highland Ave.* 404/872–2822 $–$$) looks conspicuously out of place among the tonier upscale establishments. Who cares? The enormous stacks of hotcakes and tantalizing omelets are the cure for overactive Saturday nights and hyperactive kids, while no other spot in Virginia Highland delivers the goodies: South-ern staples like chicken-fried steak and fried green tomatoes.

**Murphy's** *(997 Virginia Ave. 404/872–0904 $$)* started life as a wine-and-cheese emporium, then became a bakery that expanded into a restaurant. There is still a bakery counter, and the breads remain scrumptious. Their Sunday brunch is phenomenally popular, with inventive pancakes and almost definitive French toast. The simple yet elegant interior—whitewashed wood, Georgia red brick walls, potted plants galore—remains happily sunstruck throughout the day. And whether it's chipotle lime-cured salmon or sweet corn pancakes, everything is prepared with a deft, light touch.

**asian...** For years, **Surin** *(810 N. Highland Ave. 404/ 892–7789 $–$$$)* was Atlanta's Thai standard-bearer, while several pretenders came and went. More authentic spots have appeared, yet it remains a civilized dining experience. The arty room is stunning, with bright blue tablecloths, black-and-white photos, and vividly hued Thai wall hangings contrasting with the original tin ceiling and wood floors. As for their food, crispy basil rolls sing with freshness, while the shrimp *masaman* is a deft blend of sweet, sour, and hot ingredients, including lemongrass and chilis.

**Panita Thai Kitchen** *(1043 Greenwood Ave. 404/888– 9228 $–$$$)* is a sumptuous, sensuous dining experience. The decor is erotically charged (a red back room features hand-painted trees, vines, and peacocks in a mural taken from an Omar Khayyam love story). The food is equally seductive. Dishes like eggplant soaked in tamarind or Thai sweet sausages complement familiar items like pad thai.

The name **Good Harry & Sons** *(820 N. Highland Ave. 404/873–2009 $–$$$)* hardly inspires thoughts of sublime sushi, yet the fish is fresh and flavorful (with dollar specials nightly and inventive maki rolls). The menu's unusual "One from Column A" approach allows you to mix and match Italian, French, Japanese, and Thai dishes. But there are no vetoes on this culinary Security Council. The space is both warm and cool, with mustard and brick walls, old piping, and hallucinogenically hued paintings.

## coffee... Cafe Diem (642 N. Highland Ave. 404/607–7008 $ ) is Atlanta's most bohemian coffee shop, at least judging from the intense reading and agonized hair-raking that goes on here. Poetry readings and eclectic performers animate many a weekend night. The decor features ochre walls splashed with blues-concert photos, and tables painted lavender or covered with road maps and postcards. There's a lovely small patio where you can dine on anything from *tapenade* on toast to veggie burgers.

**Alon's Bakery** (1394 N. Highland Ave. 404/872–6000 $) serves up the best bread in Atlanta (banana nut bread) along with lemon raspberry mousse and velvety chocolate cake sinful enough to merit the seventh circle of hell. They also whip up scrumptious sandwiches like garlic-roasted lamb, and do a proper tuna Niçoise. Be forewarned, though; there is no place to sit and munch.

**San Francisco Coffee** (1192 N. Highland Ave. 404/876–8816 $) is a remarkably soothing place to sip your espresso, with exposed brick walls and large picture windows overlooking the activity on North Highland, that attracts the gamut of Highland hoppers, from nose-ringed artists to legal eagles studying briefs.

**Virginia's** (1243 Virginia Ave. 404/875–4453 $$)is ideal

for that romantic after-dinner capuccino or a restful brunch. Faux gaslights, exposed brick and yellow stucco walls hung with rotating art exhibits, and plush red velvet draperies give it a vaguely bordello-ish air. The shimmering "jungle" patio with its goldfish pond and bamboo-twig awning is more restorative than Prozac. With over 20 coffees and nearly 40 teas on tap, it's the spot of choice for harried suburban moms, gay muscle boys, Emory students cramming for exams, and your garden-variety urban hipsters who read *Granta* (the stacks offer an impressive selection of papers, periodicals, and learned reviews) or do the crossword to unwind.

**cuban...** The scene at **Mambo Restaurante Cubano** (*1402 N. Highland Ave. 404/876–2626 $$*) is as sizzling as the name implies. The interior is delightful, with metal palm-tree fronds, works by emigré Cuban artists, and seafoam formica tables. The kitchen turns out fab sangria, *ropa vieja*, and flan.

**french...** If you haven't broken bread during Sunday brunch at **Babette's Cafe** (*471 N. Highland Ave. 404/523–9121 $$$*), you haven't dined in Atlanta. The menu changes periodically, but signature dishes include Babette's Benedict (brioche toast topped with beef tenderloin, two poached eggs, and sun-dried-tomato hollandaise) and the shrimp, spinach, and *crème fraîche* omelet. At dinner, owner/chef Marla Adams tantalizes with good, hearty, rustic cuisine: cassoulet (lamb, duck, sausage, and chicken with white beans in a lamb sauce) and homemade pastas like portabello tortellini and artichoke ravioli. And yes, there are occasional recreations of the menus from the book/movie *Babette's Feast*.

*yum.*

**fusion...** By any standard, **Dish** (870 N. Highland Ave. 404/897-3463 $$$-$$$$) is exalted. The witty, sexy decor features Dr. Seuss colors: chartreuse walls in the front section, blueberry by the restrooms, as well as sultry Georgia O'Keeffe-esque hand-blown suspended lamps and black-and-white photos of trendily alternative gay and interracial couples that contrast with the original hardwood floors and beams. Clever "blasted" brick openings give it an enticingly raw, provisional look. Debs in black strapless gowns, strapping rugby-playing attorneys, and androgynous sylphs all photogenically await their close-ups and tables. Witness the tuna tartare over crispy rice cakes in red chili oil, cilantro, and mango; or silken red pepper and mascarpone tortellini with fresh corn and arugula. The wine list is admirably ballsy, with lesser-known varietals like Viognier taking center stage. *also!*

**Indigo Coastal Grill** (1397 N. Highland Ave. 404/876-0676 $$-$$$) transports diners to Key West, with bleached-wood shutters and an enormous tropical aquarium. The imaginative food is as colorful as a piñata: Any dish showers you with flavor favors. Chiles rellenos (stuffed with grilled chicken, apples, cranberries, golden raisins, garlic, and cinnamon and crowned with tomatillos, red pepper coulis, queso, feta, cilantro, and toasted pumpkin seeds) is an ingenious symphony of tastes, with a deceptive delayed after-burn. The Ancho-Chile Tortilla Soup is extraordinary. Even brunch offerings transcend mere egginess.

**Harvest** (853 N. Highland Ave. 404/876–8244 $$$) jump-started the warming to global cooking in Virginia Highland. How else to define a menu that blithely hops from honey-pecan chicken with buttermilk mashed potatoes to braised lamb shank (falling off the bone) with white beans, roasted vegetables, and red wine jus, to Chinese five-spice duck? They're abetted by a fine selection of mostly affordable California wines. The patio is phenomenally popular for brunch, the interior quite cozy with wicker and antique furnishings duplicating a bygone era of hospitality.

**Seasons' Bistro** (654 N. Highland Ave. 404/233-1344 $$) is an unusual blend of Greek coffee shop and sleek wine bar (the grape leaves stencilled on the yellow walls are a lovely touch). The diverse menu presents a U.N. of dishes, all filtered through a thick Marlboro Lite haze. Everything from duckling in raspberry-orange glaze to peppered tuna with baby bok choy and ginger black-bean sauce is expertly prepared and served by a chummy wait staff.

**Terra Cotta** (1044 Greenwood Ave. 404/853–7888 $$$–$$$$) calls itself a cross-cultural bistro, which would be pretentious were its decor and cuisine not so innovative. Black chairs and black-and-white photo exhibits artfully accent the walls and brick-red ceiling. Scott Annand's food skips from one influence to another without missing a beat. The delicate flavor of the buttery batter-dipped sea bass is perfectly offset by the crunchy black lentils and infusion of sherry vinaigrette. It's heaven on terra.

The coveted patio seats at **Tiburon Grille** (1190-B N. Highland Ave. 404/892–2393 $$–$$$) comprise one of the most relaxing settings in Virginia Highland. The theme is Atlanta goes Santa Monica, with high ceilings, muted track lighting, and terra cotta walls. The food isn't as memorable as the mood, but dishes like halibut crusted with horseradish make the ideal accompaniment to the fine wines.

**italian...** Surprisingly, there are no exceptional Italian restaurants in Virginia Highland, especially for more refined regional cuisine. However, if you're just looking for Neapolitan fare at fair prices, you can't beat **Everybody's Pizza and Pasta** (*1040 N. Highland Ave.* 404/873–4545 $–$$). Its handsome interior is all exposed brick and wood beams, with rotating artworks. The lasagna and fettuccine alfredo are excellent, but the pies really stand out, with unusual toppings including pesto, roasted red peppers, and rosemary potatoes; roast chicken, peanuts, and sprouts; and shrimp artichoke with honey-roasted garlic.

**Camille's Little Italy** (*1186 N. Highland Ave.* 404/872–7203 $$) hits the spot for robust Italian, all Mamma Mia, *mangia*, and garlic. The place is appealingly clichéd, including the red-check tablecloths and candles in straw Chianti flasks; thankfully they call it a "red tomato sauce," not *pomodoro*.

If Camille's proves too boisterous, **Capo's Cafe** (*992 N. Highland Ave.* 404/876–5655 $$) is a hideaway whose latticed archways and paintings of chefs contribute to the simpatico ambience. The menu isn't adventuresome—Chicken *Diable* (mushrooms, cream cheese, basil, dijon mustard, and brown sugar) is as creative as it gets—but it's solidly if blandly prepared. Capo's really scores as a date place when the more fashionable eateries demand an hour's wait. Its dark atmosphere is enhanced by Frank, Tony, and Ella on the sound system, setting a romantic mood.

## mexican/southwestern... Tortillas (774 Ponce de Leon Ave. 404/892–0193 $) is a bare-bones spot where the clientele and staff have even more 'tude than the spicy burritos. Band advertisements ("Drummer needed for punk ska group") are plastered everywhere. The sound mix segues from Ravi Shankar to Nine Inch Nails. The upstairs, painted in playground-bright red and green, is the only concession to a decorative scheme. Grad students arguing semiotics and burly bikers scarf down quesadillas and "new-style" burritos like chicken pesto or pork and spinach. Tofu is extra.

**Caramba Cafe** (1409D N. Highland Ave. 404/874–1343 $$) is run by the Prieto family, who make everyone feel at home. A stylish setting, margaritas with a punch, and healthful preparations (100 percent vegetable oil, lean beef) keep regulars shouting "¡Olé!"

## steak... Highland Tap Steak Cellar (1026 N. Highland Ave. 404/875–3673 $$–$$$) is a wondrous throwback to the 1950s, when meat ruled the dinner table. The bar is nifty, along with the original piping and stone-and-brick walls that look as if they could grow moss. It doesn't hurt business that they make the best damned martinis in Atlanta, with no fuss or frills. The rib-eyes and New York strips are prime, the country brunches define "hearty," and the appetite-challenged can pick at cayenne chicken salad or shrimp and basil pasta. What more could anyone want from a meat-and-potatoes diner?

## vegetarian... Soul Vegetarian (652 N. Highland Ave. 404/875–0145 $–$$) is unexpectedly opulent for a vegan

joint, with old gilt mirrors and bronze bar stools, cherry red walls, black-and-white-check tile floors, and flickering candles at dinner. Completely cholesterol-free choices include lentil burgers, batter-fried tofu filet with tartar sauce, and kalebone in pita with cucumber. Regulars range from Rastafarians to pouty, anorexic skinheads: That soybean ice cream has a loyal following.

# bars

Virginia Highland's taverns define the term "neighborhood bar": Most are dimly lit, laid-back, unpretentious spots where everybody knows your name. Though many gays live in Virginia Highland, this isn't the place to take a walk on the Wilde side. Nor are people looking to get plastered or take meetings à la Buckhead. It's just a friendly, mixed crowd that encompasses rednecks with tiger tats, a few nubile Goth chicks with pierced navels, and (especially at the restaurants) extremely pretty people who look like they could play bit parts in "Dawson's Creek," "Party of Five," or "Melrose Place."

**Atkins Park** (*794 N. Highland Ave. 404/876–4279*) is the city's oldest licensed tavern (est. 1922). A shrine to Atlanta's history (photos of Fokker biplane crop dusters, the original Coke plant, and the *GWTW* premiere), its logo is a phoenix, representing both town and neighborhood rising from the ashes. Bars don't get much cozier than this: original tin ceiling, exposed piping, leaded-glass partitions, brick walls, and naugahyde booths. The food ain't too shabby either (try the signature house black-bean and roasted-tomato soup and homemade cheesecakes). As the evening wears on, expect to see overgrown frat boys getting sozzled on Jägermeister.

**Moes and Joes** (1033 N. Highland Ave. 404/873–6090) is a fixture, as are many of the barflies (not that this is a Charles Bukowski kinda nabe). Slightly dive-y and popular with Emory students. From the red naugahyde banquettes and Pabst Blue Ribbon neon sign to the mix of tattooed truckers and pony-tailed professionals, it's utterly authentic.

**Darkhorse Tavern** (816 N. Highland Ave. 404/873–3607) draws two distinct crowds. Locals enjoy the downstairs, all classic wood, brass, and Deco frosted glass. Later in the evening, live bands playing ironic theme songs for alienated youth and a high-fiving, head-banging collegiate-stomp set take over the upstairs. The names, all pretenious, take on youthful alienation and angst, saying it all: American Tourist, Custer's Last Band, Glass Candle Grenade.

**Limerick Junction** (824 N. Highland Ave. 404/874–7147) is a near-genuine Irish pub: wooden arches over the bar, shamrocks on the doorpanes, sepia paintings of Limerick, old pound notes plastered everywhere, and Guinness on tap. The open-mike nights roust a roster of characters who perform everything from unmetered poetry to R&B ballads, mostly badly, but often with gusto.

They don't go to **Taco Mac** (1006 N. Highland Ave. 404/873–6529) for the Mexican grub. Nah, it's for buffalo wings and beer, dude, with dozens of suds on tap or by the bottle. The place could use a good scrubbing, but the Emory students and late-20-somethings who pine wistfully for their collegiate days in between preparing briefs are usually clean-cut and freshly laundered.

# music/clubs

Virginia Highland is not Clubland, period. Granted, several bars offer live music, and there's one classic blues joint. Otherwise, the action, such as it is, lurks in Poncey Highlands. Generally, the nabe attracts a drinking, not a dancing, crowd.

Like any institution, **Blind Willie's** (828 N. *Highland Ave.* 404/873–2583) has its detractors. But it's hard to argue with soulful acts like Maria Muldaur, jazz pianist Mose Allison, and the wailing harmonica master James Cotton—he taught "I Got My Mojo Workin'" to Muddy Waters. Photos of the entertainers hang on the maroon walls, a virtual Who's Who of the Blues. A postcollegiate crowd masses outside waiting to get in, while regulars include Mick Jagger when he's in town.

The entertainingly downmarket burlesque house **Clermont Lounge** (789 *Ponce de Leon Ave.* 404/983–3196) makes the Cheshire Bridge establishments a couple of miles north seem posh. The bar itself is standard-issue, with neon beer signs, yellowing nudie pinups, dimly lit booths, and Patsy Cline on the jukebox. The gals are generously endowed, their figures a relic of some hip-happier time. More likely to empty your wallet than steal your heart, they look like tattooed Russ Meyer castoffs. (You probably won't get rolled, though a couple of hours will cost a surprisingly hefty bankroll.) It's all strip and no tease: a lap dance is $10 to $20 depending on the lady, the crowd, and the time. Obviously, don't expect dishy broads; zaftig is the charitable term (there's one who can actually crush a beer

can between her breasts). The exception is Blondie, a stat-
uesque peroxided black woman who struts her stuff in
front of the club, as leeringly provocative as a Crumb cartoon come to life.

**MJQ Concourse** (*736 Ponce de Leon Ave. 404/870–0575*)
sits like an afterthought on the unofficial border strad-
dling Midtown and Virginia Highland, which has no other
true dance club. It attracts sunken-cheeked rejects, not
quite as hyperactive (and, as rumor has it, hypodermic-
jabbing) as the crowd down the street at the Gothic
Masquerade. DJs Sinceelay and Gnosis command a huge
following for their savvy blend of tribal, dub, and hip-hop.
No wonder the crowd looks skeletal: They're burning off
plenty of calories. Despite its aggressive industrial edge,
there are a few dark nooks, where couples necking in the
shadows resemble gaunt El Greco figures.

# buying stuff

Virginia Highland's shopping scene is wonderfully variegated, appealing to every taste and budget, from beer to
De Beers. It's always stylish, whether retro, contemporary,
haute, or funk: a neighborhood made for accessorizing
your body or your home. Nowhere else in Atlanta will
you find such a range of earrings, vests, lingerie, per-
fumes, end tables, vases, and wind chimes. Anyone
infected with the collecting bug will have a field day.
Blessedly, there's barely a hint of a mall. In fact the word
boutique seems freshly minted here. Everything is one-
of-a-kind, even if the goods inside are remarkably eclec-

tic, with an aromatic whiff of the New Age. Just take the kitsch and the granola earnestness with a grain of salt.

## antiques... Sharonlewisshed (1060 St. Charles Ave. no phone) carries "functional with a K" antiques, like Smith Corona manual typewriters, old tricycles, camphor bottles, Mexican and Guatemalan wood *santos*, heavy Romanian leaded glass bowls and objects, Russian icons, and Chinese screens, not to mention odd odds and ends like insect-shaped earrings. Even the interior design gets into the act: The floors are covered with yellowed periodicals.

**20th Century Antiques** (1044 N. Highland Ave. 404/ 874–7042) is appropriately named: Every design school in the last 100 years seems to be represented here, either as antiques or reproductions. Jetson-esque '50s furniture, art deco vanities and "Thin Man" martini sets make the window displays among Atlanta's most eye-catching.

## books & records... Reader's Loft (1402 N. Highland Ave. 404/881–6511) traffics in self-enlightenment and enrichment. The shelves offer a broad spectrum of books and CDs on runes, tribal fetishes, crystals, the tarot, and the like (as well as some of the actual items). An ethereal metaphysical vibe pervades the space, aided by soft New Age music, incense, and the soothing sounds of the wind chimes and broken-ceramic tinkling fountains for sale. You can even schedule a psychic reading or research the best place to study meditation, channeling, or how to cast a love spell.

**Corner CDs** (1048 N. Highland Ave. 404/875–3087) is a tiny storefront filled with the jeans-and-reversed-baseball-cap set who flock to Dave Matthews Band concerts; Stevie Nicks and Eric Clapton are still worshipped here.

## clothes... Bill Hallman Boutique (792 N. Highland Ave. 404/876–6055) sells footwear distinctive enough to turn anyone into a fetishist, from leopard-print sandals to high platform vinyl boots made for walking and stomping.

**Rapture & Bang** (1039 N. Highland Ave. 404/873–0444) is as close to haute couture as Virginia Highland gets. Perhaps alternative evening wear is more like it: Looking for a sheer black chiffon number with strategic beading? You can design your own Audley shoes, choosing between heel style, leather type, and color. Bang stocks the men's GQ/Maxim counterpart, including snazzy linen suits and stylish hats.

**Psycho Sisters** (1052 St. Charles Ave. 404/892–7340) specializes in used clothes on consignment: everything from flappers' feather boas to glitzy sparkle-dusted sunglasses to vinyl skirts to used Levi's (some with great "Flower Power" patches, others that still smell of biker cologne—diesel and dirt). Many vintage threads are indeed threadbare, but who can resist leather halters? It even racks up top labels, from Giorgio Armani and Banana Republic to Betsey Johnson and Donna Karan.

**Highland Hemp & CDs** (842 N. Highland Ave. no phone) attempts to put the high in Highland, giving you more bang for your bong. As the sign painted on the wall reverently asserts, "Hemp is a plant that has been in the service of mankind for over 8,000 years." Duds is the right word for the T-shirts ("Grow in Peace"), but the Hemptown label of casual clothes offers fine lounging or gardening clothes in earth tones. Stop by when you need hemp oil (an analgesic), hemp fiber paper (nice rough texture), stickers ("dependable psilocybin mushrooms"), and CDs from rock to reggae.

**Earth Angel** (*1196 N. Highland Ave. 404/607–7755*) caters to the frilly Southern belle with a wink, carrying the ultimate in traditional wedding garb, antique-lace veils, beribboned bonnets, embroidered ballet slippers, linens, lace, even lingerie with ethereally sensual appeal.

## gifts... **Jules Jewels** (*1037 N. Highland Ave. 404/875–2047*) showcases the broadly humorous paintings of Jules Burt (for example, a smiley heart entitled "dance your art out"), as well as wildly patterned furnishings, hand-painted picture frames, refrigerator magnets that could appeal only to collectors' magnificent obsessions—it's a loud but joyful grab bag of whatever catches Burt's eye. This is the original location; there's an outpost store in Buckhead.

**Common Pond** (*996 Virginia Ave., N.E. 404/876–6368*) bills itself as an "environmental awarehouse," which sounds a tad affected. It's co-owned by Indigo Girl Emily Saliers, so a Lilith Fair mentality prevails. Ecologically sound recycled tchotchkes include purses fashioned from rusted license plates (you don't want to throw your spare change in there) and handmade chests created from fallen branches. Soaps, candles, cards, blouses, even buddha fountains complete the inventory. You pay more for these slightly precious goods, but hey, it's for a good cause (a percentage of profits on some items goes toward various charities and environmental organizations).

**Metropolitan Deluxe** (*1034 N. Highland Ave. 404/*

892–9337) is the preeminent gift shop, selling high-end bed linens, aromatherapy paraphernalia, candles, cutesy cards, even some lovely furniture downstairs, both reproduction and hand-painted.

**Right Up Your Alley** (842 N. Highland Ave. 404/ 874–8401) carries an almost terrifying range of objects: froufrou cat collars, menorahs, aboriginal "dreamtime" papier mâché bowls, wire cowboy hats. Some of the metalwork and ceramics are lovely, but there's plenty of cheesy, questionable taste on prominent display here, too (signs like "Grandfathers are Just Antique Little Boys" or "John Lennon and Yoko Ono: The real tragedy of this relationship is that John had a better butt").

## home furnishings & accessories... You can't

help but get a buzz walking around **The Eclectic Electric Gallery** (1393 N. Highland Ave. 404/875–2840). The literally luminous works, many of them functional, utilize every kind of light, including fixtures, neon, candlesticks, and lamps. The artists incorporate various materials: wood, blown glass, fiber optics, metalwork, paper, and objets trouvés like artifacts and old machine parts. No wonder owner Kim Smith calls the lamps "heirlooms" and "sculpture."

Funky yet functional could be the motto for **V. Reed Gallery** (780 N. Highland Ave. 404/897–1389), which raises junk to an art form. Trinkets from around the world are displayed haphazardly, along with rotating "exhibits" of whimsical hand-painted furniture, wonderfully hued and textured pottery (dig the "Alice on acid" tea sets), unique jewelry, beguiling Christmas ornaments, even children's furnishings as Keith Haring might have designed them.

**Back to Square One** (1054 N. Highland Ave. 404/815–9970 $) is a haven for folk art, including tire swings fashioned into rocking horses and old cabinets stripped down to their original green buttermilk paint. They also serve homemade ice creams: Just ring the cowbell for service.

**Providence** (1409 N. Highland Ave. 404/872–7551 $) celebrates wallowing in sensual luxury, whether it's scented candles and potpourri, old gilt chairs, beaded handbags, or lamps swaddled in velvet.

**Chef!** (1046 N. Highland Ave. 404/875–2433 $) sells all your dining needs, from jammin' javas to smoking stogies, and groovy kitchen stuff (marvelous fruit glass art), including every kind of skillet and mug imaginable. It also holds cooking classes conducted by top Atlanta chefs.

# sleeping

As a primarily residential neighborhood, Virginia Highland offers a limited lodging selection: In fact, there's just one noteworthy B&B in Virginia Highland proper and two semitransient hotels in SoPo/Poncey Highlands.

> **Cost Range** for double occupancy per night on a weeknight. Call to verify prices.
> $/under 75 dollars
> $$/75–125 dollars
> $$$/125–175 dollars
> $$$$/175+ dollars

The sprawling 1927 **Highland Inn** (644 N. Highland Ave.

# for a special night...

Where would a respectable Southern city be without a welcoming B&B, let alone one straight out of *Architectural Digest*, like **Gaslight Inn** *(1001 St. Charles Ave., N.E. 404/875–1001 $$$–$$$$)*? Jim Moss and Stephen Pararo (the latter is a noted Atlanta decorator) are the congenial owners; enjoy a sherry in the sitting room (outfitted with VCR, TV, piano, CD player and delightful hand-painted globe lamps) as they tell you about Virginia Highland's rich history. The detail work of Stephen's design, even in the public rooms, is eye-catching without seeming too busy. Inspired touches include china-jar-lid doorstops, old window shutters mounted as cheap-chic art, and trophy vase lamps; the dining room contains one of only four working gas chandeliers in Atlanta. The rooms are overflowing with fresh flowers in season from the Charleston-style interior courtyard. The Rose Room (named for Stephen's mother) has a hand-painted rose headboard rice bed with corniced Battenburg lace canopy, and rose tracery in the bathroom. The Carriage House contains two equally magical accommodations, including the Garden Room (with Lexington shuttered headboard, armoire—and its own secret garden blooming with hydrangeas, azaleas, camellias, and pink dogwood). Amenities include fireplaces, whirlpools, and steam showers in some suites.

**404/874–5756 $$)** has 100 rooms, nearly all with private baths, TVs, and air conditioning; studios also have microwaves and mini-fridges. The mattresses may be too soft, but the rooms have a shabby integrity, with maroon or jade rugs and old opera and gallery posters in gilt frames adding a note of class. The clientele ranges from European students on a budget to long-term resident seniors.

You might want to motor away from the **Clermont Motor Hotel** *(789 Ponce de Leon Ave.* **404/874–8611 $–$$)**, despite the lobby's faded elegance with gilt lamps and mahogany tables. It's little more than a halfway house/transient residence filled with seedy, suspicious-looking characters who seem to have popped out of an Elmore Leonard novel (without the snappy dialogue, though). In fact, strictly off the record, many a gal working in Clermont Lounge, the basement nudie joint [see **bars**], confides she "wouldn't stay there if they paid me." Still, it's cheap and relatively sanitary. More than the edges have frayed, but lodgings (including furnished apartments) include cable TV, central air, and private baths; there are even homey touches like carved wood headboards (though you have to wonder if they were left behind when the last patron was evicted). Nightly rates are low, but the Clermont's strictly for broke novelists desperate for inspiration.

# doing stuff

Virginia Highland isn't a big tourist draw—except, of course, for its shops and restaurants. It's a haven for the visual arts, however, boasting more galleries per square foot than anywhere else in town, save perhaps Lower Buckhead's Bennett Street. Thankfully, the gallery openings aren't as bejeweled and "mwah, mwah, look at *moi*" as they are in glossy Buckhead.

**Callanwolde Fine Arts Center** *(980 Briarcliff Rd. 404/ 872–5338)* is a revivifying retreat. Exhibits run from all-American (quilts, both traditional and unconventional; "Animalscapes" of wild animals frolicking, sleeping, and hunting) to apple pie gone sour and spoiled ("Homemakers of the American Dream," a series of oils by James Wakeman depicting the subservient roles women played in '50s and '60s advertisements). Built for Coca-Cola heir Charles Howard Candler, the house is a 1920s gem, one of the few examples of true Gothic-Tudor in Atlanta. The interior gleams with walnut wainscoting and marble-and-stone fireplaces. But the rooms are mostly devoid of furnishings: This isn't a museum, but a working arts center, with regular classes in ceramics, painting, photography, etc. Check it out at Christmastime when the decorations are breathtaking.

**Modern Primitive Gallery** *(1393 N. Highland Ave. 404/892–0556)* showcases high-priced works that often resemble glorified farm implements given an S&M-dungeon gloss (several works—with titles like "Binding for Quadricep Totem"—incorporate burlap bags, rusted hooks, ropes, steel, and wood; leather and feathers or hair and ceramics are often fetishistically combined). **The Marcia Wood Gallery** *(1198 N. Highland Ave. 404/885–1808)*, as one recent brochure noted, "examines the dilemma" in which landscape and regional artists find themselves at the end of the millennium.

**Right Brain Gallery** (664 N. Highland Ave. 404/872–2696) specializes in mixed-media works; owner Barbara Dobkin is credited with coining the term SoPo to describe the revitalized section of Highland just south of Ponce de Leon. Dobkin delights in creating environments; for her, art does not exist in a vacuum. Hence, a collection of pastoral scenes will be accented by ornamental flower boxes and wrought-iron patio furniture.

**Fine Line Gallery** (624 N. Highland Ave. 404/872–3229) is rapidly becoming a premier showcase for first-time artists working in various media. The simple space is crowded with up to 10 exhibits of photographs, paintings, ceramics, and prints at a time; resident artist Lea Rizzo's studio adjoins the exhibit space, and she enthusiastically answers questions about emerging artists on the scene.

**Aliya/Ardavin Gallery** (1402 N. Highland Ave., N.E. 404/892–2835) displays a variety of generally overpriced but occasionally audacious works by local artists, ranging from abstract to representational (often distorted à la Eric Fischl), and informed by pop-culture detritus. If you're buying, it's generally more reliable for exquisite ceramics and glasswork. The openings are Virginia Highland's splashiest.

**spectating...** Aside from the clubs listed above, there are few concert or dance spaces and no theaters to speak of in Virginia Highland. If you enjoy the sight of the well-heeled and well-groomed, with the occasional ostentatiously over-the-top fashion statement, then people-watching qualifies as an artistic endeavor.

**Callanwolde Fine Arts Center** [see above] offers a series of classical and jazz concerts throughout the year, as well as traditional Christmas carols during the season. **The Atlanta Boy Choir** (1215 *Ponce de Leon Ave.* **404/ 378–0064**) doesn't quite match Vienna's, yet if boyish sopranos handling Handel like pros appeal, you can't do much better.

# body

The body beautiful is worshipped in Virginia Highland as religiously as it is elsewhere in Atlanta, but the pastors don't expect such generous donations in the collection plate. Still, it's closer to Buckhead than L5P: There are no tattoo emporia, and the colorists are more expert in giving an auburn rinse than an electric-blue crew cut. The key word here is "natural," as in wholesome, environmentally sound, organic: you know, oatmeal masks and invigorating rosemary-oil rubdowns.

Nothing like good marketing: Students of Buckhead's chichi **Van Michael Salon** apprentice at the salon's Virginia Highland outpost (778 N. *Highland Ave.* **404/874– 6604**), which cunningly labels them "new talents." Twenty dollars gets you an aesthetically pleasing tease and some teasing banter.

How hip is a salon called **Key Lime Pie** (806 N. *Highland Ave.* **404/873–6512**)? Even the decor rejuvenates: old hardwood floors, grillwork on the walls, chartreuse sofas. The salon uses the plant-based Aveda products; they'll customize and freshly blend oils and masks from various floral and herbal essences. Everyone slinks about in black (in Chinese thought, the color of creativity, not menace), waxing, hydrating, and exfoliating with ultimate professionalism. Hairstyling is surprisingly reasonable, and any service comes with a delicious perk to perk you up: a complimentary stress-relieving treatment, usually in the form of a neck massage.

**Natural Body Spa** (*1402 N. Highland Ave. 404/872–1039 $*) offers not only the expected pedicures, poundings, and pore-cleansings, but a whole range of products—sold in the separate shop—to make you glow, including do-it-yourself wooden massage tools and lines of aromatherapy. All products, including Aveda, Kiehl's, and Israel's Ahava (made from Dead Sea minerals), are environment- and animal-friendly. Men aren't given the brush-off either, with a special line of spa massages, facials, and sports massages specially designed for the male metabolism. Give your feet the salt scrub and paraffin treatment, followed by reflexology, and you'll be walking on air—and not Jordans.

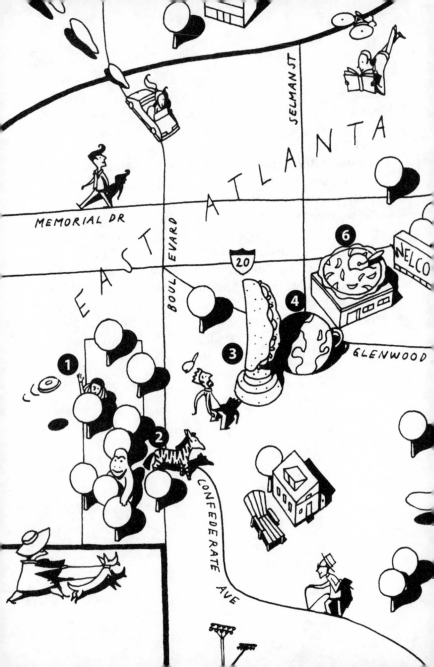

# east atlanta

Currently the big buzz in Atlanta's urban renewal movement, East Atlanta is being transformed "faster than a speeding bullet—and there were plenty of those a few years ago," as one resident cracks. Traveling south from Little Five Points along Moreland Avenue, you first encounter run-down housing and apartment complexes; then, as the bridge over Interstate 20 nears, there are check-cashing joints, wino shops, cheapo fast-food joints, and

5

N

FLAT SHOALS AVE

ORMEWOOD AVE

turn page for map key

shabby grocers. The southern approach from I-285 is almost surreal, with collard green stands alternating with hubcap hustlers and crack dealers in Atlanta's black southside. Yet just south of I-20 and east of Moreland, centered at the intersection of Glenwood and Flat Shoals avenues, sits a funky grouping of shops and cafes reinvigorated by hardy settlers hoping to make this once-forgotten corner of Atlanta something special again. It's an incongruous sight—white suburban types parking their SUVs in front of a trendy gallery, as a caravan of black youth boom by with their bass-heavy rap tracks. So far, the pierced, tattooed crowd hasn't invaded.

While many of East Atlanta's restaurants, bars, and galleries rely on moneyed customers who live outside the immediate neighborhood to keep them afloat, the area's revival cruises along because the prices of surrounding houses are cheap—for now. The vanguard consists of adventuresome late 20-somethings—people who actually work for a living and renovate their houses themselves: the kind of yuppies that are proud of their calloused hands.

Living "in town" is desirable again, yet Downtown, despite its "loft" renaissance, has never been considered a residential address. So, as Atlanta grew and the upwardly mobile wanted to live in the city, they trekked east into inexpensive, seedy neighborhoods that had rotted when their inhabitants fled to the 'burbs. These older neighborhoods

| map key | | |
|---|---|---|
| | 1 Grant Park | 4 The Gravity Pub |
| | 2 Zoo Atlanta | 5 The Shade Gallery |
| | 3 Burrito Art | 6 Grant Central Pizza |

were renovated, and in the process, their business districts revitalized. Of course, real estate skyrocketed and prospective new homeowners were forced to look elsewhere, preferably on the fringe of the newly renewed "hip" area. The young and/or middle-to-upper class influx back to the city has constantly migrated east in this manner, neighborhood by neighborhood, from Inman Park to Candler Park to Grant Park to Decatur, and so on. Intriguingly, the African-American middle class followed this progression even further east, without making inroads to the north in L5P, Virginia Highland, or Buckhead. Nowadays, someone who might not be able to afford that renovated Victorian-ized bungalow in Grant Park can likely afford the ditzy ranch-style brick home in nearby East Atlanta. Still, prices are rising, at least 30 percent altogether since 1996. It's now common to fork over $200,000 for a moderate-sized home, although a few fixer-uppers can still be found for well under $100,000.

Situated a few miles southeast of Downtown Atlanta, the area can be divided up as follows: First, there's Grant Park, a residential neighborhood surrounding a 100-acre park where most of the homes date back at least 70 years. Grant Park's original settlers were wealthy, so many older houses here are rambling Edwardian mansions. There are also many newer subdivisions near the park, where smaller houses predominate. It's not unusual to see stately, immaculately restored homes abutting decaying termite nests, contributing to an excitingly provisional, "in-process" feel. The residential mix is 50/50 black and white. Several small businesses anchor the park's western and eastern borders, Cherokee Avenue and Boulevard, while a bleaker, more urbanized area prevails to the north on Memorial Drive You may occasionally hear gunfire at 3:30 a.m., an unpleasant reminder that, yes, you're living in the city.

Just north of Moreland and east of Boulevard lies the historic Cabbagetown district. This was Atlanta's first industrial settlement, populated by families Jacob Elsas brought in from the North Georgia Appalachian mountains to work at the Fulton Bag & Cotton Mill, which he built in 1885. The mill closed in 1970, but many of those white families and their descendants still live in the old two-story wooden homes. In the past few decades they've been joined by creative types; today probably more artists and musicians live in Cabbagetown than in any other area of Atlanta. Members of little-known bands as diverse as Smoke, Cat Power, the Rock*A*Teens, and the Gold Sparkle Band prowl the streets along with the shirtless rugrat offspring of former mill workers. Cabbagetown's face is receiving yet another lift, as the mill has been renovated into luxury loft spaces, attracting a distinctly junior corporate element to the area. One wonders how much longer Cabbagetown can keep its unique heritage alive.

Finally, going east on Memorial and then south on Moreland, there's East Atlanta proper, centered around the corner of Flat Shoals and Glenwood. Unlike Grant Park and Cabbagetown, it wasn't originally "planned" as a suburb; this is reflected in its architectural diversity, ranging from late '40s and '50s brick ranch houses to older, larger, Victorian-style homes to semi-mansions on several acres of land (originally farms, before the acreage was sold off and divided into smaller lots). An indigent black neighborhood, whose more prosperous denizens fled further east toward Stone

Mountain, its humble abodes form the new urban frontier for brave yuppies and bohemians. This white gentrification has produced a 50/50 ratio—where one half owns a disproportionate amount of the top businesses and real estate. "Inverse carpetbagging," one longtime civil rights activist calls it. (There's occasional friction: several African-American Baptist ministers have waged campaigns to rid the neighborhood of the very guppies who are helping restore and raise property values.) Now, yards are being cleaned up, homes are being renovated, there's less litter, and long-decaying businesses are reinvigorated by the new ones; the Kroger grocery store on Moreland Avenue, which has been a hole for years, is undergoing a million-dollar makeover. And violent crime is decreasing— although burglaries and drug-related violations are still common. But, some longtime residents of the area feel that it's losing its flavor, and that the people wanting to transform it into an exciting, vibrant place are in fact the ones working to make it just another suburb. Albeit one with double decaf Sumatran French Roast lattes.

# eating/coffee

You may wonder why some Atlantans call the East Atlanta dining scene "up-and-coming"; Moreland Avenue near Interstate 20 is nothing more than fast-food hell. And even when the new "gentry" get a hankerin' for a Big Mac, they'll usually bypass the Moreland drive-thrus for something in another part of town. They're probably just tired of getting their orders screwed up by brain-dead teens.

Once you make it to Glenwood and Flat Shoals, however, you'll find a colorful array of arty, innovative restaurants and cafes, most of them on the expensive side. Natch, they're trying to lure young trendoids from Virginia Highland, Midtown, and Buckhead, where money flows more freely. The neighborhood hasn't gentrified to the point where restaurants here can depend primarily on local residents— they NEED to attract people from other parts of town. But whether you live in the 'hood or are just passing through, chances are, if you haven't checked out the main drag in the past month, there'll be something new and audacious.

**Cost Range** per entree
$/under 10 dollars
$$/10–15 dollars
$$$/15–20 dollars
$$$$/20+ dollars

**barbecue... Barbecue Daddy-D'z** (261 Memorial Dr. 404/222–0206 $), just a tad northwest of the area, garners many votes for best barbecue in Atlanta. The place looks like a twister totalled it—a screen porch that's lost its house— and the surrounding urban wasteland hardly whets the ol' appetite. But one bite of Daddy's melt-in-your-mouth meats makes the surroundings seem positively bucolic. They baste/smoke/marinate the beef, chicken, pork, and turkey just right, with your choice of hot or sweet sauces. The hot is the perfect mix of tang and fire, but disregard the surly stares and tell them to slop it on liberally—they skimp on the stuff if you don't prod 'em. Of course, you get white bread, potato salad, and baked beans for sides. The family that owns the place hails from Chicago, and Cubs, Bulls, and da Bears blare on the tube. Adding to the Chi-town flavor, they book some local roadhouse blues bands on the weekends.

If that ain't authentic enough for ya, get down to the heart of East Atlanta. There's always a group of kids on the corner of Glenwood and Flat Shoals with a smokin' barbecue vat, peddling the stuff on the street. It's addictive.

**coffee...** As much a catalyst for community change as it is a coffeehouse, **Sacred Grounds** *(510 Flat Shoals Ave. 404/584–5541 $)* was the first new East Atlanta business to worship at the younger, hipper altar. This was over three years ago, and today the respected cafe is so busy, it's doubling in size for 1999. It's a mellow "hanging out" place, with comfortable mix'n'match furniture and established local artists showing everything from primitive-looking folk art to modern photography—all of it, including handcrafted tables and chairs, for sale. Art openings, acoustic sets, and poetry readings bring out a neo-Beatnik crowd. The delicious coffees emphasize natural, healthful ingredients: They exclusively use organic beans from Olympia, Washington, soy milk and fat-free condensed milk, and granulated cane juice for sweetener. They also sell some delicious homemade cookies and pastries—in fact, the owners operate a cake business on the side, called Cake Walk.

**mexican...** The wall behind the front cash register at the original **Burrito Art** *(1259 Glenwood Ave. 404/627–4433 $)* displays some of the silly questions the staff is continually being asked. Sample: "What is that rolled-up thing that everyone is eating?" Okay, so the burritos here could hardly be called traditional. Meats such as jerk chicken and pork tenderloin mix with black beans, cheese, and sour cream to add a gourmet touch. The location is cramped, but cozy; rotating paintings by local artists, often resembling Rorschach ink blots, are for sale on the walls.

**pizza...** **Grant Central Pizza & Pasta** (451 *Cherokee Ave.* **404/523–8900 $$**) is a classy tavern in the heart of the Grant Park neighborhood, with pizzas bordering on the obnoxiously gourmet ("Yes, we roast the red peppers first," said one prissy bohemian staffer of a veggie version), sandwiches, and pastas, along with a comfy little bar area. Best bets are usually the nightly dinner specials (often a salmon or mussel dish) and the lasagna of the day. The larger sister location in East Atlanta, **Grant Central East** (1279 *Glenwood Ave. 404/627–0007 $*), emphasizes the pizza and subs, eliminating the pasta dishes altogether. Wooden booths line the walls, with tables cramming the floor. Many swear the pizza is better at this location, due to larger dough-mixing bowls, or something. Whatever . . . it's darn good.

**sandwiches...** **Hungry Rush'in** (1287-B *Glenwood Ave.* **404/622–0707 $**) is a combination deli, grocer (although they no longer carry fresh produce and the beer selection sucks), and wine merchant. Favorites on the ever-changing menu include the chicken-salad croissant (not overwhelmed by mayonnaise), flaky yet firm Chilean sea-bass cakes, and feta-stuffed chicken breasts, all prepared on site that morning. While there are a couple of small tables near the front window, most folks get their meals to go, and lingering over coffee is not encouraged.

**southern...** Pricey but worth it, **Edible Art Cafe** (*481 Flat Shoals Ave.* 404/586–0707 $$$) specializes in offbeat variations on Southern dishes, or as they like to call it, "gourmet soul food." Owner Deborah Berry's main business is catering, and the diminutive restaurant (eight tables), with abstract African-style designs on the walls and seductive R&B softly playing, acts as an in-house testing ground. Don't worry—everything passes muster (and mustard greens), from the appetizers (pan-fried shrimp grits, barbecued chicken spring rolls) to the entrees (the marinated fried chicken, served with pungent sweet potato–apple chutney, is miraculously ungreasy). Sides include mac & cheese and collard greens.

**variety...** Everyone leaves with a doggie bag at **Heaping Bowl & Brew** (*469-A Flat Shoals Rd.* 404/523–8030 $$), whose "one-dish meals" are piled high in virtual buckets (hence the name of this quirky, always busy eatery). Specialties include linguini with zesty tomato-wine-herb marinara sauce, thick juicy rib-eye with dill potatoes—and the massive mass-appeal favorite (white chicken meat with veggies in a lemon garlic sauce over noodles). Non-bowl items satisfy and sate, too, namely the spicy turkey burger and the catfish burrito. If you somehow have room for dessert, try "Izzy's banana pudding"—as the menu puts it, "the best trailer park dessert you will ever have." Who's Izzy? That would be Izzy Semrau, the owner's mother and the executive chef. As far as the "brew" part of the Heaping Bowl experience, go on Tuesdays and Thursdays for the best deal in town: all draft beer, including Guinness and Bass, is two bucks a pint.

A pioneer of the Cabbagetown fine-dining scene, the comfortable **Cabbagetown Grill** (*727 Wylie St. 404/525–8818* **$$**) resembles a Santa Fe refuge(e) with stone, stucco, and wood in browns, grays, and deep blues. Several glass windows are hand-painted, creating a wonderful play of color and light when the sun streams in. The petite covered patio is packed during warmer months. The selection is small yet varied and expertly prepared, ranging from comfort (meatloaf sandwich with cheese and two fresh vegetable sides) to continental (Seafood Papillote—parchment-baked phyllo stuffed with salmon, portabello mushrooms, tomatoes, carrots, zucchini and other veggies, topped with pineapple beurre blanc). For Sunday brunch, the banana pecan waffles sure are heavenly, as is the Crab Cakes Benedict.

Just south of East Atlanta proper is **Zesto** (*1181 E. Confederate Ave. 404/622–4254* **$**), part of an Atlantan drive-in chain institution. Cholesterol hogs go wild here: revered white-trash specialties include the Footlong Hot Dog Basket, the Chubby Decker (a gooey gourmet Big Mac dripping with cheese and mayo), and celestial salted crinkly fries. Just to show they can go upscale, the menu trots out tuna steak sandwiches and almond chicken salad. And the hot fudge brownie deluxe makes an excellent oral substitute for any other craving. All this in a grungy, retro diner that seems like it sprung straight out of *American Graffiti*.

# bars

Until a few years ago, an East Atlanta bar was defined by a few frankly dangerous druggy dives or by brown-bagging a 40 at the grocery store and guzzling it on the sidewalk. Times change, and now virtual fern bars, most with kitchens, sprout every few months. In addition to the following (all of which, save for the Crazy Horse, have opened since late '97), most restaurants like the Heaping Bowl and Burrito Art have small, personable bars for drinking and/or eating and/or socializing.

The otherwise nondescript **Flatiron** (520 *Flat Shoals Ave.* **404/688–8864**) occupies East Atlanta's neatest location, in the narrow, triangular-shaped corner of an old building at the corner of Flat Shoals and Glenwood avenues. It provides those prized neighborhood hangout staples: a cathedral ceiling, a decent selection of beer and wine, and a varied jukebox running the gamut from Elvis to Ella. The pub grub (burgers, tuna melts, quesadillas) is worthy, if not spectacular, and the "Ultimate Dip" (chili, black beans, melted cheddar, jalapeños, tomatoes, red onions, and sour cream, served with chips) can feed two or more.

Occupying a space where a salon called The Hip Hop Barber Shop once styled cornrows for aspiring Ice T's, **The Gravity Pub** (1257 *Glenwood Ave.* **404/627–5555**) is the newest addition to the East Atlanta drinking derby. Sip beer or cocktails at the bar, or grab a booth for cozier encounters. A little "reading room" sits at the rear, although you'll be hard-pressed to see anyone actually reading. As a sentimental homage to the previous tenants, there's a lonely old barber chair sitting by the bookshelves.

Unlike the previous two homey drinking holes, the bilevel **Fountainhead Lounge** (485 *Flat Shoals Ave.* **404/522–7841**) goes out of its way to be stylish. The look is sparse and space-age, with nothing adorning the red-and-black walls; the lighting is dim cubicle white, and the furniture as sleek and mannered as the Buckheaders and cocktail fanatics venturing ever deeper into the urban jungle for adventure. The high-priced beer, wine, and liquor selection is probably larger than the rest of the nabe's bar lists put together. In short, you can pretend to be in some swank New York or L.A. nightspot, as you sip Manhattans, compare stock portfolios, and silently worry about your Beamer being broken into outside.

The same can't be said for **The Crazy Horse Bar & Grill (687 Memorial Dr. 404/523–5495)**, north of East Atlanta near Cabbagetown and Oakland Cemetery. Rather tough and redneck-y, it resembles Dottie's before they started booking rock bands [see **music/clubs**]. Pickup trucks and broken bottles dot the parking lot, and the specimens inside are mostly grizzled, loud, and rowdy. Newcomers should probably keep to themselves and observe.

# music/clubs

Since East Atlanta's transformation from a place trendoids didn't care about to a hip and happening destination, the snooty "Neighborhood Business Association" has inevitably formed, trying to control what homeowners do with their yards and what entrepreneurs do with their businesses. They want to mold the area into something clean and livable, i.e., somewhat sterile. Despite the numerous empty storefronts in and around East Atlanta, live-music clubs are considered "undesirable," due to the "undesirables" they bring in. For example, Grant Central East was planning to add live music, and even built a small stage before they were pressured by the business association to abandon the idea.

One hope could be the E.A.R.L. (East Atlanta Restaurant & Lounge), a planned music club on Flat Shoals Avenue that is being renovated on the site of a former furniture showroom. The people behind the club own the building, so they should be able to avoid harassment by the neighborhood fun police—if they ever get the room open, that is. They've been working on it for well over a year.

The adventurous music fan in East Atlanta has to motor to get revved up by live music. The thoroughly unassuming **Dottie's Food & Spirits** (307 Memorial Dr. 404/ 523–3444), on the north edge of Grant Park, is really the only music club in the immediate vicinity. A former country roadhouse and pool hall, they started booking local underground rock bands several years ago and now the blue-spiky-haired leather-jacket crowd mixes with the old-timers who still drink—and work—here. It's about the size of a couple of double-wide trailers (well, OK, it is a couple of double-wide trailers), and the sound system is usually something less than crappy, but damn, this can be a fun little dive on the weekends! Assuming, that is, you haven't abandoned your adolescent tendencies. People tend to get trashed, stumble, and slobber all over everybody else at this place. That's why they say Dottie's oozes "character."

The bookings at **The Moreland Tavern** (1196 Moreland Ave. 404/622–4650) are so sporadic and underground that it has yet to make much of an impact as a genuine music hangout. Over the years, this faded little southside shack has become a place where elderly gay men go drinking. Its atmosphere somehow brings to mind both "Petticoat Junction" and an opium den, i.e., dark and seedy, but almost everyone you meet is very friendly and very Southern. In addition to local rock bands, they'll sometimes have outrageous drag shows in the wee hours. It's rarely packed, even when there is live entertainment.

# buying stuff

If your first impression of shopping in East Atlanta comes courtesy of, say, the Jiffy Mart on Moreland Avenue, where the top sellers are milk, cheese, and porno mags, you might never set foot south of I-20 again. Like the area's major restaurants, most of the shops in East Atlanta lie a block to the east, centered along the intersection of Glenwood and Flat Shoals avenues. Nearly all the newer shops cater to the arty crowd, offering a wacky mix of African tribal masks, antique furniture and fixtures, Southern folk art, and space-age ornaments in neon-bright plastics. Other types of businesses, i.e., clothes, records, books, etc., haven't kept pace, but it's only a matter of time—and the influx of conspicuous consumers.

**antiques... DHS** (1374 *Moreland Ave.* 404/622–1800) is Nirvana for junk-shop junkies. The wittily salacious decor alone is a hoot: Artwork from a San Francisco gay bar surrounds the perimeter (photos of men seducing each other, having sex in the backseat, fooling around in a porn theater). This is contrasted with bona fide Olympic medal stands, glorious painted marionette theaters, stagecoaches, even a wheelchair reputed to have seated F.D.R.

**Verdi O** (*492 Flat Shoals Ave. 404/880–0708*) is a combination art gallery/home-accessory/antique emporium offering an operatically extravagant selection of walnut wardrobes, cherry wood consoles, fab '50s leather recliners and ottomans, and marvelously oddball handblown, colored-glass lamps (they look like hardened lava lamps). It's the first retail space designed by Palmer Smith, Atlanta's guru of design merchandising; the clientele is suitably chichi.

## art/gifts... Traders of East Atlanta Village (485-B

*Flat Shoals Ave. 404/522–3006*) is an artsy/craftsy shop heavy on the candles. Big candles, small candles, round candles, square candles . . . basically about any size, shape, or color you want. Best-sellers include candles that float on water, ones painted in zebra and leopard-skin designs, and in the summer months, "bug-off" citronella outdoor candles in flowerpots. Traders also carries earth-child accoutrements like aromatherapy materials and handmade vegetable glycerin soap, and more practical and expensive items like velvet upholstered sofas and antique wood tables. Beware: this store is faintingly fragrant.

If you're in the market for authentic Southern folk art, yet aren't brave enough to comb the mountains searching for the actual artists (seen *Deliverance* lately?), **The Shade Gallery** (*465-A Flat Shoals Ave. 404/577–3338*) may have what you're looking for. From the well-known (Howard Finster, R.A. Miller) to the more obscure (Grace Howell's glazed clay pottery/monster heads—better than a jack-o'-lantern, and permanent!), owner and art collector John Gillett packs a fascinating crop of uniquely Southern culture into his small gallery space. While some of the more elaborate pieces by the "name" artists are priced over the top, you can get really neat smaller works for under $50. The biggest sellers? "Devil stuff," Gillett says, referring to the fixation on the horned one that seems to infuse nearly every folk artist's work.

George Jetson would feel at home at **Space Tribe Gallery Studio** (490-B *Flat Shoals Ave.* 404/688–0780), where all of the art and gifts display a futuristic pop-art/lounge bent. Many of the goods are fashioned by the more offbeat neighborhood types, such as co-owner David Bradley's hand-painted martini glasses, with their modish dots and designs. Also of note are Steve Malcolm's copper/aluminum/wood "Titan" lamp, which looks like it may take flight any moment, and David Richardson's brightly colored "alien portraits" in acrylic. Very few objects appear to have any useful function other than looking cool, but hey, sometimes that's all you need.

For a more "Third World Kmart" feel, there's **Life On Earth** (494 *Flat Shoals Ave.* 404/627–6398): Incense, Haitian carved-wood statues, Indian beads and necklaces, and special candles for Kwanza. The ambiance is cluttered but peaceful, and the quite friendly owners make much of the merchandise themselves, like their nifty bamboo incense holders and tribal masks staring you down from the walls.

**Cabbagetown Children's Center** (212 *Carroll St.* 404/222–0644) is a makeshift nonprofit thrift store/workshop/gift gallery featuring paintings, sculptures, toys, puppets, games, furniture, and unclassifiable art made by neighborhood kids, usually on the premises. When they're not busy making something that resembles Disney on speed, the imps are often hanging on your leg, pointing out their creations and encouraging you to purchase something. Future car salesmen in the making, these are kids who would be loitering in JuVee had the tirelessly philanthropic owner, John Dirga, "the saint of Cabbagetown," not provided them with a forum for self-expression.

Ray Herbert, Jr. lent his nickname to **Panorama Ray's (224 Carroll St. 404/681–2373)**, earned for the fabulous panoramic photos he took in the '50s, '60s, and '70s with his 1904 Eastman Kodak Cirkut Camera. The prints can be upwards of four, five, even six feet long, and capture incredible 360-degree scenes that often repeat the same people in different poses on the same exposure. Most of Ray's photos depict the surrounding neighborhood, in which he lived, the "Cabbageheads" who populate it, as well as many cityscapes of the Atlanta skyline. Herbert also made large folk art paintings of neighborhood characters and the city itself; several humorous depictions adorn the exterior. Ray died several years ago, but his son, Ray Herbert III, continues his legacy, cataloging and caring for his dad's old photos and taking some new ones himself.

**books...** Practically the only place to find reading material in East Atlanta outside a library, **The Village Printer (483 Flat Shoals Ave. 404/893–3944)** is a shoe-box-sized store that sells cheap used literature, but the selection's barely up to what you'd find at a neighborhood yard sale. Still, you never know . . . mostly paperback fiction, along with some biographies, travel books, poetry, and a kids/teens section.

**cds/records...** Instead of attitude-heavy indie-rock

retailers smugly selling the latest college-radio whiners, **Flat Shoals CDs & Tapes** (*496-A Flat Shoals Ave.* **404/688–4325**) provides the soundtrack to these mean streets. A closet-sized shop with all the selections on shelves behind the counter (yes, shoplifting is still a time-honored East Atlanta pursuit), it carries a mix of the hottest rap and hip-hop tracks, new and classic R&B ("best of" collections by the Isley Bros. and Cameo get prominent wall space) and gospel (the Mighty Clouds of Joy are a top-ten seller). The selection remains limited, however, especially since the tiny digs also accommodate incense, hats, shades, and other accessories.

**clothing/vintage...** The Dressing Room (*504 Flat Shoals Ave.* **404/584–2200**) is a shrine to the '70s, offering racks of used Levi's, bellbottoms with frayed peace symbols, Western wear, Hawaiian shirts, disco polyester photo-print shirts, crazy muumuu dresses, Superfly shoes, belts, purses, and so on. The colors are as vivid as they are mismatched, but that's half the fun with kitschy retro wear, right? The two hip young owners, Crystal and Michelle, will gladly take your own good-quality tacky threads off your hands, too.

They say they have the cheapest Chuck Taylors in Atlanta at **Charlie's Tradin' Post** (*648 McDonough Blvd.* **404/627– 4242**), an odd little shack just off Moreland south of East Atlanta near a federal penitentiary. At $15 a pair, it's hard to argue, as long as you don't mind 'em being marked "irregular," i.e., with minor imperfections. When you enter, you're struck by the assortment of fishing rods and knives on display. But go a little farther back, and you're surrounded by 20 tables of at least 9,000 pants stacked as high as your shoulders. A word to the wise: While most of these pants are new, many are also "unsellable," for some very obvious reasons. You take it from there. . . .

And if you happen to be shopping for the Fat Boys, you might check **Ross Unlimited** (370 Flat Shoals Ave. 404/522–4083), where they proudly carry jeans in sizes ranging from 28 to 80-plus!

## gardening...
To help hoe that weedy yard in the house you just purchased, **The Urban Gardener** (347 Boulevard 404/529–9980) offers a small but organized and comprehensive selection of plants, flowers, vegetables, and instruments of lawn destruction. A big seller is phlox, a flowery plant that acts as a ground cover on those little slopes, typical of the neighborhood yards, that are a pain in the butt to mow. While there are some froufrou gifts mixed in with the practical items (art-school whirligigs, far-too-ornate wind chimes, etc.), for the most part their inventory is fittingly down-to-earth.

## musical instruments...
Looking for a Chinese gong, a Nigerian wood oja flute, or a South Indian kanjira lap drum? You'll likely find it at **Earthshaking Music** (900 Moreland Ave. 404/622–0707), plus you'll discover a dozen other exotic instruments that hardly look as if their goal was to produce dulcet tones. The hands-on policy encourages experimentation, but you can't get too loud, as these instruments are all non-electric. The staff, which sometimes seems even more into bongs than bongos, is quite helpful and friendly—sometimes too much so. Mention one thing, and they'll eagerly display every instrument they have—"Here, play this!" "I don't wanna play that!" A

wide range of woodwind and stringed instruments are offered, but the emphasis is on percussion. A good way to add some class to your next sidewalk drum-circle session— which, alas, you almost never see, even outside the store. You're more likely to find impromptu outdoor percussion fests in Little Five Points.

# sleeping

While we'd like to say that East Atlanta and Grant Park are so exciting that no one ever sleeps, that's simply not the case. It's not a big tourist area yet, and let's face it, it's still dilapidated and dingy compared to Virginia Highland or Buckhead; most residents certainly haven't had the time or money to transform their homes into dollhouse B&Bs. The only real nearby attractions worth mentioning are Zoo Atlanta and the Cyclorama Civil War exhibit, both in Grant Park. But these aren't enough to warrant the construction of nice hotels in the area, and the East Atlanta business district's revival is too recent and unproven in staying power to have had an impact. As one local advises, "Stay with a friend: It's your only choice."

**Cost Range** for double occupancy per night on a weeknight. Call to verify prices.
$/under 75 dollars
$$/75–125 dollars
$$$/125–175 dollars
$$$$/175+ dollars

But if you're a brave soul, try **The Atlanta Motel** (277 *Moreland Ave. 404/659–2455 $*), where the front desk hands out profile sheets (a piece of paper with a featureless outline drawing of a large man) on which to fill in the details for the police in case you're robbed. Be sure to wear your bulletproof jammies! It's your basic low-low-budget motor hotel, with stained floors, roaches scurrying under the beds, and cracked ceilings, and it's definitely not worth the rate. You enter the parking lot through an Exxon station, for crying out loud. You'll do better to stop there, gas up the jalopy before the hubcaps are hoisted, and drive to Midtown so you can sleep in a real hotel.

# doing stuff

Most of the extracurricular things to do revolve around Grant Park and its immediate surroundings (don't venture too far afield on foot, however; even residents have a motto: "Keep moving and don't drive slowly"). There's plenty of history in this neck of Atlanta, but you can easily take in all this stuff on a nice day and still have time to make it to Daddy-D'z for some hot barbecue 'n' cold beer.

Just south of Interstate 20, framed by Boulevard, Sydney Street, Cherokee Avenue, and Atlanta Avenue, lies Grant Park. Its 100 acres of trees and rolling hills provide a peaceful setting for family cookouts and quiet walks, but more often than not on spring and summer weekends the roads through and around Grant Park are filled with bass-booming automobiles of young African-Americans cruising in search of the opposite sex.

Grant Park features several prominent attractions, however, including **Zoo Atlanta** (*800 Cherokee Ave. 404/624–5600*). What was a sad, overlooked zoo for far too many years has been expanded and revitalized over the last decade, and today the facilities are generally respectable. The grounds have been renovated, and the animal enclosures replicate their natural habitats. The big attraction is a gorilla named Willie B. For years, he provided an ongoing local soap opera, as zoo officials struggled to find him a suitable mate so he could procreate. The drama climaxed (as it were) a couple years back, when Willie finally got a girlfriend, and the hairy couple produced a pup.

Also inside Grant Park is **The Cyclorama** (*404/658–7625*), a 50-foot-high cylindrical painting (400 feet in circumference—you stand in the center of it) depicting the Battle of Atlanta during the Civil War. Painted in the 1880s by a group of German artists, the Cyclorama was intended to be a traveling exhibition, but that idea never got off the ground. It was saved from destruction by a group of Atlanta Samaritans, who then donated it to the city. Cleaned and restored several times, this historic building sits on a piece of land where much of the Battle of Atlanta was actually fought. The painting itself is a realistic, action-filled chronicle of the combat, tracing several key events chronologically as you move your attentions clockwise around the room. Recorded narration helps clarify and dramatize what you're seeing.

North of Grant Park and just west of Cabbagetown lies **Oakland Cemetery** (*248 Oakland Ave. 404/688–2107*), Atlanta's oldest and largest burial ground, established in 1850. It's a great place to bring a picnic lunch with a special friend on a spring afternoon, or just explore alone—you'll learn much about Atlanta's early history. Pioneering (or just filthy rich) citizens from all walks of life are buried here; their epitaphs help piece together a picture of Southern life a century ago and beyond. There are also some detailed, ornate mausoleums (many with genuine Tiffany windows!) to inspect. Among the more notable Atlantans buried here are *Gone With the Wind* author Margaret Mitchell and golfing great Bobby Jones. More than 2,500 Confederate soldiers were laid to rest at Oakland, along with more than a few carpetbaggers who adopted Atlanta as their home, but no ghostly battles have been reported.

It's more a Grant Park neighborhood oddity than anything else, but **The Robert Burns Cottage (988 *Alloway* Pl. 404/627–2941)** is on the National Register of Historic Places. Built in 1910 by the Burns Club of Atlanta, it's an exact replica of Burns' birthplace in Ayshire, Scotland. Burns, known as "the poet laureate of Freemasonry," is also the author of "Auld Lang Syne," so you might expect this gray stone house to be filled with lampshade-wearing partyers year-round. Not so. It seems perputually vacant, hence its popularity among neighborhood kids as a good place to smoke pot.

**spectating...**Why is it that Atlanta's supposedly "coolest" neighborhoods are so lacking in certain departments? Take East Atlanta/Grant Park. Not a single movie theater. Nothing notable in the way of live theater. No comedy clubs, or spoken-word venues (save for the occasional reading at Sacred Grounds). Just woefully uncultured? Maybe. But there is one kick-ass drive-in! Indeed, as of June 1998

**The Starlight Drive-In** (2000 Moreland Ave. 404/627–5786) is the only one left in the city, since the North 85 Drive-In near Tucker closed for good. Hopefully, this particular relic will stick around for awhile, as it does a pretty good business and remains in fine shape. Its six screens are always showing first-run flicks, often double features. Despite its seedy location (across from the Thomasville Heights crack-filled housing project and down the road from a federal pen), this is a great place to whoop it up with a group of friends, whether anyone pays attention to the movie or not.

Now for live theater . . . such as it is. **The Arts Exchange** (750 Kalb St. 404/624–4211), occupying an old school building, operates as an interactive learning center for the arts. They offer classes, lectures, and exhibits on visual arts and drama, and present low-budget plays, concerts, and performance art in a small, on-site theater. They'll occasionally bring in someone good, like Spalding Gray, but mostly it's amateur productions of little interest to anyone outside immediate family members.

# body

You didn't really want that flaming skull tattoo and silver eyelid ring anyway, did you? Once again, the East Atlanta Business Association rears its protective head. They will not allow tattoo parlors or piercing shops in the area: they attract ugly, weird-hair "alt" people who frighten paying customers from the other stores. You'd think those fashion fascists would recognize a shaved head qualifies as clean-cut, wouldn't you?

There are, however, a ton of dinky, old-time, mostly black barber shops with names like **Soul Zodiac Lady "D" Beauty Salon** *(465 Flat Shoals Ave. 404/525–5388)*. You'll know as you approach the storefront whether or not you'll want to have your 'do styled at these joints as you can see the (split) end results through the windows.

On the other hand, sometimes the businesses themselves decide whether or not they want to deal with you. When a stranger asks a hair snipper at **Stylistics Beauty and Barber** *(1267 Glenwood Ave. 404/622–1148)* what time they close, he'll likely be met with a blank stare, and then a half-hearted reply of "Seven." You'll be walking past the place on your way to The Gravity Pub at 10:30 p.m., and there'll be brothers in there getting their 'fros cut and chatting up the staff. Hmmm, maybe they meant 7 a.m. Or perhaps they resent the ongoing encroachment into their 'hood of all the yakity-yak yuppies, both black *and* white. Either way, this neighborhood is growing and changing, and at this point no one is going be able to stop it.

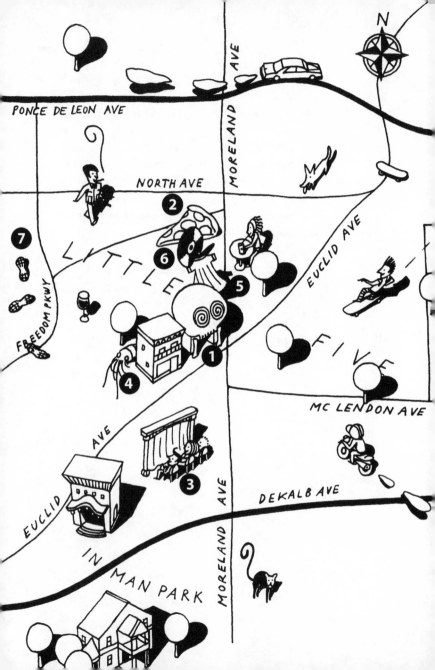

# little five points

Nose rings, dreadlocks, tie-dyes, tattoos, leather jackets, Doc Martens, bad acne, ski hats in July, perpetual scowls, and slouches. Incense and dope peddled right on the street. Flocks of slack suburban youth desperately seeking an identity (or at the very least a navel ring and a copy of the new Nashville Pussy album). One Little Five Points resident sums up his "alternative," über-cool neighborhood succinctly:

**turn page for map key**

"Depending on your age, political persuasion, and gross income, we're either a cut-rate freak show or the saving grace of a city gone increasingly corporate."

Situated east of Downtown, at the intersection of Moreland, Austin, and McLendon avenues, Little Five Points (aka L5P) is home to many of the city's more notable live-music venues, independent record stores, funky clothes shops, and cheap eats. Intriguingly, though everyone seemingly affects that malnourished albino heroin-chic look, make no mistake, this remains a predominantly white-bread (however moldy) area; most of the phat boys still hang in East Atlanta. At night, the bars and clubs are loud and bustling with rednecks and rebels-without-a-cause sticking out their pierced tongues at yuppies on slumming cruises; the post-dusk streets are generally well-patrolled by both local cops and scraggly hippies bumming for change. Although the wandering punks usually only look skinhead-fierce and violent crime is infrequent, it's still best to be alert and stay in groups.

Ironically, most of the wandering punks can't afford to live in L5P itself, which is more commercial than residential. Much of the available housing is composed of fairly pricey complex-compounds, or large pre-war renovated dwellings that fetch the usual gentrified prices. In contrast to Little Five Points's hustle and bustle, the surrounding residential areas are quiet and downright pretty. The dis-

| map key | | | |
|---|---|---|---|
| | 1 Vortex Bar & Grill | 5 | Junkman's Daughter |
| | 2 Savage Pizza | 6 | Criminal Records |
| | 3 Variety Playhouse | 7 | The Carter Center |
| | 4 The Baker's Cajun Cafe | | |

trict's face-lift has extended to the recent transformation of a large old high school building on the west end into loft apartments, bringing on fears of increased traffic, pedestrians, yuppies, and rents. Most of the kids (who look as if they rent their patch of street turf) usually drive in from Decatur and points east; the more gainfully employed bunk in adjacent looming mansions of Candler Park. Named for Coca-Cola founder Asa Candler, the neighborhood is more tranquil than the spiky circus of Little Five Points down the road. The main cross streets for business activity in Candler Park are McLendon Avenue and Clifton Road. Linked more by geography than tone or attitude, Little Five Points, Inman Park, and Candler Park each have annual street festivals that correspond to the individual flavors of those neighborhoods.

One up-and-coming area to the north, centered on North Highland, is the Old Fourth Ward. The area includes a restored 1920s brick storefront, warehouses painted lime green with red tile roofs, a working steel mill, paper plant, and salvage yard/recycling plant that is being demolished to create loft housing. Much of the commercial reclamation has been spearheaded by two of Atlanta's veteran businessmen, Dean Buckley and Jake Rothschild. Their retail store, Revival, spans four buildings, including an ice cream parlor, gourmet deli, art gallery, and office space. Revival is a metaphor for the revitalization of the district. They and their partners provide encouragement and even capital to seed the dreams of neighborhood entrepreneurs. They also helped create the Old Fourth Ward Community Garden, open to the entire neighborhood, whose mission is to foster community spirit through gardening, as well as to produce food for the homeless and indigent. Perhaps the most energizing collaboration is the Highland Bakery, a warehouse space converted into loft apartments and small businesses, whose tenants still produce bread on the premises.

Which goes to show that the L5P area remains a center of sociological ferment.

# eating/coffee

L5P's determinedly offbeat restaurants and cafes often self-consciously cultivate the air of soup kitchens gone upscale. Forget about stuffy dress codes or reservations. Many places are comfortable hangouts where you can down a few drinks, flip through one of several free weekly arts rags displayed at the entrance, and savor the no cover/no minimum local sideshow. Between old favorite institutions and new hopefuls, the fare is diverse and usually inexpensive. Service varies; it can be personable and speedy, but often you'll encounter some grunge casualty whose primary concern is how to clean out the resin in their one-hitters. And remember that many of your hosts and servers moonlight as local musicians; be kind and ask where they're gigging if you catch them in an air-guitar riff.

**Cost Range** per entree
$/under 10 dollars
$$/10–15 dollars
$$$/15–20 dollars
$$$$/20+ dollars

**american...** Rumor has it that when the bustling **Vortex Bar & Grill** (*438 Moreland Ave.* 404/688–1828 $) opened its second location in a former vegetarian cafe, several of the vegan cooks wept openly at the thought of dead cows roasting in their beloved old ovens. They didn't know the half of it. The burgers are huge and dripping with juices, while even the vegetables come fried and greasy. The sarcastic sense of humor on the menu is a nice touch: "If you ask us stupid questions, we'll be forced to mock you mercilessly." Don't let the garish oversized skull entrance intimidate you into thinking this is some kind of hard-core death-metal haunt; the interior and ambience are actually pretty tame—yuppies galore peruse the lengthy international brew list. Also worth a trip is its Midtown location.

Not in the mood for red meat and Marilyn Manson? Indigo Girl Emily Saliers is an investor in **Flying Biscuit Cafe** (*1655 McLendon Ave.* 404/687–8888 $$), owned and operated entirely by women. But the delicious comfort fare, courtesy of chef April Moon, lures discerning diners of both genders, including soigné poser/poster gay boys and upmarket families: the perfect demographic for heterogeneous Candler Park. The dinner menu changes regularly; haute Southern specialties include chicken breast dipped in buttermilk with rhubarb compote. Weekend brunch is the main attraction; expect at least an hour's wait for a table. The patient are rewarded with mouthwatering organic oatmeal pancakes, turkey meatloaf, and "pudge," a tasty mashed-potato concoction. An adjacent bakery sells fresh muffins, scones, biscuits and desserts (including chocolate-chip oatmeal macadamia-nut cookies the size of your head).

The lunch counter at **The Little Five Points Pharmacy** (*484 Moreland Ave. 404/524-4466 $*) has been jacked up into a full-fledged cafe (grub now runs toward tuna melts and meat loaf: blue-plate-special territory). This remains the place to get a genuine cherry Coke (not to mention Excedrin and Alka Seltzer) to settle post-revelry stomachs.

**The Roman Lily Cafe** (*668 N. Highland Ave. 404/653–1155 $–$$*) is transforming the Old Fourth Ward much as the Biscuit lent Candler Park credibility as a viable, revitalized area. Indeed, owner/chef Calavino Donati apprenticed at the Biscuit; her menu offers similarly innovative comfort food. A turkey and Havarti "samich" is spruced up with sun-dried-tomato garlic mayo and sunflower sprouts. Turkey poblano meat loaf is sassed by tequila jalapeño gravy. Polenta (the ultimate comfort food) adds gritty texture to seared scallops and wild mushrooms. Calavino's buzzed hair and severe wardrobe belie her exuberant greeting (the restaurant is named for her grandparents, Roman and Lily). The space is just as inventive and warm: brick walls, open kitchen, hand-painted tables with decoupage, stained glass, huge airy windows, and a fabulous mural of Fernand Léger-esque kaffee klatschers adorning the counter. An amazing find—and a bargain.

**cajun...** Bayou kitchen aficionados will drool over **The Baker's Cajun Cafe** (*1126 Euclid Ave. 404/223–5039 $*), which does an admirable job with hearty gumbo, jumping jambalaya, muffalettas, and po' boy sandwiches, plus other entrees, like eggplant lasagna and catfish. For breakfast, try the corned-beef hash, omelets, frittatas, or "*grillandes & grits,*" a carnivorous concoction of spicy beef stew and yellow corn grits, served only during weekend brunch. The owners get there at sunup, rather like that Dunkin' Donuts guy ("time to make the frittatas"?)—but the strong chicory-laced coffee, not to mention the hot pink and purple paint on the building, cut-rate Mardi Gras decor, and bold, brash paintings of food on the windows, would open anyone's eyes.

**caribbean...** Wash down the tangy, succulent Jamaican jerk chicken at **Bridgetown Grill** (1156 Euclid Ave. 404/ 653–0110 $) with an icy Red Stripe beer. Also of note are the black-bean burger, hummus, vegetable plate, and pork chops. Nearly everything comes with wondrous bread and pineapple butter, steaming sides of black beans and rice and cucumber salad, and blinding smiles from the friendly wait staff. The pretty back patio is usually crammed with a gamut of types: blond dreadlocked musicians, gaunt Trent Reznor wannabes, Courtney Love grunge goddesses, henna-rinsed Lilith Fair aficionados, and junior execs in suits and ties.

**coffee...** **Aurora** (468 Moreland Ave. 404/523–6856 $) offers basic java. No fancy frills, no four dozen syrup-derived varieties, no overpriced souvenirs for sale . . . just good, hot coffee, and a small selection of cookies and pastries for dunking. The chilly decor mixes bleak sheet-metal-industrial design with country-kitchen furnishings. Check the extensive neighborhood bulletin board for something interesting to do once you're wired. For a great hangout scene, also try the locations in Midtown and Virginia Highland.

Inman Park's **More Than Coffee** (110 Hurt St. 404/ 577–7400 $) strives to live up to its name, serving as a "community center" for the neighborhood. The tiny cafe resembles somebody's den, offering a comfortable setting for the monthly poetry readings. Works from local artists decorate the walls, and the decent newsstand features all the latest cyberpunk/literary gazettes. Sandwiches, fruits, cakes, and bagels are standard but tasty.

**Village Coffee** (420 Moreland Ave. 404/688–3176 $) benefits from its location on the crowded main square in Little Five Points. The coffees aren't bad, and the edibles range from fair to fairly good. Turkey, ham, and tuna salad prevail; a wilder option is a lamb gyro. But the best thing about this place is its outdoor seating, where you amuse yourself people-watching while you sip your caffeine.

**cuban... La Fonda Latina** (1150 Euclid Ave. 404/577–8317, 1639 McLendon Ave. 404/378–5200 $) is a hugely popular local chain, owned and operated by the entrepreneurs behind Atlanta's beloved Fellini's Pizza joints, Mike Nelson and Clay Harper. The latter is also a studio owner, musician, and all-around character-about-town. Cuban sandwiches, quesadillas, and black beans and rice are primo, as is the house specialty, paella, a traditional Spanish mix of rice, vegetables, seafood, and pork. The smaller location on McLendon, in Candler Park, is cramped and crowded, but the Euclid Avenue outpost is soothing and airy; sun and moonlight pour in through the transparent roof over the outdoor courtyard.

**italian...** The chefs at **The Patio** (1029 Edgewood Ave. 404/584–8945 $$) serve hefty portions of delectable mid-priced Spanish-Italian fare. Everything is made fresh, from pizza to pasta (wonderfully garlicky staples like linguini with clam sauce). They're open for dinner only, except on weekends, when their frittatas are gobbled up during brunch. The Old-World-style atrium patio, lit up with tiny lights at night, is so cozy you'll want to spend the night.

**Fellini's Pizza** (422 Seminole Ave. 404/525–2530, 1634 McLendon Ave. 404/687–9190 $) has become an Atlanta institution, with six locations all over town. Each offers inexpensive, savory slices and dopey local-musician staffers (they even work rhythmically: Watch the way they spin pizzas, almost in harmony). They stay open late for post-rock-show munchers—till 2 a.m. every night except Sunday, when the ovens cool at midnight. The patio at the McLendon location, popular with families, is almost always full during the spring and summer. **Savage Pizza** (484 Moreland Ave. 404/523–0500 $), however, is a more-than-adequate substitute. The food's slightly more expensive, but they do deliver if you live in the 'hood, and the pies are more decadently gooey than the flavorful thin-crust Fellini's offerings (the two could easily revive the New York-versus-Chicago pizza debate).

**mexican...** Though **El Myr** (1091 Euclid Ave. 404/588–0250 $) is tiny and dim, the atmosphere is jovial, and the burly Tex-Mex burritos fill many a local band member's belly. When the crowds overflow to the small outdoor patio, you can find solace at the inside bar, where the margaritas flow late into the night. The high-quality, high-octane tequila shots at **Gringos'** (1238 Dekalb Ave. 404/522–8666 $$) will knock you on your *culo*. The authentic Central American dishes—chiles rellenos (stuffed with pork, chicken or beef) and barbecued pork—have just the right amount of seasoning, zinging with fresh cilantro, habañero, poblano, tomatillo, or tamarind. Portions are huge; you may have to be rolled out. The patio is packed weekends, so expect a lengthy wait.

**middle eastern...** Belly dancers? Tarot card readings? Cornish hens? Get thee to **The Casbah Moroccan Restaurant (465 N. Highland Ave. 404/524–5777 $$$)**. Tantalizing lamb dishes, couscous, and kebabs tickle your palate, while sultry swirling damsels jiggle their tummies and spin scarves amid sensual puffed pillows, velvet drapes, and embroidered banquettes. For lighter, less expensive fare (no belly dancers here; maybe the prices at the Casbah function as a hidden cover charge) try the quaint **Olive Bistro (1099 Euclid Ave. 404/582–0029 $)**. The olive-oil-seasoned eggplant and tabbouleh are perfectly pungent, while the hummus and falafel taste ultra-fresh (they even soak their own chickpeas). **Marco's Pita (1105 Euclid Ave. 404/588–0777 $)** is an ideal pre-theater dinner stop, being adjacent to 7 Stages theater and the Variety Playhouse. Marco himself serves up several varieties of pita sandwiches (the Italian and seafood editions get high marks), as well as falafel and veggie burgers. The secluded patio makes for surprisingly romantic tête-à-têtes, given the long, skinny, crowded room.

# bars

Drinking is a favorite pastime in Little Five Points, but unlike the cheesy McBars you'll encounter in yuppier, busybody Buckhead, most of the folks you'll meet in these watering holes are neighborhood locals who know the bartenders on a first-name basis, as well as other customers stumbling through the doors. Oddly, rowdiness is rarely a problem, though putting one foot in front of the other can be. That's what taxis and liver transplants are for, right?

**The Euclid Avenue Yacht Club** (1136 Euclid Ave. 404/ 688–2582) is nowhere near a boat, let alone a body of water. Still, a case could be made that their 20 draft beers and 150 bottled varieties (plus or minus) could float any passing vessel. A motley assortment of local types have seemingly grown roots here. Example? Meet "315," an artist/roamer who's here every freakin' night, it seems. ("I hated the name Billy," is all he'll allow about the name.) Maybe the regulars are hooked on the superior bar food. Many say the grilled cheese is orgasmic; others prefer the turkey delis or cheesesteaks. Odd note about the Yacht Club: Every Sunday afternoon, dozens upon dozens of chunky bikers park their Harleys out front and spend the day inside drinking beer . . . . No one really knows how this clad-in-leather-and-chains-tradition began. Nobody asks, either.

**The Austin Avenue Buffet** (918 Austin Ave. 404/ 524–9274) is the place to go before you head to the Star Bar [see **sidebar**] for a night of cowpokin'. With cheap workingman's beer, Waylon and Tammy on the jukebox, and plenty of old-time regulars who'll talk your ear off if you treat 'em kindly, you can't go wrong. Local country bands occasionally play here on weekends, but this isn't a late-night place—you'll be thrown out before midnight (or before that if your chinos look too pressed). As for eats, let's just say the Buffet isn't exactly known for its buffet (chips, ham & eggs, crackers, hot dogs).

For more conventional drinking environs, **The Brewhouse Cafe** (401 Moreland Ave. 404/525–7799), with its large outdoor patio, is a popular hangout in the warmer months. Beer specials often change by the hour, so keep your ears open. And avoid the food. For something with a tad more dignity, **The North Highland Pub** (469 N. Highland Ave. 404/522–4600) offers grub and libations for those who stumble slightly off the beaten path to North Highland Avenue. And to hobnob with old-timer local politicos and liberal journalists, head to **Manuel's Tavern** (602 N. Highland Ave. 404/525–3447), a journalist hangout founded by longtime Dekalb County government czar Manuel Maloof. Nearly everyone here smokes cigars and grouses about the glory days of the Democratic Party. Sam Nunn fans, take note: It's within spitting distance of The Carter Center.

# music/clubs

By any barometer, Little Five Points is Atlanta's live rock 'n' roll hub, for local and national acts alike. While music venues and dance clubs elsewhere in town sprout up and vanish with dizzying frequency, most Little Five Points venues have survived and thrived for years. Each club has its own distinct personality, and in many cases, its fiercely individual clientele. If you're into more than one style of noise, you'll be right at home jumping from one seedy yet comfy club to the next. In most cases, weekday shows start around 9:30 p.m., while weekend gigs get rolling between 10 and 10:30 p.m.

**The Point** (420 *Moreland Ave.* 404/659–3522) is a good, all-purpose rock club that in many ways serves as the centerpiece of Little Five Points itself. Holding more than 300 colorfully adorned bodies when they shoehorn 'em in, The Point remains Atlanta's Point Zero for both emerging alternative rock acts and promising local bands. Sunday afternoons are reserved for all-ages punk shows, a popular weekly ritual. Not in the mood for loud music? Too bad: The upstairs bar is just as crowded and twice as noisy. The patrons look pretty rough here, as do the employees. Most are pussycats deep down. Maybe.

Feelin' full of youthful angst? **513** (513 *Edgewood Ave.* 404/223–5132) loads the stage with sweaty, pissed-off punk, hard-core, and ska bands. The sound is terrible and the surroundings are bleak. Most shows seem like amateur night in a friend's basement while the parental units are away for the weekend. At least it isn't squeaky-clean "Party of Five" and "Dawson's Creek."

**The Masquerade** (695 *North Ave.* 404/577–8178) plays the same type of live music, along with industrial, metal, and alternative-rock bands. This huge, imposing space is housed in a multi-level old mill. Live bands play upstairs in "Heaven," sometimes competing with the throbbing din coming from below: "Hell." That's where the goth-looking dance-club part of Masquerade thrives (black halter tops and pierced navels prevail; beware the possibility of unintentional hypodermic jabbings). Here, you'll shake like a zombie to the pulsing electronica, '80s retro, swing, and more (each night has its own theme). Meanwhile, an in-between "Purgatory" area offers pool tables, video games, live DJs, and a bar. During warmer months,

## redneck underground

Headquarters of Atlanta's "redneck underground," **The Star Community Bar** *(437 Moreland Ave. 404/681–9018)* has more character—and more characters—than any other club in town. From the swanky retro fittings of the Little Vinyl Lounge downstairs to the jumpin' shenanigans upstairs, something here's guaranteed to loosen the buckle of even Bible Belt thumpers. Other than Tuesday night's popular disco with Afro-star DJ Romeo Cologne, this is a live-music venue—roots/rockabilly icons like Link Wray and the Flat Duo Jets pack 'em in, while swingin' Kingsized (featuring Vinyl Lounge bartender Mike Geier) and nutty drunks Truckadelic (with Star Bar soundman extraordinaire Joe Hamm and the club's pants-dropping, pierced-penis-exposing mascot-by-default Billy Rat) are local favorites. Housed in an old bank building, the "vault" at the Star Bar is now an appropriately tacky shrine to Elvis, where lovers swoon to the jukebox and make wishes while lobbing coins toward the golden toilet seat. The Star Bar itself seems haunted by the ghosts of the area's larger-than-life musicians and crazies who have passed away recently, like songwriter/guitarist Gregory Dean Smalley and beloved poet Deacon Lunchbox. A great place to get loopy on cheap Pabst Blue Ribbon.

Masquerade's large backyard transforms into a makeshift live-music park.

The comfortable, aptly named **Variety Playhouse** (**1099 Euclid Ave. 404 / 521–1786**) offers touring bands from a wide swath of genres in an intimate theater setting with superb acoustics, though most bookings skew toward the "adult alternative" end of the scale, whatever that is. Think Richard Thompson, Wilco, Victoria Williams, Ray Davies, et al. Most shows start early: 8 or 9 p.m.

# buying stuff

Little Five Points offers eccentric shops catering to the more artsy, subversive wing of urban society. There are dozens of wacky clothes stores peddling everything from secondhand threads to auto-erotic clubwear (nothing you'd wear to the office, of course, though you'll look abfab hanging out on the corner with your pals). Many of these apparel emporia also venture into jewelry, gifts, and cosmetics, of the highly glittery variety. As you might expect, the independent record stores in Little Five Points concentrate almost fetishistically on the kind of fringe recordings that prompt blank stares when inquired about at the chain stores. And then there are those curious, "anything goes" places that seem to lack any theme whatsoever. Outside of some of the fancier items of clothing, prices are pretty reasonable.

**books...** **A Cappella Books** (**1133 Euclid Ave. 404 / 681–5128**) is tailor-made for the reader of dog-eared tomes. The size of a large den, the shop offers shelf after shelf of quality used books in a sedate environment that encourages browsing. The specialty here is out-of-print works, most hand-picked by owner Frank Reiss. Plenty of cool music and pop culture manifestos, plus a large section dedicated exclusively to Beat Generation writers (Burroughs, Bukowski, Kerouac, et al.). **Charis Books & More** (1189 Euclid Ave. 404/524–0304) in Candler Park is a cozy, independent feminist bookstore, and the only one of its kind in Atlanta. Staffed mainly by volunteers, the store features a generous list of difficult-to-find books, including a wide selection of feminist magazines, lesbian titles and unique children's books. They often host speakers, open mike nights and discussion forums. **In Character** (1647 McLendon Ave. 404/378–1130) focuses exclusively on theater, film, and performing-arts books. The casual room serves as a meeting place for the community's aspiring actors and filmmakers. In addition to screenplays, sheet music, and stage plays, they stock publications on directing, costume design, makeup, stage direction, criticism, and more.

## cds/records...

Contrary to its name, **Criminal Records** (466 Moreland Ave. 404/215–9511) specializes entirely in CDs, except for a few indie 7-inch vinyls: new and used music catering to the "gimme-indie-rock" crowd. Other forms of alternative pop media are represented, too, including books, 'zines, and a healthy dose of comics. Bespectacled owner Eric Levin offers live performances and "meet & greets" with local and touring national acts at the store. The much older **Wax 'n' Facts** (432 Moreland Ave. 404/525–2275) has been drawing music fans to Little Five Points since the mid-'70s. This overstuffed store is usually packed with people flipping through bin after dusty bin of vinyl and CDs. It houses a good import selection, plus shirts, posters, mags, a few collectibles, and a venerable staff full of cranky wackos, whose musical knowledge approaches "Jeopardy" champion status; they rarely have to check the inventory on the computer. They know every inch of the store. Candler Park's **Full Moon Records** (1653 *McLendon Ave.* 404/377–1919) sells used music almost exclusively. While you won't find the selection of some other retailers, would-be DJs and nostalgia junkies will howl at the prices—all CDs are $7, while most LPs go for $3.

**Satellite Records** (447 *Moreland Ave.* 404/880–9746) offers dizzy techno-heads scads of vinyl (and some CDs) in all the genres of the moment: breakbeat, jungle, trip-hop, trance, etc. The in-house turntables are constantly commandeered by spiffy spinners testing out the beats, and owner Tommy Sunshine (that's right) is a prominent local DJ himself, often hosting parties across the street at The Point.

Right around the corner, the smaller **Rewind Records** (1120 *Euclid Ave.* 404/827–9463) has less of a selection, but between these two stores any DJ should be able to dig up the dance tracks they're craving.

## clothes/new... Junkman's Daughter (464 *Moreland Ave.* 404/577–3188) has probably clothed everyone in Little Five Points at some point during the '80s or '90s. The queen of L5P retro duds started out in a smaller location on Euclid Avenue back in 1982 selling mostly secondhand items, but since the store relocated to this bigger (but still jam-packed) space several years back, it has focused on new attire, cool gifts, toys, trinkets, books,

shoes, and other elements of survival. Many display clothes seem more like Halloween costumes than sensible streetwear, but some manage to make fashion statements in a stage whisper rather than a scream.

The aptly named **Throb** (1140 Euclid Ave. 404/522–0355) purveys devilish, skintight, often strategically ripped or transparent men's and women's clubwear in the front of the store, and more daring leather and fetish sex gear, handcuffs, straps, and so on in the back. Sexy? Scary's more like it! Throb also carries the usual silver jewelry items, pipes, bongs, and other smoking accessories for stoners.

If you're looking for fun, tacky clubbing clothes, you'll find fulfillment at **Wish** (447 Moreland Ave. 404/880–0402). The '70s do the hustle with the '90s in this colorful boutique, and frankly, it's hard to tell them apart. Far earthier are the items at **Atlanta Hemp** (1645 McLendon Ave. 404/370–1717). Everything in the store (socks, dresses, hats, shirts, overalls, sandals, sneakers, bags, etc.) is made at least in part from our friend the hemp plant. Taking the gimmick to the next level, they recently added a fridge stocked with hemp-seed ice cream ... let's just say Baskin-Robbins has nothing to worry about.

When you want to draw attention to your feet, step into **Abbadabba's** (421-B Moreland Ave. 404/588–9577). The outrageous boots, stylish sandals, and an extensive lineup of Birkenstocks and Doc Martens aren't as wild as the clothes in their other Atlanta stores, but this is still the best place in the area for cool shoes. Looking to top off your outfit with a temporary 'do? **Fifi Mahoney's** (1152 Euclid Ave. 404/681–3434) traffics in silly wigs, hats, and accessories. But the specialty here is cosmetics; their line of glittery lipstick and nail polish, Cookiepuss, a fave of drag queens at Backstreet and strippers on Cheshire Bridge Road alike, is made—guess where—in Atlanta.

## clothes/vintage... Stefan's (1160 Euclid Ave. 404/ 688–4929) is easily Atlanta's classiest vintage clothing store. The threads are in uniformly excellent condition, and you can find some bargains—just don't expect Salvation Army goods or prices. The emphasis here is on dressier items, and the selection of menswear is better than the ladies'. The focus at **Frock of Ages** (1653 McLendon Ave. 404/ 370–1006) is on frilly dresses, hats, and jewelry, although they do sell a few ties. Browsers beware: This place smells like mothballs.

## food... You won't hear an animal scream at Little Five Points' only real supermarket, **Sevananda** (1111 Euclid Ave. 404/681–2831), which caters to a granola crowd with organic fruits and vegetables, whole-grain breads, rice, unrefined sugar desserts, homeopathic supplements, and plenty of God's gift to vegetarians: tofu. It also happens to be Atlanta's only community co-op, serving 1,300 members. (Its other claim to fame: In its previous incarnation, it was the Piggly-Wiggly supermarket featured in the movie Driving Miss Daisy.)

## gifts/art... For some authentic country-and-western supplies, take a ride into **West of Heaven** (424 Moreland Ave. 404/577–8775). The Patsy Cline and Hank Williams, Sr. portraits here reveal the store's redneck heart, but like the merchandise at an all-night Stuckey's gift shop, it's

never done in a condescending manner. Proprietor
Texanne also sews up her own authentic cowboy threads
for local honky-tonkers. Aside from the owner's own
sequin-studded clothes, the usual cowboy/girl getups are
here, from boots and hats to spurs. Giddyup!

Moving from country to worldly we have **Soulkiss** (1149
Euclid Ave. 404/525–9668), whose traditional and exotic
baubles, bangles, and beads hail from around the planet.
You can walk out of here with Czech glass hairclips,
Indonesian scarves, Middle Eastern belly-dancing beads, or
Siwa virginity disks. For a more focused experience, check
out **African Connections** (1107 Euclid Ave. 404/589–
1834), a small but enlightening presentation of modern
and tribal art, furniture, and musical instruments.

**Donna Van Gogh's** (1651 McLendon Ave. 404/370–1003)
is a delightful art boutique in Candler Park, specializing in
the work of talented, idiosyncratic local artists like Kate
Dana (whose paintings depict '50s and '60s Southern culture like soda fountains and drive-ins) and R. Land (who
creates grotesque yet humorous monster images). Almost
all the goofily humorous paintings, sculptures, and knick-
knacks are small enough to make excellent gifts.
**Boomerang** (1145 Euclid Ave. 404/577–8158) sells higher-
end vogue-ish bachelor-pad-style stuff as well as home
furnishings: candles, wall hangings, furniture, lighting
fixtures, etc., displayed in a colorful, funky manner.

The very name **Revival** (674 N. Highland Ave. 404/
581–0420) symbolizes the revitalization of the Old Fourth
Ward district. Revival is composed of different shops that
run into one another. The first restores and sells vintage
kitchen Depression/World War II-era appliances and home

furnishings, including Waring blenders and Hardwick gas stoves. Co-owner Jake Rothschild also sells his line of gourmet all-natural foodstuffs in an adjacent deli, including cocoa and preserves. Another storefront is being transformed into Jake's Ice Cream Parlor, featuring a vintage art deco 1920s soda fountain with chrome and green leatherette stools; with a patio overlooking Downtown, it will be the only ice cream emporium located directly on the bike path. Another store will house a community art gallery.

If you're driving down Edgewood Avenue in Inman Park and find yourself amid a cloud of bubbles, you've found **Bouji** (753 Edgewood Ave. 404/659–4100). Wacky pals Pierre Legault and Neal Vipperman run this odd little shop as well as create 80 percent of the items in their courtyard (the rest come courtesy of other local artists). The emphasis is on art that is both functional and unconventional. Using recycled trash like old liquor bottles, they create hummingbird feeders, oil lamps, wind chimes, bowls, tiles, furniture, and whatever else strikes their fancy. Nowadays, customers bring in things they would otherwise discard, and donate it to the boys as raw material. Oh, and the bubble machine strategically aimed toward traffic? It started as an inexpensive means to get people to notice the store. It worked, and now Pierre and Neal bring in lots of extra pocket change by renting and selling the little devils.

Bouji's neighboring store is **Urban Nirvana** (15 Waddell St. 404/688–3329), a weird little wonderland full of clay sculptures, fountains, and "garden art" made on the premises. But owner Christine Sibley gets as much attention for the animals roaming around outside as she does for the yard furnishings inside. Turkeys, goats, peacocks, and sheep are just a few of her pets.

Pee Wee Herman would have a field day in **Gazoyks** **(912 Austin Ave. 404/688–7735)**, whose shelves are stuffed with nutty noisemakers, goofball toys, novelty gags, rubber chickens, propeller beanies, and so on (sorry, no rain-coats): This is a great place for last-minute gifts of the stocking-stuffer variety. Another good stop for usually air-borne, sometimes educational playthings is **Identified Flying Objects** (1164 Euclid Ave. 404/524–4628). Whether it be kites, boomerangs, frisbees, balls, or hackey-sacks you're in the market for, I.F.O. can set you up. They also play a lot of Grateful Dead here.

**videos...** When you've outgrown the new-release wall at Blockbuster, you're ready for **Blast Off Video** (1133 Euclid Ave. 404/681-0650). The walls of this cramped room are filled with weird cult movies, sexploitation flicks, psy-chotronic fare, obscure music videos, B-movie sci-fi, experimental independent stuff, and other specimens from the soggy bog of nontraditional filmdom. The peo-ple who work here are more peculiar than the videos they stock (indie fans: Think Kevin Corrigan's brilliantly geeky turn as a video-store clerk in *Walking and Talking*).

# sleeping

Surprise. Don't expect fancy overnight accommodations. In fact, L5P's central business district and surrounding areas don't have anything remotely approaching a low-end chain hotel. For value, you're better off on a friend's couch or at the shabbier motels in adjacent neighborhoods [see **midtown** and **virginia highland**]. Several beautiful old homes in Inman Park, however, have been restored and converted into B&Bs; the prices are pretty reasonable for a comfortable stay in a lovely century-old Queen Anne Victorian house where Southern hospitality lives. They're within walking distance of the cool stuff, too.

> **Cost Range** for double occupancy per night on a weeknight. Call to verify prices.
> $/under 75 dollars
> $$/75–125 dollars
> $$$/125–175 dollars
> $$$$/175+ dollars

**The King-Keith House** (889 *Edgewood Ave.* 404/688–7330 $$) was built in 1890 by local hardware magnate George King. The wraparound front porch is a beguiling place to hang out. The congenial current owners, the Keiths, are quick to point out that their house is one of the most photographed in Atlanta, and it's easy to see why. The restoration work is immaculate, including repainting in authentic turn-of-the-century colors; the interior gleams with magnificent hardwood floors. Breakfasts are sumptuous affairs, with fresh fruit, baked goodies, and specials like banana French toast.

The facade of **Sugar Magnolia** (804 *Edgewood Ave.* 404/222–0226 $$) is less attractive (the front steps could use a new coat of paint), but the interior is chockablock with period antiques. The unabashedly romantic Royal

Room comes complete with a sunken double jacuzzi, while an efficiency cottage out back offers more privacy than most B&Bs.

# doing stuff

Most people who visit or populate Little Five Points do so because of its unique shopping and entertainment options, as well as its urban-village vibe, lacking elsewhere in Atlanta. Most activities, then, tend to center around . . . shopping and being entertained. The pale skin, thin physiques, and dopey expressions on a good portion of the inhabitants suggest the following: a) their outdoor experiences consist mainly of trying to bum smokes off passersby on the sidewalk, b) sports are the last things on their minds, and c) the idea of expanding their knowledge and cultural well-being by (gasp!)—attending a museum—brings on a cold sweat. Still, a few noncommercial alternatives to the street hassles and hustles offer opportunities for relaxation and even enlightenment.

The very names **Inman Park** (*Moreland and Edgewood avenues*) and **Candler Park** (*McLendon and Terrace avenues*) suggest soothing greenery. Indeed, these and several other small parks dot the landscape surrounding Little Five Points, providing ample opportunities for sun worship, picnics, and clandestine snuggling with someone special. The largest is Candler Park. Surrounded by woods and rolling grass-covered hills, the softball field and nine-hole golf course are the only public facilities of note in the area. Snaking its way through Candler Park is a paved biking/in-line skating/jogging path that extends nearly to the Martin Luther King, Jr. Center on the west side (and past Downtown, if you don't mind limited riding on sections of city streets) and over to Ponce De Leon Avenue on the east. This three-to-four-mile section is arguably the most traveled, especially mornings and evenings, when runners, bikers, and bladers create a spectacular parade of motion.

A real jewel is **Springdale Park** (just off Edgewood and Euclid avenues), the ultimate date spot, with paths lined with lilies spring through autumn and tadpoles, crawdads, bass, and carp skimming through the ponds.

You can even bicycle just west of Candler Park to **The Carter Center** (1 Copenhill Ave. 404/420–5100), where the Jimmy Carter Presidential Museum and Library are housed. This shrine to Carter contains memorabilia, documents, photos, and other artifacts from his term in the White House. The historical displays trace Carter's ascent from unknown south Georgia peanut boy through state politics and on to his unexpected transformation into the big cheese. If that ain't enough, two theaters screen reverential films recounting the saga. The interactive exhibits are silly, but a full-scale reproduction of Carter's Oval Office is poignant. The archives in the adjacent library are primarily of interest to historians and documentarians. If you never liked Carter, you'll probably be turned off by the saintly peacemaker image the museum pounds into your head, but the grounds are beautiful, and a charming little cafe makes this a leisurely lunchtime destination.

Still, the number one activity in Little Five Points is simply "hanging out." The majority of the activity occurs in the Plaza in the center of the business district, at the corner of

Moreland and Euclid avenues, and it is indeed a fine location for people-watching. The sheer variety of humanity on display is sport in itself, and before long you'll surely see three or four or nine other people you know. Don't ever throw away your old Nikes or Chuck Taylors—the telephone lines above the Plaza are loaded with dozens of pairs of worn-out shoes, dangling by the shoelaces, in sort of a combination ongoing art project and final resting place. Whatever . . . .

**spectating...** Sadly, the diversity of nightlife beyond live music is limited. There are no movie theaters in the immediate area, not even a tiny indie or revival sanctuary. Periodic spoken-word nights in coffee shops and clubs are dying out. More representative of the neighborhood's personality is local musician Bill Taft's occasional "Another Evening With the Garbageman" nights at the Star Bar [see **music/clubs**]. Between Taft's bouts of stream-of-consciousness storytelling, he presents edgy local bands, artists, comedians, and short films in what is truly a bizarre, homegrown variety show.

L5P does offer a handful of small, enterprising theater groups; you won't find Broadway-scale presentations but rather intimate productions of spiky new works and revivals of plays (like Ionesco's The Bald Soprano) that often perplex local audiences.

Weekends at **Dad's Garage Theater Company (280 Elizabeth St. 404/523–3141)** have become a jolly ritual for fans of improvisation. "Scandal" is their regular late-night offering on Fridays, an ongoing extemporaneously created soap opera involving a cast of woefully wicked and dysfunctional characters, including everyone's favorite, the nasty Boozy the Puppet. Late-night Saturdays, it's "Theater Sports"—competition improv at the mercy of the audience. Try and trip 'em up, which is half the fun, anyway. For something a bit headier, **7 Stages (1105 Euclid Ave. 404/523–7647)** puts on sometimes controversial, always unique, thought-provoking fare. Occasionally they'll bring in wild folks like breast-squirting, yam-squeezing Karen Finley for "special" engagements. Also of note is **Horizon Theater Company (1083 Austin Ave. 404/584–7450)**, presenting mostly locally written dramas of limited budgets and (usually) high quality. Can't say much for the uncomfortable venue, but in the Atlanta theater scene, you learn to work with what little you're given.

# body

"Am I in Atlanta or a copy of *National Geographic*?" you might ask. Tattoos and piercings *are* mainstream here: Every 20-something worth their weight in nine-inch nails has to have *something* somewhere on their body to show off to friends and worry parents. As Atlanta's alternaland, L5P has more than its share of businesses willing to help you along in your quest for permanent self-mutilation—uh, expression. Surprisingly, the hair salons don't really specialize in mohawks, dreadlocks, or spikes, preferring to remain comparatively conservative. Remember: Most tattoo parlors offer body piercings, but not all body-piercing shops do tattoos.

Candler Park's **Piercing Experience (1654 McLendon**

*Ave.* 404/378–9100) specializes in puncturing flesh: They're both highly regarded and highly sanitary. They'll put 18-karat gold, African Niobium metal, or stainless-steel jewelry just about anywhere you want, either by appointment or walk-in whim. Check out their Web site at piercing.org. **Urban Tribe** (1131 Euclid Ave. 404/659–6344) is also big with the piercing crowd, but they'll give you the ink needle, too. Any style can be rendered, but their forte is tribal (duh!) totems. **Tornado Tattoo** (464-A Moreland Ave. 404/524–0009) owner Gary Yoxen has been a mainstay of the Atlanta punk scene for years. The hulking hard-core musician, boasting a load of tattoos himself, brings in customer traffic based on his reputation alone. Others are drawn by its location in the back of the popular clothes and gift boutique Junkman's Daughter.

Likewise, the longtime owner of **Sacred Heart Tattoo** (483 Moreland Ave. 404/222–8385), Tony Olivas, has a reputation as a master of detailed body art. Sacred Heart does an exceptional job on the more intricate, fine-line style of tattoos, and although Tony rarely works out of this parlor, their other artists are uniformly good. Sacred Heart's piercing business, **Body Mind** (483 Moreland Ave. 404/222–8414), operates out of the same building.

You can meet all of these proud skin painters and piercers at the annual Atlanta Tattoo Arts Festival at the Masquerade [see **music/clubs**]. Artists, aficionados, and crazy loons who use their entire bodies as canvases convene in the horrific environs of this cavernous club—many from outside Atlanta—showing off and throwing down. Bring someone shockable and watch as jocularity ensues.

There aren't many coiffing options in Little Five Points.

Most people appear to go for the "just-rolled-out-of-bed" look, anyway. But **Headlines Hair Studio** (1147 *Euclid Ave.* **404/577–5970**) is long-established; the room is small and sparse—waits are common—but you'll most likely be pleased. They also do all that aromatherapy magic that people swoon over. Meanwhile, down the road and 'round the corner, **The Austin Avenue Barber Shop** (914 *Austin Ave.* **404/523–2324**) is where vintage chairs meet modern-industrial steel and black-and-white checkered design. The stylists are friendly and have a keen eye for what 'dos will do—on both ladies and gents.

# decatur

If any neighborhood serves as a
model of Atlanta's "New South"
inclusiveness, Decatur is it.
Offering some of the cheapest
real estate close to Downtown
Atlanta (roughly six miles
west), the town of Decatur and
its outlying areas in DeKalb
County have been colonized
by yuppies just starting
families, the African-American
middle class, and even a
few scraggly bohemian
longhairs and determinedly

turn page for map key

unhygienic L5P skinheads. Now add a healthy number of well-scrubbed students from Emory University (whose medical school is widely regarded as one of the best in the South) and a few buzz-cut gals at Agnes Scott College. Season with suburban moms in curlers who avidly peruse the latest *National Enquirer* at the supermarket . . . and you have essence of Decatur, which beyond its sleepy, placid exterior shows signs of reaching critical hipness mass.

The tradition of tolerance extends almost as far back as its 1823 founding by naval hero and local boy Stephen Decatur. In the mid-1800s, town leaders offered a free lot to anyone who would build a church of any Christian denomination (the ecclesiastic version of homesteading). Episcopal, Catholic, Methodist, and—post-Reconstruction—Baptist houses of worship sprang up and dot the area to this day. Despite all its churches, Decatur is hardly a fundamentalist stronghold. Fast forward to the 1960s, when Mayor Elizabeth Wilson led the fight to integrate the DeKalb County Public Library. Then, in August 1993, when the neighboring ultra-right-wing Cobb County Commission passed a resolution "denouncing the gay/lesbian lifestyle," Decatur's straight mayor invited Cobb County's rainbow contingent to move to his (non-red) neck of the woods. The town has become so gay-friendly that one of Atlanta's most endearing social clubs is "The Digging Dykes of Decatur," easily identified at Gay Pride rallies by

| map key | | |
|---|---|---|
| | 1  Emory University | 4  Brick Store Pub |
| | 2  DeKalb County Courthouse | 5  The Freight Room |
| | 3  Sweet Melissa's | |

their flower-bedecked plastic sunbonnets and bubble-blowing lawn mowers.

The central downtown square, Decatur Square, which abuts the imposing granite DeKalb County Courthouse, has been largely restored and teems with hip new cafes catering to a young, laid-back clientele. Of course, some old-school businesses have resisted the onslaught of gentrification, and the MARTA subway system stops right in the middle of the square, allowing big-city panhandlers to work the Decatur lunch-break crowd. By evening, however, yupsters, families, and the occasional alternative zombie reclaim the restaurants and pubs of the square and its adjacent pedestrian walkways. The police maintain a visible presence here as well, but while muggings and rapes are uncommon, car break-ins are a popular sport.

Decatur Square is bracketed by Ponce de Leon Avenue on the north, Church Street on the east, Commerce Drive on the west, and Trinity Place on the south. There are several noteworthy centers of activity within easy driving distance. Just south of the square sits Agnes Scott College; the area has a lovely campus feel, with turn-of-the-century college buildings and quiet streets lined with spreading oaks, bordered by a more raucous strip of eating and drinking joints along East College Avenue. And yet it's so trendy that scenes from *Scream 2* were shot on its campus and women's studies groups debate postfeminism with messianic zeal in nearby coffeehouses; as one student matter-of-factly observes, "If you took an informal survey, we probably have the highest percentage of lesbian enrollment in the country." Farther south is the Oakhurst area, the most yup-scale part of the neighborhood, with carefully restored 1920s bungalow houses. A few miles northwest of downtown Decatur, along North Decatur and Oxford roads, lies Emory University. The adjoining Emory Village shopping strip serves the university community as well as the surrounding Druid Hills neighborhood, where elegant, spacious, red-brick residences are fronted by handsome porches and manicured yards. Going a mile or so east on North Decatur, to its intersection with Clairemont Avenue and beyond, the area becomes less cutting-edge, more timelessly working-class suburban, interspersed with strip malls and shabby apartment complexes galore. Likewise, the farther north you go on Clairmont Road (it loses the "e" and becomes a "road" somewhere along the way), the more generic the pickings, although at the intersection with North Druid Hills Road, the Toco Hills shopping center offers signs of gentrification.

All in all, the historic center and surrounding blandness remind one of a Mayberry that has boomed in population. But the cast of characters certainly extends beyond Barney Fife, Floyd the barber, Goober, and Aunt Bee (although, come to think of it . . . did she ever marry? Maybe she'd feel right at home and even find a companion!).

# eating/coffee

You'll encounter the widest range of cuisine in the colorful cafes around Decatur Square, whose atmospheres range from lively-chatty to cozy-romantic, and where prices remain moderate. Closer to the colleges, the usual cheaper beer-and-a-slice hangouts predominate (oddly enough, there's very little fast food), alongside some more adventure-some dining spots. Standard attire is rarely fancier than unripped jeans and a shirt that isn't drenched with motor oil.

**Cost Range** per entree
$/under 10 dollars
$$/10–15 dollars
$$$/15–20 dollars
$$$$/20+ dollars

# american... The Crescent Moon (254 W. Ponce de Leon Ave. 404/377–5623 $) serves breakfast and lunch all day, as well as vague daily lunch specials, i.e., Thursday is "pasta day," offering a mystery pasta (usually something recognizable like spaghetti and meatballs) and a drink for $4.95. The killer dishes are the huge stuffed spuds—whole potatoes packed with the likes of smoked chicken, 'shrooms, mozzarella, and barbecue sauce, topped with half a second potato. This monster also comes in a veggie variety. Locals swear the pecan pie here is Atlanta's best.

**The Food Business** (115 Sycamore St. 404/371–9121 $$) is a loud, tri-level restaurant filled with eager eaters day and night thanks to quirky juxtapositions of fresh ingredients. For breakfast, the Crabcake Benedict is recommended, as is the Calico Scramble (eggs scrambled with zucchini, yellow squash, tomato, and goat cheese). Hot and cold sandwiches dominate the lunch menu; all are quite tasty, and served on freshly baked honey grain bread. For dinner, diversity is the key: Rosemary chicken salad, filet mignon, and mu-shu chicken burritos are all solid choices. A glass display case of desserts entices even the calorie-conscious, with sweet-potato-pecan pie, blue-berry pie, and a Kahlua brownie tart among the quite delicious choices.

**Mick's** (116 E. Ponce de Leon Ave. 404/373–7797 $$) is part of a popular local chain whose menu offers a little bit of everything. While the only standouts are the Cajun Crawfish, the Andouille Sausage with Spicy Cheese Dip, and the desserts (the Oreo Cheesecake or Heath Bar Ice Cream Pie merit cheating on your diet), nothing screams "Stay away!" either. The interior of each Mick's is different; this one has the feel of a stately old Southern home, with three rooms and a patio. Sunday brunch is big with the white-haired after-church crowd, who wonder aloud if they dare have a mimosa rather than iced tea with their Eggs Benedict (hollandaise on the side).

**Sweet Melissa's** (127 E. Court Sq. 404/370–1111 $$) resembles a souped-up, stylish diner, with red-and-blue neon lighting, mirrored walls, black-and-white checkerboard tablecloths, and an old-style lunch counter. Lunch and dinner are ordinary, offering little more than basic sandwiches and chips, and the occasional pasta special. But Sunday brunch draws crowds for the omelets you design yourself from a list of farm-fresh ingredients. Whatever you order, be sure to get a side of cheese grits. A light jazz combo plays during Sunday brunch, adding a classy touch.

**cajun...** Bayou transplant Leslie Lester brings her Grandma Grace's spicily authentic recipes to **Ya Ya's Cajun Cuisine** (426 W. Ponce de Leon Ave. 404/373–9292 $$$). The food, while quite good, wouldn't make Emeril Lagasse sweat. Best bets are the crawfish étouffée, the fried shrimp platter, and Grace's Au Gratin, a soupy seafood mixture bound together with baked cheeses. Meat lovers will enjoy the jambalaya, with its big, BIG hunks of chicken, shrimp, and pork, while the gumbo will clear your sinuses. Bright green and scarlet accents and fishing nets give Ya Ya's the odd air of a Christmas party at a coastal crab shack. Adding to the festive atmosphere are a few older local blues guys, like Chicago Bob Nelson, who play on weekend afternoons and evenings.

**coffee...** You enter the **Church Street Coffee House** (*205 W. Ponce de Leon Ave. 404/378–5002 $*) through a small courtyard patio (delightful on cooler evenings). For those who abstain from the chains, this hole in the wall is the best coffeehouse in the area, with a laid-back vibe, plenty of reading material, students and hipsters hanging out, and decent java. Poetry readings featuring both established and little-known wordsmiths from the Atlanta area take place the second Tuesday night of every month.

**Café & Gelato** (*308-B W. Ponce de Leon Ave. 404/373–9468 $*) caters to coffee connoisseurs as well as gourmet ice cream fans. Sip a French Roast Kona or Guatemala, and enjoy the rich Italian gelati and sorbetti. They also serve sandwiches, Euro-style cakes and pastries, and bagels. Not an especially cool place to hang out, but the food and drink are of a higher standard than most java joints.

The out-of-the-way upstarts at the simply named **Joe** (*707-B E. Lake Dr. 404/371–1113 $*) are hoping their brave foray into beany brews will help revitalize a rundown little area called Oakhurst just west of Decatur. Indeed, lots of creative young urban pioneers are moving into the small, affordable houses, in the hope that new cafes and businesses will follow. At the moment, Joe is it, but this clean, sunny little pastry & latte shop is doing quite well. The owners used to be stagehands for local rock 'n' roll concerts, and you'll spot some of the all-access passes they've acquired, for everyone from Dan Fogelberg to Nine Inch Nails, under the glass counter where you order.

**continental...** The breezy wraparound outdoor patio, glass-walled interior, and frilly touches such as hand-embroidered pillows, lace curtains, and lots of potted plants lend **Zac's Cafe** (*308-I W. Ponce de Leon Ave. 404/373–9468* **$$$**) the air of a cross between a greenhouse and Grandma's parlor. The food is a cross between Southern and Continental. The rosemary-scented pork tenderloin, served with fluffy, intensely flavored mashed sweet potatoes, is downright heavenly. Other fine signature dishes include the Jambalaya pasta and the deservedly beloved meat loaf crowned with barbecue sauce and bacon, which achieves near-gourmet status. "I raised three daughters on it," says co-owner and mom Lyodene Haley sweetly. "I chop up the onions and green peppers real fine, and I put oatmeal in it instead of bread crumbs, because I read it on an old Quaker Oats box years ago."

Contrasting with Zac's sunlit gaiety, the mood at **The Supper Club** (*308-H W. Ponce de Leon Ave. 404/370–1270* **$$$**) is exotic and romantic (it's one of the few places in family-happy Decatur that does not welcome children) and seasoned with a quirky Art Nouveau feel, with strings of fairy lights along the walls, elegant antique lamps, brown velvet curtains, and copper-top tables. The constantly changing menu is concocted by owner Michelle Niesen, who was inspired to open this bistro after hosting a series of themed dinner parties at her Inman Park apartment. Regular favorites include the fish kebabs, pork tenderloin, steamed mussels, and Ms. Niesen's extraordinary signature dish: wild shitake mushroom pancakes covered with sun-dried-tomato butter, balsamic reduction, and sauteed spinach served over linguini. A specific wine is suggested for each selection (there is a tiny wine bar just as you enter). Reservations are a must in this minuscule boîte; fortunately it's open late by Decatur standards, though Ms. Niesen once snipped over the phone, "We close whenever we feel like it." By day, the Supper Club's premises are turned over to a casual breakfast and lunch place called **Bill E. Goat's Coffee & Cantina**, which is under completely different management. (The java and burritos are perfectly decent, but certainly not worth a detour.)

**french...** Travel back to the Old World at **Café Alsace** (*121 E. Ponce de Leon Ave.* 404/373–5622 $$$), a quaint little bistro whose robust fare hails from the Alsace-Lorraine region of France, where German and French cooking are happily married. Quiche Lorraine is a specialty (hello!) but also try out the Goat Cheese Wedding Salad (two varieties of cheese and large enough for two), Crevettes et Couscous (shrimp and ham in sauce over parmesan couscous), or Spaetzel à l'Alsacienne (noodles baked with ham, onions, cream, and cheese). There can be a line around the block here on weekend nights.

**Violette** (*3098 Briarcliff Rd.* 404/633–3323 $$–$$$) is easily the most romantic restaurant in the Emory area; every other table seems to hold frat brothers about to pin (yes!) their sorority sisters or older couples beaming at this charmingly retro scene in the dim flickering light. The food is both fairly priced and inventive: Witness pork tenderloin studded with caraway seeds and juniper berries or leg of lamb with honey-cumin sauce served over couscous, the sweetness and heat in perfect counterpoint to the savory meat.

**italian...** You're practically embraced by the staff when you stroll into **Bundos Market** (113 E. Court Sq. 404/ 687–9461 $$$). Luckily, the food is just as agreeable, with the creamy white-wine sauce (a house specialty) adorning everything from baked salmon with scallops to pasta carbonara and mussels linguini. Nightly specials, such as Bundos Chicken (boneless breast stuffed with spinach, onions, tomatoes, and feta cheese) and the veggie lasagna (a big hit with the health- and animal-rights-conscious Decatur crowd), are highly recommended. They bake their own bread, and it's so good you'll want an extra basket. The narrow, undistinguished interior doesn't make for very romantic dining, so try to snag one of the coveted outdoor tables.

**mediterranean...** Quick, name a restaurant where you'll find Jello mold and cottage cheese salad, moussaka, and filet mignon on the same menu. Welcome to **The Square Table** (129 E. Ponce de Leon Ave. 404/373–9354 $) a low-key mainstay of Decatur Square that keeps chugging away amid the plethora of newer, more chic surrounding restaurants. This place doesn't appear to have been been remodeled since it opened 28 years ago, and you've gotta have a soft spot for any restaurant outside of Waffle House or Big Boy that puts pictures of its food on the menu. Owners Roula and Speros Millas emigrated to the U.S. from Greece in the '60s, and yes, traditional Greek dishes liberally infiltrate the menu. Besides the usual baklava, Greek salads, and gyros, a different Greek special is offered every day—witness *pastitsio* (the sublime Attic version of macaroni and cheese, with white sauce, feta, and ground beef). Adding a bizarre touch, the gracious elderly Southern ladies who work there will gently correct your Greek pronunciation, while mangling it themselves.

## mexican... Burrito Art (1451 Oxford Rd. 404/377–7786 $$) offers even more unusual wraps. Offbeat but succulent examples include Grilled Pork Tenderloin (with a touch of sherry), Asian Meat Loaf, and Grilled Eggplant. The original East Atlanta branch has more character (and characters), not to mention art on the walls, but this place does a brisk biz among students and yupsters alike.

## middle eastern... The presence of Emory students cramming and professors marking papers makes **The Cedar Tree** (1565 N. Decatur Rd. 404/373–2118 $) resemble a campus commons during lunch, for which they offer tasty, inexpensive falafel, tabbouleh, baba ghanoush (baked eggplant with sesame paste), and grape leaves with hummus. Carnivores will enjoy the chicken or lamb souvlaki and gyro platters. While the food is unusually good, The Cedar Tree looks like any plain ol' sandwich shop. In fact, it shares the space with **Jason's Pitza** (404/373–2122 $), which has successfully cross-bred pizza with pita sandwiches. Stuffed between two thin, round pita layers, you

can get your choice of toppings . . . er, fillings. Chicken is a big favorite, with florentine, Alfredo, Thai, pesto, and curry varieties; for vegans there are such selections as the zesty, colorful zucchini, tomato, and garlic combo. The most unusual items are the surprisingly good dessert "pitzas" stuffed with bananas or strawberries: Middle Eastern bread meets Mom's apple pie, sort of.

**pizza... Oz Pizza** (309 E. College Ave. 404/373–0110 $) is operated by former employees of long-established local chain Fellini's, and indeed, it's sometimes easy to forget you're actually someplace different. The slices and salads are virtually identical (and luckily, very good), the colorful slapdash interior is arranged with low-budget practicality in mind, and you could swear the dreadlocked bass player behind the cash register took your order at a Fellini's two months ago. He probably did. If anything, this joint is reminiscent of Fellini's when they were a scrappy upstart trying to wean Atlantans off Pizza Hut in the '80s, and their food is all the better for it.

In the Emory Village area, **Everybody's Pizza** (1593 N. Decatur Rd. 404/377–7766 $$) is so pie-in-the-sky good, it's even merited raves from the "Today" show and The New York Times. The thick-crust whole pizzas (no single slices here) are classics, made with fresh chewy dough and a choice of more than 30 toppings. The delectable pizza-crisps—extra-extra-thin-crust 13-inch pizzas—are becoming increasingly trendy among families, Emory students, and singles alike; try the florentine and garlic-sesame chicken varieties. A table on the covered outdoor patio, complete with soothing fountain, is worth the wait.

**southern...** A wildly popular lunch destination for students, downtown Decatur office workers, and nearby neighborhood dwellers, **Our Way Cafe** (303 E. College Ave. 404/373–6665 $) is one of Atlanta's biggest bargains. Affable servers dish out mounds of Southern-style grub from steaming tubs cafeteria-style. The vegetables are something you'd expect Aunt Bee to bring out at suppertime—sweet potato casserole, honey-glazed carrots, collard greens, mashed potatoes—while the meat specials (baked chicken, barbecued pork, meat loaf, etc.), which are uniformly delectable and thankfully almost never overcooked, change daily. You can roll out of here stuffed to the gills for under $5.

Big Greg of **Big Greg's Barbecue** (1479 Scott Blvd. 404/378–6041 $) played football for the University of Georgia, and his lip-smacking barbecued chicken, beef, and ribs are hearty enough to satisfy any linebacker's protein needs. The place is little more than a shack gussied up with pennants and pigskin memorabilia, but it rocks like a frat house full of jocks. Big Greg's also serves a delicious—if heavy—country breakfast.

Just northwest of the Emory campus, **Dusty's** (1815 Briarcliff Rd. 404/320–6264 $) serves up mouthwatering barbecue, cobblers, and chicken wings to a slightly schizoid clientele divided between raucous undergrads and retired couples; the heavenly hickory scent and lively chatter waft a couple of blocks down the road.

**thai...** **Thai Chilli** (2169 Briarcliff Rd. 404/315–6750 $$) sizzles with the superlative food of chef/owner Robert Khankiew, who jumpstarted the Thai craze in Virginia Highland at Surin. Here, the plates are more colorful than the plain but softly lit room. Boldly flavored dishes include delicately flaky salmon in coconut-milk green curry and marvelously crunchy basil rolls in plum sauce. The staff is exceptionally attentive to kids, and although most dishes are appropriately fiery, they'll suggest milder choices for tender palates.

**vegetarian...** Located in the Rainbow Grocery, where you can pick up your supply of rice cakes and soy milk on the way out, **Rainbow's Restaurant (2118 N. Decatur Rd. 404/633–3538 $)** prepares healthy fare on the premises. In addition to the de rigueur veggie burgers, soups, and meatless chili, you can also wolf down a guac sandwich, vegetable quiche, or strawberry-banana smoothie. And they have a tasty, extensive salad bar, with hummus and homemade dressings. The best deal is the plate of brown rice topped with steamed broccoli, zucchini, carrots, and other veggies, which goes for a whopping $2.95.

# bars

Decatur is a good place to make an early night of it (young families abound). Most drinking troughs close up by midnight or, if you're lucky, 1 a.m. But don't let this give you the impression that Decatur is completely un-happenin'. There are plenty of establishments in which to kick back and hoist some brews; they're just usually a little more conservative (and less trendy) than your typical Atlanta nightspot. Avoid getting too rowdy—the local fuzz don't suffer fools gladly.

Might as well start with the best. The English-pub-like

**Brick Store Pub** (125 E. Court Sq. 404/687–0990) is one serious drinking bar. They offer a modest selection of 20 draft and 40 bottled beers, and only the good stuff: imports and microbrews personally selected by the owners. The most commonly available barleypop you'll find is probably Bass or Guinness; otherwise, be brave and take a chance on a crazy Belgian brew like Hoogstraten Poorter, or St. Sebastian Ale. Add to that 15 varieties of single-malt scotch, plus lotsa top-shelf bourbon, Irish whiskey, and cognac, and you've got the makings of a woozy cab ride home. Good food, too—try the fish & chips.

Sound too classy for you? Then stutter-step about 40 yards south through the square to **The Grog Shop** (121 Sycamore St. 404/687–9353), where you'll find a big TV tuned to ESPN, dollar-a-game pool tables, darts, table hockey, loud music, and cheap cold beer, including pitchers at $4 a pop. Yes, the place is kinda dumpy, and a little too bright on the inside (it puts the hole in watering hole) but it's okay for an unassuming little neighborhood bar. Some people swear by the food here. Others just swear.

For the serious pool shark, **Twain's Billiards and Tap** (211 E. Trinity Pl. 404/373–0063) is the tavern of choice. There are two large rooms of billiard madness: one for smokers, one for non-smokers. Here's the skinny for any would-be Minnesota Fats: Unfortunately, you pay by the hour instead of by the game. Darts are free and beers inexpensive ($2 for a Bud, cheaper when they're running specials). Large selection, too—around 100 bottled beers at any given time, and 25 drafts. In addition to the pool rooms, there's a large den-like lounge with lots of comfy sofas and tables, board games, and an outside patio.

**Trackside Tavern** (313 *E. College Ave.* 404/373–9170), right next to Agnes Scott College and usually open until 3 or 4 a.m., is where the employees from the other bars go after work for several more hours of party fun. Trackside has the friendly, young slacker vibe lacking in Decatur's other pubs. Any drinking hall with a foosball table rates high marks, plus they have air hockey and cheap coin-op pool tables. They *do* offer Jägermeister on tap, for you boozers harboring a death wish; otherwise the selection is standard. Trivia Night is on Tuesdays; it's rowdily competitive, since the questions are easy and you have a fighting chance of winning a few drinks on the house. Food? Pickled eggs, my friend. And sandwiches.

# music/clubs

Decatur is home to Emily Saliers and Amy Ray, aka the Indigo Girls, and due to their massive popularity, the small list of live-music venues in the Decatur area caters solely to the acoustic crowd. In the wake of their rise to fame in the '90s, literally hundreds of budding Amys and Emilys have sprouted up in Decatur; many more relocated here hoping for a little coattail action (much like what happened in Athens after R.E.M.'s ascent up the charts). Ray's own independent record label Daemon has released several CDs by some of the more interesting acoustic and non-acoustic musicians she's hyped (check out Daemon's diverse local all-star rendition of "Jesus Christ Superstar" for a good overview). Many other songwriters have either released their own albums, or like Michelle Malone and Natalie

Farr, been signed to out-of-town labels (New York-based Velvel, in both cases). The general consensus is that Decatur's acoustic scene peaked about three or four years ago, but it's still the best part of Atlanta in which to catch up-and-coming local folkies and touring national artists.

**Eddie's Attic** (515-B N. McDonough St. 404/377–4976) is regarded around the country as one of the best listening rooms for acoustic music. Owner Eddie Owen used to manage the Trackside Tavern when the Indigo Girls played there back in the '80s, and has remained pals with them ever since. Hence, it's not unusual to see Amy and/or Emily climb onstage to jam with songwriter friends, or do their own set (which invariably packs the house, no matter how secret they try to keep it). A steady parade of local minstrels is the club's bread and butter, headlining most weeknights and weekends, but Eddie usually brings in a few national touring acts every month, such as Richard Buckner or John Gorka. Housed on the second and highest floor (hence the name) of a building on the south end of Decatur Square, the unadorned space—hardwood floors, wooden chairs, tiny tables, and a small bar—helps focus attention on the stage. Several signs remind you to keep silent during the invariably quiet performances, and you'd better obey them, lest you get a thunderous "Shhhhhhh!!!" from across the room. If you can't resist yapping, there's a nice deck set off on the other side of the building, with a pair of pool tables and a dining/hanging area. Many performers do early, all-ages/nonsmoking sets at 7 p.m. in addition to the regular 9:30 p.m. slot.

**The Freight Room** (301 E. Howard Ave. 404/378–5365), over near Agnes Scott College, mixes up the genres a bit more, expanding beyond singer-songwriters to include bluegrass, country, folk, and blues musicians. Popular local artists like Grace Braun and the Vidalias have graced the small stage, as well as national acts like the Freighthoppers and Shawn Phillips. Mostly, though, lesser-known but invariably solid artists headline. The Freight Room has a regular clientele of mostly older neighborhood types who've had it with the somewhat clique-ish Eddie's crowd. Housed in a century-old train depot right on the tracks, the Freight Room also serves some passable food that you can eat out on the old loading platform. And like Eddie's, the Freight Room is an early club compared to the rest of Atlanta—most shows are going by 9 p.m.

Decatur does have its naughtier side, and it's on ample display at **Guys and Dolls** (2788 *Ponce de Leon Ave.* **404/377–2956**), Atlanta's only club offering both female *and* male strippers. There are separate sections for male, female, and even gay male oglers. A favorite of bachelor and bachelorette parties and the occasional discreet local bigwig, Guys and Dolls strikes a median between the posh, stuck-up Gold and Cheetah clubs and the seedier establishments along Cheshire Bridge Road [see **sidebar** in **south buckhead**]. Keg parties, two-for-one covers, $1 wings, and $1 lap dances also draw a barely legal crowd.

# buying stuff

Other than a few unique, upscale gift boutiques, most shops in the Decatur Square area stand in dismal, frustrating contrast to the booming restaurant and cafe resurgence. The offerings get somewhat brighter, especially around Emory Village, beyond the central district, but even there nothing compares to the shopping in Buckhead, Virginia Highland, or Little Five Points. Despite the influx of yuppies and ever-present students, stores that specialize in anything more left-field than you'd find in a mall seem to alienate the masses. The situation should improve as this area of Atlanta continues to grow and prosper.

## books... WordsWorth Booksellers (2112 N. Decatur Rd. 404/633–4275) is a large independent bookstore that draws fiscally challenged students in droves thanks to its proximity to Emory University, good selection, and great bargains. Thousands of titles are marked 75 percent off in the discount room. (William Shatner's *Tekwar* anyone? Naahh...) There are also 4,000 computer-related books, a large selection of CD-ROMs, and a 10,000-title children's area, not to leave out art, history, science fiction, mysteries, classics—basically books, books, books, from floor to ceiling. Though it sounds overwhelming, there's also a small reading area with comfy sofas and a table— a relaxing haven.

## cds/records... Wuxtry (2096 N. Decatur Rd. 404/329–0020), an offshoot of a popular Athens institution, is a typical cluttered independent record store, whose knowledgeable, opinionated employees have seemingly been working there since the beginning of time. In vinyl, the used records outnumber the new, while the ratio of old to new CDs is about even. Either way, whether you're looking for some obscure underground noisemonger or just the

latest Sonic Youth, the gang at Wuxtry will happily help you out. Unlike most of the few similar stores dotting the Atlanta landscape, Wuxtry doesn't really venture into comic books, T-shirts, magazines, or other artifacts of youth culture, sticking exclusively to music. In the mid-'80s, Wuxtry and L5P's Wax 'n' Facts were "it" for indie stores in Atlanta—and to this day, they remain respected bastions of coolness.

## clothing/vintage...
Like its sister store in Little Five Points, **The Clothing Warehouse** (2094 N. Decatur Rd. 404/248–1224) offers rack after rack of secondhand jeans, corduroy pants, sport jackets, hats, and scarves—the only difference being that in Little Five Points, this kind of thing is passé, whereas out here it's more or less the only game in town. The selection of vintage dresses is among Atlanta's largest, and with more than 500 pairs of jeans to flip through, you'll surely find at least one that flatters. The most fun, however, is examining the gaudy '70s ultra-thin polyester shirts. It's like excavating the ruins of an alien civilization driven to extinction by extended exposure to clashing colors.

## gifts...
Looking for an attractive but ultimately useless wedding gift for that cousin you haven't seen since junior high? You'll probably find it at **By Hand South** (112 E. Ponce de Leon Ave. 404/378–0118), a fine crafts gallery in downtown Decatur. It's the sort of place where you're always afraid you're gonna break something: The majority of the merchandise consists of decorative painted bowls, glassware, vases, and jewelry, plus some dried flower arrangements to pretty things up a bit. The neatest works

## dekalb farmer's market

The freshest experience in Decatur is the magnificent **DeKalb Farmer's Market** (*3000 E. Ponce De Leon Ave., 404/377–6400*), open every day from 9 a.m. to 9 p.m., a veritable cornucopia of ultra-fresh produce, not to mention boutique regional cheeses, breads, etc. The market is a Decatur must-stop. International goodies, from Korean daikon to Caribbean *dasheen* (a bitter spinach-like leafy vegetable), are arrayed in row after tempting row in a 140,000-square-foot space. Flags from Australia to Zambia hang from the ceiling; the staff sport name tags identifying their home countries and what languages they speak. And of course, there's a superlative salad bar, alongside a cafeteria serving up ultra-cheap ethnic eats, from samosas to satays. Seating is basic— white plastic tables and chairs—and the shopping-cart derby rages around you; still, what a wonderful deal for under 10 bucks. The people-watching is pretty damn fun, too.

are the colorful animal sculptures made out of old gardening tools—rakes, hoes, trimmers, etc.

Perhaps they picked up those tools down the street at **Garden Topia** (418 Church St. 404/378–2929), a designer garden shop set in a large old home on the square. No bags of manure lyin' around here, but you will find fancy sprinklers that double as yard art, plus hand-painted flowerpots, organic soaps, and wind chimes. If that all sounds a little too New-Age-y, well, they do carry shovels and trowels. Gardening shirts, hats, and shoes also account for much of the inventory, but most popular are the offbeat items made by local artists, such as Ann Stewart's stained-glass-in-stone mosaic birdbaths.

**Rue de Leon** (131 E. Ponce de Leon Ave. 404/373–6200) carries some gardening items, but this high-end gift shop's major focus is imported antiques, especially from France (where owner Catherine Krell's daughter lives): primarily authentic, finely crafted furniture, plates, glassware, and vases. Can't afford a $300 Lalique bud vase? The painted candles are very nice, and comparatively inexpensive. Or buy some potpourri for your mother. All moms love potpourri—it's been documented somewhere.

*Sabi* is West African dialect (a mix of Spanish, Portuguese, French, and tribal tongues) for "to know," and **Sabi Fine Things** (308F W. Ponce de Leon Ave. 404/377–5630) is certainly an education in traditional West African cultures. Nearly everything here comes from that region, including crafts, clothes, percussion instruments, and home furnishings. The most fascinating items are the children's toys and games: The elephant hand puppets made from cloth and gourds from the Republic of Benin are delightful, while the Mancala, a game played with seeds or shells, helps teach about the seasons. The owner's sister lives in West Africa and operates three stores there, so the stock is constantly replenished.

The festive **Alice's Wonderland** (3005 N. Druid Hills Rd. **no phone**) has the feel of a neighborhood yard sale gone goofy. There's no real theme here, just an assortment of fun "stuff": disco wigs, used records, movie posters, gaudy fake jewelry, books, tacky furniture, collectibles, funky clothes, etc. That "Saved by the Bell" body lotion and bath soap collection you've been dying for, well, here 'tis, right next to the cowhide chair with actual bull's horns forming the arms and backrests.

# sleeping

Despite its growth, Decatur has yet to be established as a significant tourist or business destination in itself, and it's too far from Atlanta's major highways to attract road travel business. Thus, Decatur doesn't offer a wide assortment of hotels, and most are fairly standard, run-of-the-mill jobs, albeit relatively inexpensive. A classy, renovated old hotel would be welcome in Decatur Square—unfortunately, there is none. Most visitors, it seems, either stay with friends or relatives or choose more stylish accommodations closer to Atlanta. The minor exception is the Emory University area, whose hotels see significant convention business (especially medical gatherings).

**Cost Range** for double occupancy per night on a weeknight. Call to verify prices.
$/under 50 dollars
$$/50–75 dollars
$$$/75–100 dollars
$$$$/100+ dollars

The most contemporary lodging in Decatur is the

**Holiday Inn Select** (130 *Clairemont Ave.* 404/371–0204
**$$**), where the lobby alone looks bigger than any other
nearby hotel! They tend to get a lot of business-related
guests, the large on-site convention center being a big
selling point. Nice indoor pool, too. The rooms are, well,
high-end Holiday Inn, in muted pastels and florals. The
Citrus Grove restaurant and Argyle's lounge offer dining
and imbibing opportunities, but you'll find more fun and
variety right up the street in Decatur Square.

At the other end of the hotel food chain is **The Relax
Inn** (245 *E.* Trinity Pl. 404/378–1122 **$**), a bland, low-
budget motel that's a tad frayed. Actually, it's not bad if
you're not planning on spending too much time there and
aren't trying to impress anyone. The sheets, though not
Egyptian cotton, are freshly laundered, and the plumbing
works. They even have HBO and The Movie Channel—life
could be worse.

If you're really on a budget and have a sense of adven-
ture, you might want to try **The Atlanta Dream Hostel**
(222 *E.* Howard Ave. 404/370–0380 **$**), likely one of the sil-
lier places you'll ever stay. Like a combination hippie fun-
house/artist's zoo, the private rooms are not so subtly
themed (the Jesus Room has a black velvet Last Supper on
the wall as well as a hologram of the Virgin Mary) and a
pet peacock struts amid the metal sculptures, fountains,
and Elvis shrine in the backyard garden, which the hostel
shares with the equally zany St. Agnes Tea Garden (under
renovation at press time—let's hope they keep the selec-
tion of nearly 50 teas and creative pasta/sandwich menu),
a wondrous spot housed in an old barn and owned by the
same people, John Makar and John McGuinness. As with

most youth hostels, the majority of the cheaper rooms are shared by up to six occupants. And you must have either a student I.D. (national or international) or a foreign passport to stay here.

**The Emory Inn** (1641 *Clifton* Rd. 404/712–6700 $$) caters mainly to guests of the school, prospective students, and outpatients from Emory's hospital, which, with its academic foundation and proximity to the Centers for Disease Control, is one of the country's finest facilities for state-of-the-art health care. The Inn has 107 rooms, a pool, and a nice patio area. It's actually quite a tranquil spot, abutting 14 acres of woodland. The lobby, lounge (with working fireplace), and rooms are charmingly cozy for a business hotel, with Shaker-style knotty pine furnishings. The Emory Garden Cafe is a delightful oasis of bamboo and wicker. In-room amenities include Spectravision pay-per-view flicks, irons, and hair-dryers.

Even more attuned to the needs of the business traveler, if somewhat soulless and antiseptic, is **The Emory Conference Center Hotel** (1615 *Clifton* Rd. 404/712–6000 $$$), a more upscale experience with a concierge, bell staff, and restaurant. This 200-room hotel attracts primarily corporate conferences and meetings, as well as guests of Emory. Both of these hotel facilities are operated by Emory University.

Boy, does it ever look ugly from the outside, with its pea- and pine-green color scheme and el-cheapo concrete motor lodge design. However, the interior of **The University Inn** (1767 *N. Decatur* Rd. 404/634–7327 $$$–$$$$) has been significantly upgraded in recent years. It's now a relaxing little motel with rooms that are neat and clean, if plain, and all are non-smoking—you'll find an ashtray outside every door. There's no restaurant, but the rooms have microwaves, and plenty of good eats await you down the road at Emory Village. Although this hotel is not affiliated with Emory, it does attract a large customer base from parents of students and hospital outpatients.

# doing stuff

Those looking for extracurricular activities in Decatur actually have a decent range of choices, especially in spring and summer and around holidays, when there always seems to be some sort of event happening in or around the Square. Spring and fall bring the Concerts on Decatur Square, a series of weekly outdoor concerts centered around the community bandstand kiosk in the center of the downtown square. Families bring picnic dinners to these popular Saturday-night concerts, featuring a variety of palatable, middle-of-the-road musical entertainment (jazz, pop, bluegrass, oldies, etc.) provided by local talent. Additionally, the Blue Sky Concerts lend a little pizzazz to lunch breaks every Wednesday at noon during the same months, May and September. It's during these times that the area really takes on a small-town, neighborly feel.

The Fernbank cluster of museums, just off Ponce de Leon Avenue between Decatur and central Atlanta, also offers an interesting learning outlet for kids and adults alike. Home to Atlanta's only IMAX theater [see **spectating**], **The Fernbank Museum of Natural History** (767 Clifton Rd. 404/370–0960) is housed in a soaring stone-and-brick building with spiral staircases and towering columns. The museum's major permanent exhibit, called "A Walk Through Time in Georgia," is basically a chronological history of the earth itself, with 17 galleries recreating landscapes such as the limestone caverns of the Cumberland Plateau and the swamplands of Georgia's Barrier Islands. Meanwhile, "Spectrum of the Senses" is an interactive, hands-on experience (over 60 rotating exhibits include a life-size kaleidoscope, for example) that's deservedly a favorite with children and teens. Other notable sections include the Caribbean Coral Reef Aquarium and the World of Shells.

A related but separate facility, **Fernbank Science Center** (*156 Heaton Park Dr.* 404/378–4311), is located a mile or so closer to downtown Decatur. Home to one of the country's largest planetariums (very cool for stargazers; call for showtimes), the Science Center also has an observatory with telescope, open Thursday and Friday evenings when the sky is clear. When out-of-the-ordinary cosmic phenomena (comets, asteroid collisions with Jupiter, etc.) occur, the telescope becomes a popular after-dinner show for science nerds and swoony daters alike.

The interior of Emory University's **Michael C. Carlos Museum** (*571 S. Kilgo St.* 404/727–4282), partly housed in a 1916 beaux-arts gem, was redesigned in 1985 by renowned architect Michael Graves, who then fashioned a 35,000-square-foot postmodern addition. The Carlos houses Emory's extensive antiquities collection, painstakingly assembled and expanded since 1875. Originally showcasing artifacts from the "Cradle of Western Civilization," it now has a massive collection of indigenous art from Asia, Oceania, North America, and sub-Saharan Africa.

It also has Egyptian mummies, illuminated manuscripts, Etruscan coins, cuneiform tablets, amphorae, jewelry, and statuary from Costa Rica to Cyprus—practically everything but King Tut's tomb—and that's just the permanent collection. Add in rotating exhibits like works on paper by Rembrandt, Degas, and Kandinsky, and you have easily Atlanta's most varied and exciting museum. Finally, you don't have to wait for special months to enjoy the ongoing happenings at **Agnes Scott College** (141 E. College Ave. 404/638–6400). There are always student art exhibitions, recitals, dance and music performances, planetarium shows (they have one too, although it's not nearly as nice or large as Fernbank's), theatrical events, etc. Most are free and open to the public, and are held on campus in the chapel or the auditorium.

**spectating...** Decatur and its surrounding areas have few unique choices in the viewing department, but those few are at least worth venturing outside for, and two in particular warrant a trip across town.

Topping the list is **The IMAX Theater** at The Fernbank Museum of Natural History [see **doing stuff** ]. If you've never experienced an IMAX film, you really should check this out—the six-story-tall screen puts you as close to being inside the action as two-dimensional technology permits. Most of the films are nature-oriented documentaries, with such epic subjects as Mt. Everest, the Amazon, the deep mysteries of the ocean, outer space, etc. Dangling a carrot for the chic cocktail culture crowd, Fernbank presents "Martinis & IMAX" on Friday evenings, where you can swill beer, wine, and yes, martinis (sold on the premises, and not half bad) while mingling about the beautiful Fernbank Museum grounds prior to the movie. Now, if that ain't a classy idea for a date, what is?

**The Toco Hills Theatre** (3003 N. Druid Hills Rd. 404/325–7090) is unique not only in that it is an old one-screen theater inside a shopping plaza, but also because of its spacious size. Sadly, of the 700 seats, probably 670 go unfilled for most showings. While the Toco Hills Theatre doesn't show art films exclusively, neither does it go in for the latest blockbuster action flick. Mostly, it brings in critically acclaimed foreign, independent, and mainstream fare that goes otherwise overlooked. The sound system has just been boosted, adding greatly to your viewing enjoyment. The interior, however, doesn't appear to have changed in 25 years, with its tan wood panelling befitting a '70s porn house (not necessarily a defect).

Live theater choices are slim. The most notable productions usually occur at **Neighborhood Playhouse** (430 W. Trinity Place 404/373–5311), which, as its name suggests, utilizes little-known local talent in nearly every facet of its productions: as actors, stagehands, and sometimes, writers. Housed in a nondescript brick building, Neighborhood Playhouse usually presents six productions per year, each running for five to six weeks. At least two musicals are staged every year, with suspense yarns, farces, and plays based on classics like To Kill a Mockingbird or Little Women filling up the roster. As the 170-seat theater attracts a sizeable older crowd of season-ticket holders, you won't see too many "edgy" or experimental works at the Neighborhood Playhouse.

Those productions are reserved for **The Discovery Arena**, a smaller room located within the Neighborhood

Playhouse facilities. Recent presentations include *Kiss of the Spider Woman*, *Mating Habits of Mammals*, and the seasonal original *Twisted Christmas*, which is, as its name suggests, a humorous, nontraditional Yuletide tale of mirth and woe. The Discovery Arena is a small black box of a room, holding 75 or so semi-comfortably in a open-seating arrangement. It also doubles as a children's playhouse, **The Explorer Kidz Theater**, where fractured fairy tales like *The Ugly Duckling: Beauty's Not All It's Quacked Up to Be*, and *Cinderellie-Mae* are staged for the rugrats. These are often more entertaining than the main productions.

In addition to these sparse film/theater offerings, several nearby malls offer the usual multiscreen cinema circuses.

# body

Decatur is hardly the place to go if you're looking to get your butt pierced or your tongue tattooed. Most of the local inhabitants seem to have outgrown such behavior anyway. Gyms are also in surprisingly short supply. But several clean, semi-hip salons and barber shops can sculpt your follicles into shape (no Marine cuts or Bride of Frankenstein dos). While none really stands out, they're staffed by friendly, helpful folks eager to get you looking as stylish as possible.

The best place on the square is **Ruta Baga (121 E. Court Square 404/377–8900)**, where the two stylists, John and Heather Rusnak, are a friendly husband-and-wife team. They couldn't hire anyone else if they wanted to, since the cramped room is sized more like a kitchen than a salon.

Still, the unusual carved-wood globe lights are a nice touch, and you can trust the Rusnaks—they style each other's hair, and they always look spiffy!

For cheap, try **Cut Zoo** (2106 N. Decatur Rd. 404/636–5380), one of three locations in the Atlanta area. A mere $8.75'll get you fixed up, and if you sacrifice the fine attention to detail and embellishments you'll get in more posh salons (no aromatherapy or glasses of wine here), the price is right and the staff is usually young and pretty wacky.

Near Emory, **Village Hair** (1540 N. Decatur Rd. 404/378–6511) is a four-chair barbershop that gets a steady stream of students from the university, though many students opt for the familiar chain shop **Supercuts** (1583 N. Decatur Rd. 404/371–0896) across the street.

If you're still desperate for a piercing and are too lazy to drive eight minutes to Little Five Points, you could try **Today's Fashion** (139 Sycamore St. 404/378–2011) on the square, or as the dilapidated, deteriorating wooden sign above this tacky joint reads, "day's ashion." See, right there, there's a little hand-scribbled brown cardboard sign in the front window: "We pierce ears & nose." Uhh . . . I wouldn't recommend it, Sparky.

# off the edge

## georgia's stone mountain park

This imposing 825-foot-tall outcropping is the world's largest exposed granite slab. Apparently, it was just sitting there waiting for officially sanctioned graffiti, which was provided by a towering bas-relief originally conceived by John Gutzon Borglum (of Mount Rushmore fame) in 1923. Several squabbles and sculptors later, a carving— 190 feet wide and 90 feet high—was finally completed by Roy Faulkner and Walter Kirtland Hancock in 1970. This is the Rushmore-is-less version: Carved heads portray Jefferson Davis, Robert E. Lee, and Stonewall Jackson.

The sight certainly gives a rush, especially during the kitschy but nonetheless impressive laser-and-pyrotechnic shows on summer evenings. More than 6 million people visit the surrounding 3,200-acre park annually; other attractions include a train chugging around the base of the mountain; a paddleboat; a 19-building "Antebellum Plantation"; hiking trails; waterskiing, waterslides, and fishing on the 363-acre lake; various historic centers and museums; crafts shops; even horse-and-buggy tours.

# buford highway

Most towns have their neatly compartmentalized ethnic enclaves. Not Atlanta. But along Buford Highway, zooming northeast of Buckhead all the way into the boonies, Asian, Mexican, and even African restaurants sit beef-cheek-by-pork-jowl with strips malls and car dealerships. The fare at these unprepossessing spots is the most adventuresome in town. Stalwarts include the Ethiopian **Abbay** (3375 Buford Hwy. 404/321–5808 $–$$); Korean **Seoul Garden** (5938 Buford Hwy. 770/452–0123 $); the Peruvian **Machu Picchu** (3375 Buford Hwy. 404/320–3226 $–$$) and the Middle Eastern **Lawrence's Cafe** (2888 Buford Hwy. 404/320–7756 $–$$). An enormous oil portrait of T.E. Lawrence complements the gyrating belly dancers at the latter.

# west end

This tranquil area (comprising a section just west and southwest of Downtown) is arguably the first African-American middle-class residential neighborhood in Atlanta. Today, the Atlanta University Center, including the campuses of the prestigious, historically black Spelman and Morehouse colleges, dominates its northern half. The southern part is a collection of Victorian, Edwardian, and Beaux Arts mansions, where many prominent black Atlantans made their homes during segregation. There are three must-sees. Alonzo Herndon, who founded the Atlanta Life Insurance Company in 1905, built a Neoclassical beauty whose stately colonnades ironically recall antebellum plantation great houses. The **Alonzo F. Herndon Home** (587 *University Pl.* 404/581–9813) now functions as a tribute to his entrepreneurial skills; the lavish decor, including rococo gilt-trim walls, Empire and Louis XV–style furnishings, would have been considered exorbitant even by rich "white" standards of the time. The **Hammonds House Galleries** (503 *Peeples St.* 404/752–8730) is located in the former home of respected African-American anesthesiologist and art patron Dr. Otis Hammonds. Hammonds died in 1985; the building includes his remarkable collection of Haitian and African tribal art, and serves as a resource center for black artists worldwide. Finally, there's **Wren's Nest** (1050 *Ralph David Abernathy Blvd.* 404/753–735), the former home of *Uncle Remus* author Joel Chandler Harris. Harris was a white journalist enthralled by the African folktales of Brer Rabbit told in slave quarters throughout the South. The books gained wide popularity, attracting such fans as Teddy Roosevelt and Mark Twain; the former presented Harris with the stuffed great horned owl perched over the study door. African-American storytellers keep the tradition alive summer afternoons.

# atlanta's upmarket 'burbs... marietta, roswell, vinings, sandy springs

KFC's 30-foot-tall Big Chicken is the cherished landmark in Marietta, capital of Cobb County just to the northwest of

Atlanta. Cobb County was once a shining example of the red, white, and blue (that's redneck, white trash, and blue collar), but Marietta has become increasingly upscale, as evidenced by its five National Register Historic Districts, including renovated antebellum and Victorian mansions, churches, and the turn-of-the-century town square lined with antique shops, fern bars, eateries, and even a theater. Another symbol of the gentility is the **1848 House** *(780 S. Cobb Dr. 770/428–1848 $$$–$$$$)*, an innovative Southern restaurant whose verdant gardens and period furnishings provide a reminder of traditional Southern hospitality.

Several miles northwest of Buckhead, atop a crest of rolling hills and small mountains banking the Chatta-hoochee River, sits Vinings, a historic neighborhood that strives to retain much of its turn-of-the-century look and charm despite becoming a thriving residential, shopping and restaurant district. Antiquing and dining prevail. **Soho** *(4200 Paces Ferry Rd., Ste. 107, 770/801–0069 $$$–$$$$)* is a stylish New York–themed bistro specializing in fusion cuisine. But by far the best eating experience in Vinings is along the Chattahoochee at **Canoe** *(4199 Paces Ferry Rd. 770/432–2663 $$$–$$$$)*. If the weather's nice, be sure to get a table on the patio, where you overlook a lovely riverside garden.

Roswell also sits atop a ridge overlooking the Chatta-hoochee. Due north of Atlanta, straight from Buckhead up Roswell Road (which—go figure—becomes Atlanta Street in Roswell), it has the look and feel of an old Southern mountain town (founded in 1839 by Roswell King and his son, Barrington), where blue-blooded families still live in ornate antebellum homes (at least those that haven't been converted into event facilities; elaborate weddings are held throughout the town). Docents in period dress from the Historical Society provide guided tours to sites such as Bulloch Hall, home of Teddy Roosevelt's mother, Martha Bulloch. In the town square, artsy-craftsy shops and restaurants surround a small, open park. **The Public House** (605 S. *Atlanta* St. 770/992–4646 $$$$), serving an elegant assortment of Southern-influenced variations on pork chops, prime rib, and even duck, is the most established eatery around here, while **Chaplins** (555 S. *Atlanta* St. 770/642–6981 $–$$) is more of a burger 'n' munchies beer hall, though a pleasant place to hang out after antiquing. **Weems & Associates** (565 S. *Atlanta* St. 770/641–8846) carries an impressive selection of 18th- and 19th-century American antiques, and offers restoration services. **Cynthia Aiken** (55 Park Sq. 770/552–7550) offers less furniture, more collectibles at her nearby antique shop, while **Rose Cottage** (11 Maple St. 770/993–1996) specializes in old-timey toy bears and dolls.

Far cheesier delights await due south of Roswell, in Sandy Springs. A heavily trafficked corridor of strip shopping centers and franchise food, it inexplicably features a cluster of drinking holes catering to party-hearty suburbanites. Junior execs on the prowl reach critical mass at such perpetually packed bars as **American Pie** (5840 Roswell Rd. 404/255–7571) and **Good Ol' Days** (5841 Roswell Rd. 404/257–9183). Booze and cruise heaven.

# transportation

**airport:** Hartsfield Atlanta International Airport, 404/530–6600

**buses out of town:** Greyhound, 232 Forsyth St., S.W., 404/584–1731

**public transportation:** MARTA, 2424 Piedmont Rd., 404/848–5000

**taxis:** Checker Cab, 404/351–1111; **Atlanta Yellow Cab**, 404/521–0200

**trains:** Amtrak, 1680 Peachtree St., N.W. 404/881–3065

# emergency/health

**fire department:** Atlanta City, 675 Ponce De Leon Ave., 404/853–3333; **Decatur**, 230 E. Trinity Pl., 404/373–5092; **Fulton County**, 3977 Aviation Cir., 404/505–5700; **DeKalb County**, 3630 Camp Cir., 404/294–2345

**police:** Atlanta City, 175 Decatur St., 404/853–3434; **Decatur**, 420 W. Trinity Pl., 404/377–7911; **Fulton County**, 130 Peachtree St., 404/730–5700; **DeKalb County**, 3630 Camp Cir., 404/294–2000

**pharmacies:** Little Five Points Pharmacy, 484 Moreland Ave., 404/524–4466; **Kings Drugs**, 2345 Peachtree Rd., 404/233–2101

**hospitals:** Piedmont Hospital, 1968 Peachtree Rd., 404/605–5000; **Emory University Hospital**, 1364 Clifton Rd., 404/712–7021; **Grady Memorial Hospital**, 80 Butler St., 404/616–4307; **Northside Hospital**, 1000 Johnson Ferry Rd., 404/851–8000

**babysitter/day-care service:** A Great Night Out, 2347 Drew Valley Way, 404/633–3329; **Wonderful World of Children**, 1316 W. Peachtree St., 404/881–6668

# media/information

**newspapers:** (daily) **Atlanta Journal-Constitution**, 72 Marietta St., 404/526–5151; (free weekly) **Creative Loafing**, 750 Willoughby Way, 404/688–5623

**radio stations:** WNNX (99.7 FM) modern rock; WKLS (96.1 FM) rock; WHTA (97.5 FM) hip-hop; WRAS (88.5 FM) college/alternative; WRFG (89.3 FM) community/diverse; WABE (90.1 FM) NPR/classical; WREK (91.1 FM) college/diverse; WGST (640 AM/105.7 FM) news/talk; WGKA (1190 AM) diverse

**tv stations:** ABC: WSB Ch. 2; FOX: WAGA Ch. 5; NBC: WXIA Ch. 11; WB: WATL Ch. 36; CBS: WGNX Ch. 46; UPN: WUPA Ch. 69

**convention & visitors bureau:** Atlanta Chamber of Commerce, 235 International Blvd., 404/880–9000

**January: King Week**: At various Downtown locations, mostly at the King Center. Celebrations and activities honoring slain civil rights leader Martin Luther King Jr., centered around his Jan. 15th birthday.

**March: St. Patrick's Day Celebrations**: Parades and partying in Buckhead and Downtown. **Great Decatur Beer Festival**: Slap down a minimal cover charge, then sample a generous assortment of micros and specialty brews in Decatur Square. They also do it in October.

**April: Freaknik**: Gigantic spring-break booty call for students of black colleges nationwide. Basically a roving cruising party, with no discernable direction. **Atlanta Dogwood Festival**: Large outdoor celebration in Piedmont Park, celebrating the arrival of spring. Vendors, food, local bands, balloons for the kids. **Inman Park Springfest and Tour of Homes**: Street festival among the grand Victorian homes of this revitalized in-town neighborhood. Walking tour brings you inside some of the nicer digs. **Sweet Auburn Springfest**: The beats are pumpin' at this large urban street festival, in a historic, traditionally African-American district.

**May: Music Midtown**: Weekend outdoor music festival brings in lots of superstar acts, as well as many regional and local favorites. Upward of 200,000 people attend this annual drunken nuthouse. **Atlanta Jazz Festival**: Established headliners along with up-and-coming jazz acts attract crowds to free shows in Piedmont and Grant parks. **Decatur Arts Festival**: A multi-day event celebrating the visual and performing arts. A film festival runs in conjunction, screening local works.

**June: Atlanta Film and Video Festival**: Independent flicks of all kinds, including many local films, at various screens around the city. **Virginia Highland Summerfest**: Outdoor street festival, with all kinds of specialty vendors, food, and local bands. **Gay and Lesbian Pride Festival**: Multi-day festival centered around a lively parade through Midtown. Music and other entertainment color Piedmont Park.

**July: Peachtree Road Race**: Even if you left your running shoes in the closet, this Fourth of July 10K run attracts hordes of enthusiastic spectators as it winds its way from Buckhead to Piedmont Park. The rest of the Fourth offers parades and fireworks displays throughout the city. **National Black Arts Festival**: Celebrating the spectrum of African-American music, dance, theater, and more, in various venues around town.

**September: Candler Park/Lake Claire Art & Music Festival**: Neighborhood street fest is a laid-back, funky affair, with loads of local bands. **Montreux Atlanta Music Festival**: World music festival is patterned after the famous one in Montreux, Switzerland, offering free concerts in Piedmont and Centennial parks. **Nexus Art Party**: Indoor/outdoor shindig at Nexus Contemporary Art Center has a different theme each year, with music, dancing, and drinking.

**October:** AIDS Walk: Spirited charity walk through Midtown benefits various AIDS research and support organizations.

**November:** Peachtree International Film Festival: Relatively young but rapidly growing fest showcases indie films of all kinds.

**December:** First Night Atlanta: Family-themed no-alcohol New Year's Eve street party all around Midtown. For boozers, there are plenty of New Year's options elsewhere in the city.

## eating/coffee

## bars/ music/clubs

## buying stuff

## sleeping

## doing stuff

## body

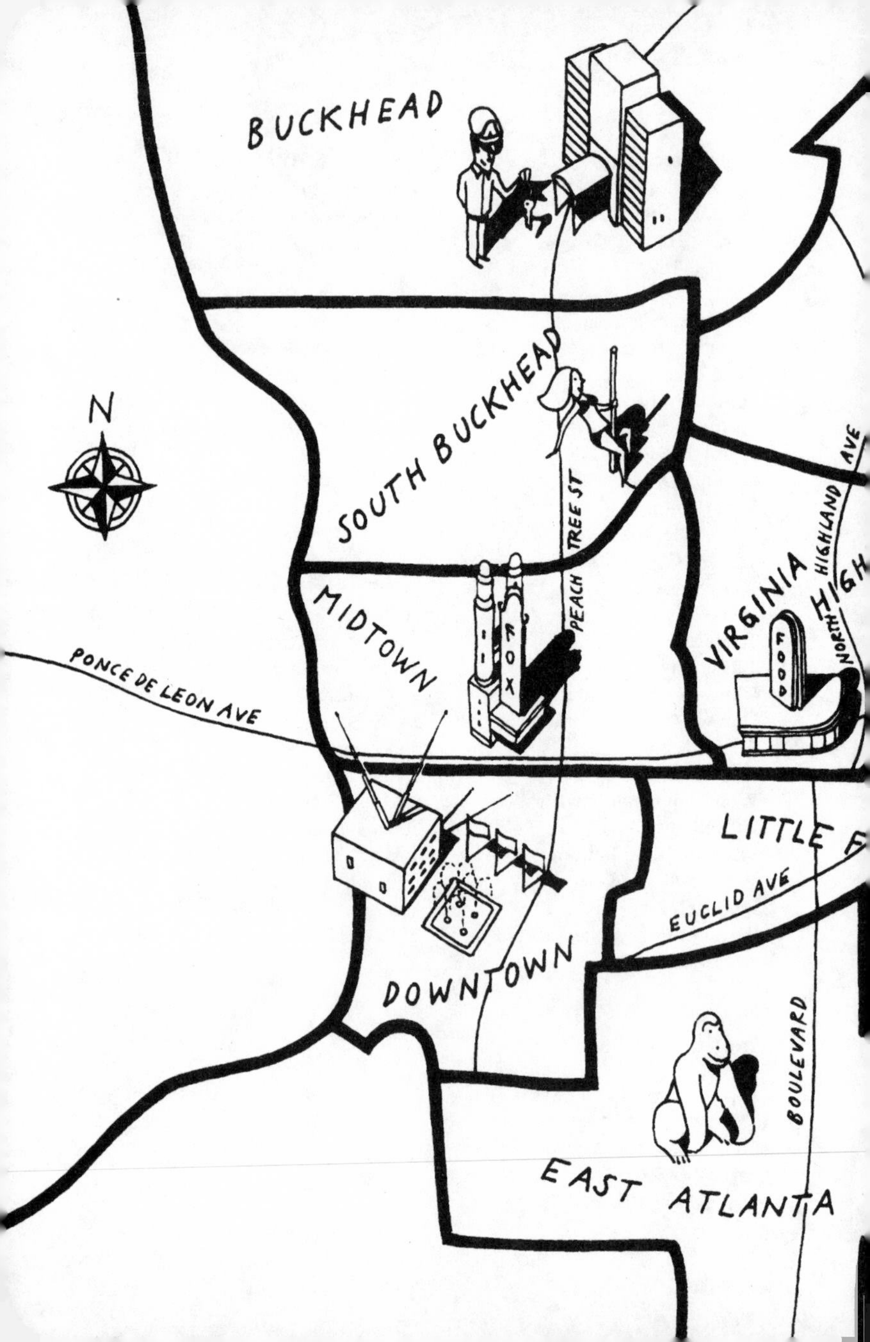
BUCKHEAD
SOUTH BUCKHEAD
N
MIDTOWN
PONCE DE LEON AVE
PEACH TREE ST
FOX
VIRGINIA
FOOD
NORTH HIGHLAND AVE
HIGH
LITTLE F
EUCLID AVE
DOWNTOWN
BOULEVARD
EAST ATLANTA